ATHEISM KILLS

The Dangers of a World Without God —
and Cause for Hope

BARAK LURIE

CT3 Media, Los Angeles, CA

For permission requests, write to:

CT3Media, Inc.
12100 Wilshire Boulevard, 8th Floor
Los Angeles, CA 90025
www.ct3media.com/

Jacket design by Ben Lizardi

Printed in the United States of America

Ordering Information:
Special discounts are available on quantity purchases by corporations, associations, and others. For details, contact the publisher at the address above.

Atheism Kills / Barak Lurie —1st edition

ISBN: 978-0-9995139-1-0

For my father and mother, Ranan and Tamar Lurie

TABLE OF CONTENTS

FOREWORD

By Dennis Prager

Here's a riddle:
What do you get when you combine a lawyer, a first-class mind, exhaustive historical research, compelling human stories, moral passion, and grappling with the greatest issues of life?

The answer: *Atheism Kills* by Barak Lurie.

This book does not focus on "proofs" of God's existence. Though a strong believer in God, I have never sought proofs of God's existence—simply because I don't believe that such proofs exist. If God wanted His existence known the way we know that a cell or a mountain exists, presumably He would have made His existence as provable as that of a cell or a mountain. Moreover, we can only prove that which is completely contained within the natural world. And, by definition, God transcends the natural world. He did, after all, create it.

What we do have here are arguments – arguments that are so logically powerful that I have to conclude what the eminent contemporary thinker, Charles Krauthammer, an agnostic, said to me when I asked what he thought about atheism.

"I believe," Krauthammer said, "that atheism is the least plausible of all theologies. I mean, there are a lot of wild ones out there, but the one that clearly is so contrary to what is possible is atheism. The idea that all this universe—what is [the atheist argument]: It always existed? It created itself *ex nihilo*? I mean, talk about the violation of human rationality. That, to me, is off the charts."

And Krauthammer is not only an agnostic; he is someone who was rendered a quadriplegic by a diving accident while a very young man in medical school. If anyone might be expected to embrace atheism, it would be a man with a brilliant mind, trained as a scientist (at Harvard, a thoroughly secular institution), to whom life dealt a severe and unfair blow at a young age.

What Barak Lurie offers here is, in my opinion, more important than "proofs" of God's existence. Instead, he proves something else—the consequences of atheism. And those consequences are precisely reflected in the title of the book: atheism kills.

There are, of course, fine individuals who are atheists. There were undoubtedly fine people who believed in the pagan gods who demanded child sacrifice. The existence of fine atheists says nothing about atheism, any more than the existence of fine Aztec believers argued for Aztec religion. Atheism is the subject of this book. And Lurie is right: Atheism kills. It kills people, civilizations, beauty, meaning, order, happiness. If something is good, atheism will eventually kill it.

That's why this book is important. People need to know both the logically inevitable consequences of atheism and its historical record, which starkly bears them out. This is not mere theory.

Atheism Kills is a robust, relentlessly interesting, and intellectually invigorating read. But it is also – and perhaps most of all—a *cri de couer*, an impassioned cry from the heart. Lurie is worried about civilization, and cares deeply about human suffering. Those are the reasons, I suspect, that he devoted so much time and effort to writing this book. And every one of us who reads it is the beneficiary of his noble and massive effort.

Without God, everything is permitted.
— FYODOR DOSTOEVSKY

If God did not exist, it would be necessary to invent Him.
— VOLTAIRE

INTRODUCTION

A student was taking helicopter flying lessons. After some weeks, he started begging his instructor to let him have his first solo flight. The instructor was wary but eventually agreed on one condition: The student had to radio him every 1,000 feet to make sure everything was okay.

So the student agreed and the big day came. He began flying normally and soon, as promised, radioed in at 1,000 feet and confirmed: "All good."

Then, at 2,000 feet, the student radioed in again: "Everything is fine, but it's getting a bit cold."

But before he reached 3,000 feet, the instructor saw from his position on the ground that something horrible was happening: the helicopter had just stopped mid-air. Soon, it began a horrifying descent. Then it plummeted and crashed.

The crash destroyed the helicopter, and set it aflame. But the student miraculously managed to crawl out alive. He had broken bones and burns everywhere on his body.

The instructor ran to him. "Oh my God, what happened?" he cried out, when he reached him.

"I told you it was getting cold," the man answered. "So I shut off the giant fan."

So it is when we shut off God from our lives, when we no longer understand God's central role in the creation of our civilization. We no longer ascend. We may hover for a while, but ultimately, we can only look forward to a very brutal end.

You walk across a dusty field, the cold and dry wind biting at your face. You approach the stone well of atheism. You reach it, and peer down. The only thing that comes back at you is blackness.

You drop a stone and wait to hear it reach the bottom, but no sound returns. You lower a water bucket, hoping that you'll pick something up. But when you raise it, there is nothing.

Atheism offers nothing but its own emptiness. It offers no nourishment for the body nor the mind. No hope, no laughter, no joy, no beauty, no sense of purpose, and no sense of a world beyond our own. It has never created a song or innovated new technology. It has never inspired anyone, nor caused anyone to aspire to anything positive.

The atheist will proclaim that no one has died in the *name* of godlessness. While that is technically true, it is a meaningless point. More meaningful is that millions have died *because* of godlessness. Atheism kills.

The ranks of the godless have swollen, and the devil has been smiling. He's known all along that to foment evil, he need not create an equal and opposite force to goodness. He need not even tempt you with evil thoughts or sinister voices in your head. He need not tell you to worship him as some "alternative" god.

No. All he would need to do is persuade everyone that God isn't important. After that, he can exploit your instinctive need to matter, your need for purpose. And once he's done that, you'll just give the devil your soul, without any fight at all.

Worse yet, you won't even know you're doing it.

In the movie *Pulp Fiction*, the John Travolta character Vincent Vega explains the differences between Europe and America: "It's the little things," he says, such as how they call the Quarter Pounder a "Royale with Cheese," and how Europeans use mayonnaise on French fries instead of ketchup. ("They drown them in that shi*t", he says).

Even though Vincent was thinking in his own limited pedestrian terms, the "little differences" apply to our civilization at large. And what seem to be "little" differences have a way of becoming "big" ones: We've gone from when society considered skin magazines seedy (men would even receive their *Playboy* magazines in the mailbox in brown wrappers), to a world where women proudly upload sex videos of themselves to random porn sites for free—it seems their main motivation is the thrill of getting as many "views" as possible (and gaining "fame" that way). Many states and countries have now legalized marijuana and other hallucinogens. Acceptance of low-level crime (prostitution, gambling, drug use, vandalism, and even urinating in public) is also on the rise.

Distinctions are fading, from something as trivial as casual and formal attire at work and church, to the more significant distinctions: man and woman, child and adult, honor and shame, and good and evil.

The world now seems to try to now take out God altogether from our lives and even our history, as if God had never been part of it at all, or at best a relic of a quaint but irrelevant past. If there is a devil who seeks to undo God, he could not have done it in a better way.

Our new world seems eager to undermine religious institutions, clubs, or symbols that promote religious identity and values—even the Boy Scouts. This new world demands that the government take down crosses that might exist on public lands—no matter how historical they may be.[1] At every turn, our new world seems to try to stop displays of nativity scenes and even decorative lights in public places during Christmas. You are to say "happy holidays," not "Merry Christmas," lest you offend anyone. Some towns have even disallowed Bible studies in private homes, on the pretext that such studies constitute a "business assembly" that needs a license from the local city hall.[2]

Allowing private prayer in schools is unacceptable, and even praying after touchdowns in high-school football games has become the subject of legal attack. But if you "take a knee" and don't show respect to the American flag during the playing of the national anthem at that same game, that's no problem. In Los Angeles public schools, students can talk back and yell whatever "willful defiance" they want at their teacher.[3] They can wear a T-shirt with virtually any offensive language they want—except if you wear something with the American Flag or something religious. That may be hate speech, you see.[4]

But it's not all bad for the teacher: she can teach anything she wants (including how horrible America is and how to put on condoms). She just has to make sure not to talk about God or religious values, or the many contributions Christianity and Judaism gave to civilization. Because that would be going too far.

Christians and Jews have become defensive when they express their faith. America itself has also started looking at itself as a flawed, and even evil, country. Instead of focusing on liberty, truth, loyalty, self-reliance, and standing up to true evil, the moral discussion has centered on environmentalism, climate change and promoting the pursuit of visual and physical sexuality to extremes we've never seen before. Women wear leggings which seem to showcase every crack and line in their bodies; a "hook up" culture has developed, where you have sex first and maybe grab a coffee with each other later; schools teach about gays and gay sex (but don't worry, it'll be in age appropriate ways); and the media now seeks to identify people less on their values and more on their skin color or the nature of their sexual proclivities.

Fewer schools and parents advocate timeless moral precepts. They may appreciate them, but such morals remain unsung, nonverbalized, and irrelevant abstractions—like the notions of infinity, black holes, or what the last digit of Pi might be.

What feeds this new paradigm in our society? The fading of God. It's like when Scotty beams Kirk off the *Enterprise* on *Star Trek*. There the captain goes—from solid to translucent . . . to gone.

"I am an atheist, but thank God no one else is."

This was my mantra when I was an atheist in my youth. Strangely, not once during this time did I consider its internal contradiction. But within it lay the kernel of what I was to realize quickly enough: a world without God is a world where free will, the individual, morality, beauty and even time have no real meaning. Civilization itself cannot exist. Atheism as a *governing* ideology has led to only one of two things: chaos or horrific evil. Usually multitudes die. Not the kind of multitudes you show with a long list of names. It's more the kind you show with statistics or a number, with lots of zeros after them.

"But look at me," the atheist now protests. "I'm an atheist, and I'm a good person."

Yes, and there were good Communists, too. So what? communism as an actual *governing* ideology has usually ended with the gulag, mass executions, or at best forced labor and reeducation camps. It usually ended with mass graves, where the bones of hundreds and thousands of corpses intermingled with each other, one indistinguishable from the other.

As we show in our first chapters, Godlessness has resulted in far more mayhem and murders than all Judeo-Christian religious institutions combined. There is no comparison. Virtually every culture that has rejected God has collapsed or engaged in horrific mayhem. By contrast, virtually all cultures grounded in the Judeo-Christian tradition have flourished.

The atheist does not appreciate that whatever he believes to be good is the product of thousands of years of the Judeo-Christian mindset. It is notion of God which has provided the foundation to our moral understandings, to our sense of law and justice, to our sense of progress and innovation, and even to the meaning of time. God has been the nourishing soil that has allowed civilization itself to grow. Take Him away, and civilization soon withers.[5] Or, if you like, civilization becomes the hapless Wile E. Coyote, who has unwittingly chased the Road Runner over a cliff, soon realizing nothing is beneath him: You notice the poor guy always kind of hovers in the air a few seconds, just before he plummets to his doom.

But the atheist, benefitting as he does from this exquisite moral code which literally took thousands of years to develop, now rejects God as unnecessary. He argues humanity no longer needs God, like a butterfly no longer needs its cocoon. This metaphor fails, however, because we will *always* need Him, like the tree always needs its soil.

It's more as if the atheist argues the following: Yes, my parents raised me. Yes, they protected and fed me. But now I am a grown man. Because I don't need my parents to sustain me anymore, parenthood itself is no longer necessary—for anyone.

How did we get to this point? Atheism's history is revealing: atheism was virtually nonexistent throughout the centuries, until it gained great traction in Europe during the Age of Enlightenment, particularly with the French Revolution.[6] It then gained greater currency in Germany with writers Friedrich Nietzsche and Karl Marx, the latter of whom wrote his famous contemptuous quip that religion was the "opiate of the people."[7]

As godlessness grew more acceptable, it eventually coincided with Charles Darwin's notion of evolution and its root premise, "survival of the fittest." The elites of society saw in evolution an opportunity to repurpose civilization itself. They soon demoted individuality, freedom, and the very sense of our infinite worth in the eyes of God. Such notions seemed no longer relevant, even primitive. What mattered was growth, strength, and progress.

Soon the rejection of God became so influential that some governments adopted it as state doctrine. Your worth to society's collective agenda was what made you valuable. Never mind that a dictator would decide that agenda; freedom was far too dangerous to leave to the individual. Freedom and individualism had been quaint, but the modern era now demanded more sensible, "command-and-control" measures.

This idea of the whole being more important than the individual in turn led to communism. Soon Eugenics came into fashion in America, which then bolstered progressivism, fascism and Nazism.

All these ideologies (as well as communism) only delivered devastation upon the earth. None of them offered any of the benefits they had promised.

And yet we don't often discuss *why* that is so.

It is telling that, up through the mid-nineteenth century, even the brightest of doctors and scientists had failed to understand that it was tiny invisible microbes that caused so much of the sickness and death that plagued the earth. They thought foul odors, imbalances of the mind and body, and/or spirits caused the maladies they treated. It didn't dawn on them that a simple protocol of hand-and-arm scrubbing could drastically reduce such deaths.

Similarly today, we often point to peripheral characteristics of communism, fascism, and other forms of totalitarianism as the cause of their horrors—things such as nationalism, scapegoating of minorities, and a leader's charisma. But such things describe only the *tools* of such monstrous regimes, not the thing that animates them in the first place. Many fail to understand that godlessness might have been the invisible pathogen that enabled the horrors of the twentieth century and beyond—and which promises more horror if we don't address it. Sadly, godlessness seems to remain that unrecognized pathogen, no matter how horrifically it continues to metastasize.

And so godlessness grows. Just like Hitler's Nazi party consisted at first only of a fringe group of extremists but seemingly harmless miscreants, atheism is now gaining a foothold as never before. Church attendance in Europe, where Christianity had blossomed and propelled Western Civilization to where it is today, has now dwindled so much that a Netherlands church repurposed itself as an indoor skate park. In America, fewer and fewer Christians feel the need to attend church (in 2007, churches were closing at a net rate of 3,000 churches per year).[8] Their primary reason? They perceive that God and faith are no longer relevant to their lives.[9]

But as we shall see, Europe is learning the costs of abandoning God. Power always abhors a vacuum, and people crave structure. Hence it is no surprise that radical Islam—with its own violent but purposeful structure—now seems to be gaining a foothold throughout Europe. And without the passion of belief in the Judeo-Christian God, there will be nothing to stop it.

All this having been said, atheists seem to know they still must offer something to believe in, as if they intuit there must be a purpose somewhere within them. So they champion something called Humanism, an ideology that we should all strive to greatness and good works because we're . . . well, you know, human.

But humanism is meaningless, utterly outside of the actual meaning of atheism, and contrary to the devastation atheism itself must lead to. To truly live his beliefs of godlessness (the universe is random, survival of the fittest explains every human development), the atheist should eschew all notions of charity, responsibility to the community, personal responsibility, justice and truth, or any sense of obligation to past or future generations. He should respect only power. Passion, freedom, and personal growth? Why should we aspire to such things? Acting in a "good," moral, or socially responsible way is acting inconsistent with the core tenets of atheism. He's like a person who protests the presence of the police in his town, only to seek out the police the moment someone attacks him.

The atheist has not thought his own beliefs through. He believes in a world of randomness, survival of the fittest, and opportunism and power, and then proclaims the need for us to all get along and live in a world of respect, law and order, and freedom.

So, which is it? And why would an atheist even wish for a world of principles? After all, what does it matter? Why does *anything* matter? Atheism *must* lead to the get-it-while-you-can approach to everything. Let those religious fools build society for us if they want to. I'll just grab the money, sexual thrills, and toys that you've made it so easy for me to take while I'm here.

For atheists, this internal contradiction is the sand in their oil, the annoying pebble in their shoe, the *Harry Potter* Lego set that's missing a piece so you have to borrow pieces from the *Star Wars* Legos set (I have young children; trust me, it's annoying).

They want to believe in their way of understanding the world, but their minds tell them they don't want to live in it. It's cognitive dissonance, on steroids.

Either live as an atheist or do not. But you cannot receive the civilizational benefits Christendom and Judaism has given us over thousands of years, and then proclaim them as virtues of atheism. They are two radically opposite and competing ideologies.[10]

Atheism ultimately must lead to the evisceration of all distinctions and purpose, and the destruction of the pillars of society itself. And you don't need to look far for proof: wherever and whenever governments actually have adopted atheism, it has left only bodies floating face down in the river, indistinguishable from the trash and dead leaves floating with them. As we show later, the *primary core* of the vicious godless ideologies (communism and fascism) was the rejection of God.

Next, the atheist will proudly distinguish himself from the passionate zeal of the religious. He just wants to get along and not hurt anyone, he'll tell you. That sounds nice. But the fact that the atheist doesn't have passion enough to fight for his beliefs is *not* a good thing. In fact, it's part of the problem. The enemies of Western civilization—authoritarianism, radical Islam—are full of passion for our destruction. You may be interested in tolerating them, but it turns out they're not so interested in tolerating you. Better get ready to fight back with something stronger than your vanilla latte.

We need to appreciate what built civilization in the first place. We need to see that choosing God is not only a philosophical preference, like deciding which Beatles album was truly the best. God should be a complete and integrating force in our lives, so much so that every facet of what we do incorporates Him. And just attending church more often will not be enough.

I'm not talking about creating a theocracy. Far from it: state-run religions actually tend to push people away from God (compare Europe with its former state religions to America with no state religion; America remains far more religious). I am talking about our individual, personal devotion to God. Throughout America's founding and even through the early 1960s, not going to church or synagogue and working on Sundays were anathemas to who we were as Americans. In most American towns churches were literally the center of their communities, where people engaged in social functions, sought out and gave charity, and worked out their problems.

This is what we need to reteach and relearn. It starts in our families—then in our neighborhoods and, yes, in our schools. In fact, we need to speak of God *as a fact*—as real as numbers, Shakespeare, or American history.

Shocked? Don't be: What we do today, compartmentalizing God only to Saturday or Sunday mornings (if that), is the *oddity* in Western civilization's history, not the norm.

But God is not something you do when you get around to it, like cleaning out your roof gutters. If you know God, you know that God is in everything, and He permeates every aspect of your life. When you delve into it, you must come to this conclusion: Either God is everywhere and in everything we do, or He is not. There is no in-between. And you need to come to this other conclusion: whenever the world rejected God, it didn't turn out well.

Our society is slowly marginalizing God out Himself, even demonizing Him. The goal seems to be to push Him out altogether.

We must resist. Godlessness is the one overarching force that will tear the fabric of our society, because God *is* the foundation of who and what we are as a society—whether we like that or not.

Godlessness kills. It kills not only those who disagree with an all-encompassing "utopian" agenda, but it kills in almost every other way: It kills the distinctions that make up civilization itself. It kills the notion of freedom, truth and justice. It even kills our sense of a past and future.

It not only kills from the outside, but it acts like leprosy and cancer, rotting anyone who adopts it from the inside. It kills the one's sense of creativity, purpose, beauty, passion, compassion, and courage. It even kills the notion of the individual and free will.

The evidence is too strong to come to any other conclusion: Atheism is amoral, immoral, soulless and cruel. Atheism has never nourished a soul, never created anything of value, and as a government ideology has never resulted in anything other than devastation and tyranny. And perhaps most concerning for the present civilized world, it creates an environment of crippling passivity in the face of danger.

This book pursues one mission: to sound the alarm of godlessness, and to chart a course toward God. Lack of belief in God is our greatest danger. Nazism, Communism, and radical Islam were and are just some of the fires of evil that atheism both creates and enables.

There will be more fires of evil to come. But just as with any fire, if we don't have fire stations and structural procedures to fight it, the fire will consume us. An effort to understand the fire, consider the fire's feelings, "be one" with the fire, or hope that the fire will see the errors of its ways, will not be enough.

We have no choice. We must return to God.

CHAPTER I

THE NOT VERY GOOD, THE PRETTY BAD AND THE REALLY, REALLY UGLY

Five Stories

His wife was seven months pregnant with their second child when the group of thugs barged into his home and took her away. He followed them to the local hospital, where—despite his pleadings—they jammed a needle into her belly.[1]

"They grabbed my wife's body like they were grabbing a pig, four or five people holding her hands and legs and head, and injected a shot into her belly," the man said.

Ten hours later, she gave birth to a boy, wriggling and faintly crying. But the doctors in southern Hunan province would not even let her hold the dying infant, the husband said. They put the baby in a plastic bag and instructed him to pay a cleaner a small sum to bury it on a nearby hill.

The incident happened in 2011, in the Internet age and when China was walking openly and proudly on the global stage as a major power.

The story is hardly unique: In 2005, farmers in the city of Linyi, China, told the Washington Post that local authorities raided the homes of families with two children and demanded that at least one parent be sterilized. Pregnant women who already had two children were rounded up for abortions. If people tried to hide, their relatives ended up in jail.

"My aunts, uncles, cousins, my pregnant younger sister, my in-laws, they were all taken to the family planning office," one woman who was pregnant at the time said. "Many of them didn't get food or water, and all of them were severely beaten."[2] Eventually the authorities forced an abortion of this woman's fetus. Then they sterilized her, too. Often, staff members with little or no medical training carried out such operations, leading to numerous complications.

In 2012, authorities dragged a pregnant woman to a hospital in Shaanxi province and performed an abortion on her because she could not pay the $6,300 fine for having a second child. After social media posted photos of the mother—who was also seven months pregnant—on a hospital bed holding the corpse of her child, the woman's husband eventually received about $785 as compensation.

Although the government never officially endorsed and even prohibited them, forced abortions and compulsory sterilization had been an integral part of China's one-child policy since the 1980s. Local and provincial officials implementing the policy would do anything to keep the birthrate low, which they saw as a path to a promotion.

One woman with two daughters fled her home to avoid discovery of her pregnancy. When the "family-planning" team arrived at her house, they found only the woman's 80-year-old mother. They tore down the dwelling, destroyed the furniture and ruined the food, "The house vanished in just 20 minutes," the man said.

"I told the official in charge, 'This is too ruthless.'

The official replied with two simple words: 'It's policy.'"[3]

∽

In July, 2017, 31-year-old Jamel Dunn, a disabled man who had to walk with a cane, found himself submerged in a pond near his family's Florida home. He was struggling to stay afloat, just minutes from drowning.

But he was not alone. He looked over and saw a group of five Florida teens on the shore. He yelled out for the boys to help him.

Did the boys call 911? Did the boys jump in the pond to help? Did they scramble to find rope or a long stick for him to grab so that they could pull him to the shore?

No. They took out a smartphone and videoed the entire event, hoping to capture the man's actual drowning. In fact, during the more than two-minute long video, one can hear the five boys laughing as the man struggled to stay afloat. The teens told the man gleefully that he was "going to die" and they were not going to help him. At one point, one of the teen boys said mockingly: "he dead."

Dunn's sister eventually received the video, and she expressed her outrage about it on social media: "If they can sit there and watch somebody die in front of their eyes, imagine what they're going to do when they get older. Where's the morals?" she asked.

As Cocoa Police Department spokeswoman Yvonne Martinez told CNN: "The family is frustrated ... the detectives are frustrated, that we cannot hold anyone accountable for this," Martinez added. "No one deserves to go like that."[4]

∽

Marc Lépine was born Gamil Gharbi, the son of an Algerian Muslim. In 1989, Lépine walked into an engineering class at L'École Polytechnique at the University of Montréal, armed with a semi-automatic rifle and a hunting knife. He shot into at the ceiling and commandeered the class. Then he separated the men from the women. He told the men to leave.[5]

The male students complied, moving away quickly. The men remaining standing in the corridor, just outside the classroom. Even as they heard the first shots and screams and pleading from inside the classroom they had just left, they did nothing. There appears to be no evidence that the men even talked among themselves as to what they might do to stop the horror.

It would seem to last forever. The gunman killed the women one at a time, methodically, until they were all dead. It wasn't quick: he had taken his time between each kill, shooting from left to right. Once that was over, he wrote the word "shit" twice on a nearby student project he saw. Then Lépine walked out of the room and passed the men. As he went by, the men again did and said nothing.

The gunman then moved easily and without any confrontation through the building's corridors and other classrooms, finding more students, specifically targeting women. At one point he reached the cafeteria, in which about a hundred people had gathered. The crowd scattered after he shot a woman standing near the kitchen and wounded another student. Lépine shot and killed two more women hiding in an unlocked storage nearby.

As he continued his slow rampage, students and faculty hid in classrooms and dove under desks. At one point Lépine changed the magazine in his weapon and moved to the front of a classroom, shooting in all directions. At this point, a wounded student asked for help; Lépine unsheathed his hunting knife and stabbed her three times, killing her. He then exclaimed,

"Ah shit," took off a cap he was wearing, and then shot himself in the head.

In the twenty minutes which had elapsed, Lépine had killed fourteen women and injured another ten. He had also hurt four men in crossfire. No one had even tried to rush the murderer, thrown anything at him to hurt or distract him, or even yelled at him.

Even though police forces had rushed to the building and surrounded it for much of the killing spree, they had never gone in during the interminably slow melee. Many women died during the time the police were outside. Another tragedy: after briefing reporters outside, the Montreal Police director of public relations entered the building only to find his own daughter's stabbed body.

One can only imagine it now: the screams echoing loudly outside just before the murder of each new female victim, crying for mercy from the gunman, and for help from anyone who might hear them. They would be the kind of screams that would haunt anyone who survived for decades after: several students who had been present at the time of the massacre committed suicide themselves. At least two of those had left notes confirming that they committed suicide because of the overpowering distress the massacre had caused them.

The killing spree was horrific enough. But a separate horror apparently stayed with many of the survivors: that no one—not the men in the hallway nor the police outside—did anything. It seemed they had no idea what to do.

It was as if they had never received an instruction manual.

Toward the end of World War II, in January 1945, Master Sgt. Roddie Edmonds seemed like any other ordinary American soldier. The Germans had captured him, along with thousands of other Americans, during the Battle of the Bulge in late 1944. He and his men were now languishing at the Stalag IX-A POW camp near Ziegenhain, Germany.

The Wehrmacht had a strict anti-Jew policy and segregated Jewish POWs from non-Jews. On the eastern front, Germans had sent captured Jewish soldiers in the Russian army directly to extermination camps.

At the time of Edmonds' capture, the most infamous Nazi death camps were no longer fully operational, so Jewish American POWs were instead sent to slave labor camps where their chances of survival were low. Commanders had warned U.S. soldiers that Jewish fighters among them would be in danger if the Germans captured them, and told them to destroy dog tags or any other evidence that might identify them as Jewish.[6]

One evening at the camp, the German POW camp commander ordered the U.S. soldiers to present all the Jews among them early the next morning, and to have them fall out in line.

Edmonds knew what was at stake. He would have none of it. He gathered every one of the other POWs in the bunks together. A committed Christian, he had no doubt of what he would do. Huddling his men that night in the barracks, he told them in no uncertain terms that they were not going to let only the Jews fall out the next morning. Instead, as he ordered, "we are all falling out."

The next morning, true to Edmond's instructions, every single one of the POWs fell out in formation for the camp commander, as Jews.

The German commander arrived punctually. He did not like what he saw. "With all the camp's inmates defiantly standing in front of their barracks, the German commander turned to Edmonds and said: 'They cannot all be Jews.'"[7]

Edmonds replied with the words that every soldier there would remember for decades after the war: "We are all Jews here."

The Nazi officer would have none of it. He whipped out his German Lugar pistol and pressed it firmly to Edmonds head, giving him one final chance. But Edmonds only gave his name, rank and serial number, just as the Geneva Conventions required.

The tense standoff continued, with the German commander's pistol still pressed on Edmonds' temple. The commander now gave him seconds to comply.

Finally, Edmonds said, clearly and calmly: "If you are going to shoot, you are going to have to shoot all of us because we know who you are and you'll be tried for war crimes when we win this war."[8]

The German commander slowly dropped his Lugar. He then withdrew and never again pushed to separate the Jewish soldiers. They stayed in the POW camp with the others until the end of the war.

By this act, Edmonds saved the lives of more than two hundred Jewish-American soldiers. For Edmonds, it was just his duty. He hadn't even thought to repeat the story to his own family. It's a story that his son, the Rev. Chris Edmonds, discovered years after his father's death in 1985, when one Jewish soldier witness after another mentioned it to him, almost in passing.

Israel later designated him one of the coveted "Righteous Gentiles" of the world. As of the writing of this book, Congress has nominated him for the Congressional Medal of Honor.[9]

It was August, 2014, when Islamic State militia (also known as ISIS) descended upon the Yazidis in Northern Iraq. Everyone fled to the mountain, but the militants captured Peral,[10] twenty-one years old, from Kojo, Sinjar, among more than five thousand other Yazidi women. The fighters told them all to stay in the village where they would be safe, but the fighters in fact were going to sell them into sexual slavery.

Before that, the militants had forced her and the others to watch as they murdered the rest of their families. "While many remain in the evil clutches of ISIS, some have managed to escape to relay horrific tales of abuse, rape, slavery and brutal torture. In some cases, young women returned home carrying the unborn children of their captors."[11] Peral would not be one of them.

They soon took her to Syria by bus with around four hundred other girls. She did not know what village she arrived at, only that she was soon standing on an auction block.

The man who chose Peral was a very angry man. Soon after taking her, he beat her and threatened to shoot her. He took her to a farm where she and others barely ate for eight days.

She was sold again and again. Her last captors forced her into an underground location, where ISIS fighters were to rape her and many others multiple times a day, for months on end.

One day, she managed to grab a cell phone one of her captors had inadvertently left behind, after he had raped her. She looked around, terrified. But the risk was worth it. She picked up the cell phone and dialed in desperation to reach a friend.

Miraculously, she did. She told her friend her horrific story. "Track this location, and just kill us all," she pleaded. "If you know where we are, please bomb us... There is no life after this. I'm going to kill myself anyway—others have killed themselves this morning."

She said her captors wouldn't even let her go to the toilet. "Please do something," she said. "I've been raped 30 times today and it's not even lunchtime."[12]

Each of these stories will play out in some way throughout this book. They are anecdotes that reflect the dangers and emptiness of atheism on the one hand and the need for God on the other. For godlessness offers only chaos and, in the process, unwinds all the distinctions we have developed throughout the millennia that have shaped our civilization—the most important being the distinction between good and evil.

Worse yet, it is an ideology that leads inescapably to either an annihilation of all those who think differently or, at the very best, passively allows evil through the door. Why? Because by definition, atheism doesn't even recognize evil as "evil." And in so doing, that passivity helps evil grow. The only thing to save our civilization is a truly abiding belief in a God who demands goodness and justice among us, based on one guiding and clear moral set of standards. Without that, we can expect only destruction of all we have created and hold dear. And without God, as I will discuss later, there can be no wisdom. Without God, there can be no justice.

The atheist will insist otherwise: he will say we don't need God to be good. He will say he doesn't need God to recognize evil. But to say that is intellectually dishonest to the very premise of everything he believes: that there is no meaning to life itself, that everything is random, and that good and evil are merely phantom structures that society creates to keep everyone in line.

In my atheist days, I knew that in a world where everything is the result of mere randomness, the happenstance occurrence of atoms colliding with each other with no guiding principal, then no one event was "better" or "superior" than another. It would be like saying this or that action in a jungle, such as the swaying of a monkey or a leaf falling from a tree or a bug burrowing into the ground, is better than other actions that might be happening in the jungle. The jungle is the jungle, where things just happen—not good nor evil.

And likewise, in a random world, an occurrence of violent rape would be no different than the petting of a dog or the picking of a flower. All events and actions are "equal." In a world where everything stems merely from randomness, then we might as well view everything in the here and now as random, too. All choices are possible and all choices are acceptable. If that is the case, then do whatever you want in the service of your agenda. If that means killing, enslaving, or imprisoning those who disagree with you or who are weaker than you, well then . . . you do what you need to do.

It is not only that we are living in troubled times, with this or that feckless leader at the helm, and that's why we have so many problems with evil. This suggests that somehow all we need to do is elect the correct political leaders, who will be bright and savvy about how best to navigate us through the storms to a perfect economy and to perfect diplomacy with our enemies.

Here's the problem: We will never be able to fight evil without God. Only with God in our lives can we have true virtue, true compassion, true courage, and true justice. We fool ourselves if we think that a world without God can somehow remain sensible, civilized, or compassionate, let alone continue to blossom and progress. None of that can occur with atheism. But godlessness is growing.

All that atheism can offer is the gradual but inevitable descent into mayhem or, at best, the orderly chipping away of innovation, freedom, and justice. That is it. Any notion that a godless individual, much less a godless government, will somehow always know to do the "right" thing fails to realize that whatever sense he has of what is right actually has grown out of a moral code that the Judeo-Christian ethic created. He is like our student helicopter pilot in the beginning of this book, who thinks he no longer needs the helicopter blades anymore.

History and our present times should show us that God is no longer a quaint choice of belief that may give us a nice communal feeling. God is in fact a necessity if we ever hope for true human growth, if we ever hope to continue our escape from the chaos and evil of Sodom and Gomorrah.

We have talked of the inherent evils of atheism. We have proclaimed that atheism kills. Now let us show you, by the numbers.

Murder by the Numbers

Because murder is like anything you take to
It's a habit-forming need for more and more
You can bump off every member of your family
And anybody else you find a bore

...

It's murder by numbers, one, two, three
It's as easy to learn as your ABC's

...

Now you can join the ranks of the illustrious
In history's great dark hall of fame.
All our greatest killers were industrious
At least the ones that we all know by name.

— *The Police, "Murder by Numbers"*
from Synchronicity (A&M 1983)

"Religion has caused far more deaths than anything else."

Many people have trotted this phrase out as the major basis for rejecting any notion of a God. When I was an atheist, it was the first thing I threw at any believer in God. When I did, I was able to dismiss religion for the clear hypocrisy it was. There was the Inquisition and the Crusades, after all.

So many, many people killed. It was all so very wrong. Wouldn't the world be better off without religion? You know, like in that John Lennon song.

In my former atheist view, it was the end of all argument on the matter. You could almost hear the door closing on the subject; thank you for coming. We're done. Next subject, please.

It's one of those refrains people repeat so often that we begin to believe it must be true.

But is it? Like Colombo, that somewhat unkempt but annoyingly persistent crime detective of the TV series from the seventies, we begin to leave the room, but then turn around and feign a puzzled look: "But there's just one thing . . . ." In this case, only one exception.

The exception is a period of history people commonly refer to as the twentieth century. You'll see in a moment.

But first some history on atheism. While the ideology of atheism always existed, atheism didn't really gain traction meaningfully as a fashionable philosophical currency among the intellectuals until the late nineteenth century. It started among European academicians, where nihilism as an intellectual philosophy took hold. It then expanded beyond universities to the point that people began to think governments should embrace it.

Communism took hold—a devoutly godless approach to government. Where previous dictators or leaders themselves had held varying intensities in their devotions to God—some paid homage to faith only to cynically placate their masses (numerous French kings, Constantine) and others truly believed (Washington and the other founding fathers, Abraham Lincoln)—here came a new government, one that rejected God as the anchoring center of civil life.

In communism, atheism became one of the central tenets of its offering: God was out of the picture, no longer relevant. In fact, He had now become an *impediment* to humankind's advancement. Man was now finally to assume full responsibility for himself, and leave the human race's silly and destructive past once and for all.

Everyone could share in the production and reap benefits from it collectively. And everyone was to go along with the game plan. In fact, you had better go along, or the government would find a way to "disappear" you. But it would all be good and necessary when you think of the Big Picture. After all, when you are about to replace the entire edifice of humankind, there might be those who complain. And naturally drastic resolutions require drastic steps.

Atheism had grown from a seed of an idea that people talked about in abstract, arm-chair philosopher ways in their living rooms and faculty lounges. It then morphed into the large tree that was now going to provide nourishing fruit to the masses. Atheism was ready to take center stage.

Like an adolescent, however, it thought it knew everything. And like an adolescent whose parents gave him the car keys, the adolescent felt invincible; he was sure nothing could go wrong.

The communism wave spread, bringing the *essential component of atheism* with it. Eventually, communism gobbled up Russia and Eastern Europe then spread into China, North Korea, Vietnam, and Cuba. To ensure that no one would worship any gods before it, communism banned the practicing of any religion, particularly Judaism and Christianity.

Then came communism's less-obnoxious child, socialism, which also sought to mandate the equalizing of society and minimizing success through taxation and regulation as did communism, only without all that killing—communism with a happy face, if you will.

But the diminishing of God remained. After all, the more one looks to the state for structure, the less one needs God for that structure—and even more so as the notion of the right to welfare and other entitlements grew. After all, the *state* is now providing, not God. Where once it was churches and synagogues that routinely assumed the responsibility for the poor and those who might otherwise suffer dire straits, the state took over.

And it took over so thoroughly that it was soon difficult to imagine how society could survive without the state. The church still assumed its helpful and charitable role, but from the common citizen's point of view, that work seemed less significant. It became quaint. Some people still liked the idea of the state handling all their lives.

And in the process, they strained God out. He was not necessary to the general plan. In fact, He was the proverbial fly in the ointment. Man knows what we need for our daily existence. Allowing a God-centered paradigm is a danger to the main "command and control" plans of socialism.

And so communism—and fascism—set about on its mission to make God disappear. But in its process of doing so, it diminished freedom, justice, and the individual. Soon enough, it would embark upon the greatest murder spree history had ever seen. Butchery, murder, torture, enslavement, theft, rape and every other degradation and humiliation became routine and acceptable tools.

With that history, let's now return to address the atheist's charge that Judaism and Christianity has killed more than anything else. Since the charge is ultimately a question of history and math, let's first add up the killings of major atheist movements, governments and leaders. We'll then compare them to those of Judaism and Christianity and their leaders.

The Atheist Killings

The French Revolution and the Reign of Terror

Unlike the American Revolution, where the colonists fought for freedom and rights which they believed God had bestowed upon every man, the French Revolution stemmed in large part from a *rejection* of religion altogether. And atheism had gained currency and respect, thanks to the great *philosophies* of the Enlightenment and the Age of Reason, particularly Voltaire.

By the time the French Revolution began in 1789, the Catholic Church had already began reforming its excesses, including changing property holdings and clerical control of French society. Two years earlier, King Louis XVI had signed The Edict of Versailles, which gave non-Catholics in France the right to practice their religions as well as give legal and civil status.[13]

But this was not enough to appease the anti-clerical sentiment, which had festered and grown for decades before. During a two-year period known as the Reign of Terror, the episodes of anti-clericalism grew more violent than any in modern European history. The new revolutionary authorities abolished the Catholic monarchy; nationalized church property; exiled 30,000 priests and killed hundreds more. In October 1793, the new government replaced the Christian calendar with one which started from the date of the Revolution. New forms of "moral" religion emerged, including the deistic Cult of the Supreme Being and Cult of Reason.[14] The revolutionary government briefly mandated observance of the former in 1794.

It became known as the De-Christianization of France, and the new government first waged it against Catholicism, and then against all forms of Christianity. It included destruction of statues, crosses, bells and other signs of worship. In October 1793, the government enacted a law making all nonjuring priests and all persons who harbored them liable to death on sight.[15]

In August 1789, the State declared that all church property in France belonged to the nation, and ordered confiscation and sale of church properties at public auction. In July 1790, the National Constituent Assembly published the Civil Constitution of the Clergy, which stripped clerics of their special rights—the clergy were to become employees of the state. All priests and bishops were to swear an oath of fidelity to the new order or face dismissal, deportation or death.[16]

As the population viewed the Church more and more as a counter-revolutionary force, this exacerbated the social and economic grievances. Soon violence erupted in towns and cities across France. In Paris, over a two-day period beginning on September 2, 1792, the new Legislative Assembly dissolved into chaos, and angry mobs massacred three Church bishops and more than two hundred priests, later known as part of the September Massacres.[17] Authorities ordered mass drownings (*noyades*) and other mass executions in Nantes and Lyon for not consistently supporting the revolution, or if they suspected anyone of being a royalist. These executions affected priests and nuns the most.[18] Hundreds more priests went to prison.

The Legislative Assembly and its successor, the National Convention, passed anti-Church laws throughout the country. Many of the acts of de-Christianization in 1793 were motivated by the seizure of church gold and silver to finance the war effort. In November 1793, the *département council* of Indre-et-Loire even abolished the word *dimanche* (Sunday).

The Assembly also replaced the Gregorian calendar, an instrument Pope Gregory XIII had established in 1582, with a new French Republican Calendar which abolished the Sabbath, saints' days and any references to the Church. The seven-day week became ten days instead. (After difficulties in coordinating relations with other countries and what should probably have been a not-so-surprising national disdain of a longer work week, the authorities decided to re-implement the Gregorian Calendar in 1795.)[19]

The new authority held anti-clerical parades, and the Archbishop of Paris, Jean-Baptiste-Joseph Gobel, was forced to resign his duties and made to replace his mitre with the red "Cap of Liberty." Townships replaced street and place names with any sort of religious connotation to secular names. Religious holidays were banned and replaced with holidays to celebrate the harvest and other non-religious symbols. Many churches were converted into "temples of reason," holding Deistic services.[20]

While Maximilien Robespierre and the Committee of Public Safety denounced the de-Christianizers as foreign enemies of the Revolution, they nevertheless established their own new religion, the Cult of the Supreme Being. This new religion was supposed to supplant the "superstitions" of Catholicism, and the rival Cult of Reason. In June, 1794 the still-powerful Robespierre personally led a vast procession through Paris to the Tuileries garden in a ceremony to inaugurate the new faith. His execution occurred shortly afterward, on July 28, 1794.[21]

As late as 1799, France was still imprisoning priests or deporting them to penal colonies. Persecution only worsened after the French army captured Rome in early 1798, declared a new Roman Republic, and imprisoned Pope Pius VI, who would die in captivity in France in August, 1799. This changed once Napoleon rose in power, after which year-long negotiations between government officials and the new Pope Pius VII led to the Concordat of 1801, formally ending the de-Christianization period.[22]

In the end, victims of the Reign of Terror totaled somewhere between 20,000 and 40,000. While most everyone suffered, it proportionally impacted the clergy of the Roman Catholic Church the greatest.[23] Under threat of death, imprisonment, military conscription, and loss of income, about 20,000 priests were forced to abdicate and hand over their letters of ordination, and up to 9,000 of them agreed or were coerced to marry.[24]

By the end of the decade, approximately 30,000 priests had been forced to leave France, and others who did not leave were executed.[25] Any non-juring priest faced the guillotine or deportation to French Guiana.[26] By 1794, few of France's 40,000 churches remained open; the government or the mobs had closed, sold, destroyed, or converted them all to other uses.[27]

The deadly Reign of Terror ended, but it would forever subdue religion in France. Contrasting the American and French revolutions, founding father of the American Revolution Alexander Hamilton noted the abandonment of religion as a core reason for the horror that had gripped France. As he saw it, France had abandoned religion, in favor of "a gloomy, persecuting and desolating atheism."[28] The French were "...spreading ruin and devastation far and wide—subverting the foundations of right security and property, of order, morality and religion[,] sparing neither sex nor age, confounding innocence with guilt, involving the old and the young, the sage and the madman."[29]

Hamilton was prescient. As the world was to soon discover in even more horrific fashion only a few decades later, it's what atheism does best.

Stalin

At least 20 million died because of Stalin's quest for world communism, and the higher end might be much more than even that. During WWII his tactics led to the deaths of about 8 million of his own soldiers. Additionally, his armies killed about 2.8 million German, Hungarian, Romanian, and Finnish troops. Stalin's policies meant no mercy to prisoners, and large numbers died after being taken captive during the war.[30]

Following WWII, Stalin instigated a policy of terror on the German people. This led to about 2 million German civilians being murdered outright and thousands more committing suicide. Stalin enforced brutal police states on all the peoples of eastern Europe. Tens of thousands died in these takeovers. German POWs were kept in horrible conditions for as long as ten years after the war, leading to the deaths of at least 1 million.[31] The horror doesn't stop with brutal killings; the Russians conquered Berlin in 1945 and then proceeded to engage in a mass rape of up to 2 million women.[32] According to historian William Hitchcock, in many cases women were the victims of repeated rapes, some as many as 60 to 70 times. At least 100,000 women are believed to have been raped in Berlin alone, with 10,000 women dying as a result.[33]

Antony Beevor describes it as the "greatest phenomenon of mass rape in history," and has determined that Russians raped another approximately 1.5 million women in parts of Prussia and Poland alone.

When a Yugoslav politician complained to Stalin about the horrible rapes in his country, Stalin responded that it was understandable "if a soldier who has crossed thousands of kilometres through blood and fire and death has fun with a woman or takes some trifle."[34] To another who complained about the Red Army sexually abusing German refugees, Stalin reportedly said: "We lecture our soldiers too much; let them have their initiative."[35]

Stalin didn't just inflict his wrath on the Germans. Before and after the war, Stalin executed nearly a million of his own citizens, beginning in the 1930s. He forced millions more into forced labor, deportation, famine, massacres, and detention and interrogation.[36]

"In some cases, a quota was established for the number to be executed, the number to be arrested," said Norman N. Naimark from his work *Stalin's Genocides*. "Some officials over-fulfilled as a way of showing their exuberance."[37]

Hitler and Stalin were both peas in a pod: Both destroyed the lives of millions in the name of a transformative vision of Utopia. "Both destroyed their countries and societies, as well as vast numbers of people inside and outside their own states. Both, in the end, were genocidaires."[38]

Accounts tend to gloss over the genocidal character of the Soviet regime in the 1930s, which killed systematically rather than from barbarity to barbarity. In the process of collectivization, for example, the Soviet regime killed 30,000 kulaks directly, mostly shot on the spot. They also forcibly deported about 2 million to the far North and Siberia.[39]

They were called "enemies of the people," as well as swine, dogs, cockroaches, scum, vermin, filth, garbage, half animals, apes. Activists promoted murderous slogans: "We will exile the kulak by the thousand when necessary—shoot the kulak breed." "We will make soap of kulaks." "Our class enemies must be wiped off the face of the earth."[40]

The destruction of the kulak class led soon enough to the Ukrainian famine. The Soviet Government manipulated circumstances to bring on a shortage of grain and bad harvests, which soon starved the Ukrainians.[41] Desperate Ukrainians ate leaves off bushes and trees, killed dogs, cats, frogs, mice and birds then cooked them. Others resorted to cannibalism, with reports of some parents even eating their own children.[42]

Meanwhile, nearby Soviet-controlled granaries remained full, containing huge stocks of grain, which would never ship out of the Ukraine. Farm animals, considered necessary for production, received food, while the people living among them received nothing.[43]

By the spring of 1933, the height of the famine, an estimated 25,000 persons died every day in the Ukraine. Soviet authorities halted all food shipments to help the Ukrainians from abroad at the border. The Soviet Union's policy was to deny the existence of a famine, and to refuse outside assistance. Inside the Soviet Union, just using the word "famine" or "starvation" in a sentence could lead to arrest.[44]

Meanwhile, the Soviets made "useful idiots" out of the foreign press and international celebrities who visited through carefully arranged tours and photo opportunities. It worked: the writer George Bernard Shaw and other British socialites returned very impressed about the modern Kiev the Soviets had staged for them. French Premier Edouard Herriot even declared there was no famine. Walter Duranty of the New York Times sent a dispatch stating ". . . all talk of famine now is ridiculous."[45]

By the end of 1933, nearly 25 percent of the population of the Ukraine, including three million children, had perished as a result of the unique utopian vision of Soviet communism.[46]

Records are scant, and no one will ever know how many people Stalin killed. We know only that his brutal quest for power resulted in the deaths of multiple millions. The median estimates among historians is 30 million.[47]

Marxist–Leninist atheism was an integral part of the wider Marxism–Leninism philosophy which was at its core irreligious and anti-clerical, while at the same time advocating a materialist understanding of nature.[48]

Like Marx and Lenin, Stalin was an avowed atheist, leading an atheist regime and implementing an atheist ideology.[49]

Mao

What about Mao? Maybe he was that peaceful atheist we hope for.

Alas, no. Mao Zedong's policies caused the deaths of tens of millions of people in China during his twenty-seven-year reign, more than any other 20th century leader. Historians estimate his regime killed between 40 million to as many as 70 million.[50] He did so through executions, starvation, and prison labor.[51]

The Chinese Communist Party came to power in China in 1949. Mao was a devout Marxist and considered violence the only means necessary to achieve an ideal society. To that end, he planned and executed violence on a grand scale.[52]

The first large-scale killings under Mao took place during land reform and the counterrevolutionary campaign. Mao himself envisaged that "one-tenth of the peasants" (or about 50,000,000) "would have to be destroyed" to facilitate his reform.[53]

Benjamin Valentino says that Mao's "Great Leap Forward" was a key cause of the Great Chinese Famine and that Mao purposefully steered the worst effects of the famine towards the regime's enemies.[54] Mao also gave his Red Guards carte blanche to abuse and kill the revolution's enemies as they saw fit to achieve his Marxist vision.[55] Those the regime labeled "black elements" (religious leaders, conservatives, or anyone "rich") died in the greatest numbers, as the regime rationed them the least amount of food.[56] In a secret meeting at Shanghai in 1959, Mao ordered the confiscation of one-third of all grain from the countryside. He said: "It is better to let half of the people die so that the other half can eat their fill."[57]

Later, in the 1960s, Mao launched The Great Proletarian Cultural Revolution. Through this, Mao hoped to consolidate his power. The government targeted all professionals – doctors, teachers, lawyers—in a great purge of the middle classes. It even killed millions of pet cats, because the communist party saw them as dalliances of the bourgeois.[58]

It viewed anyone who might have expressed an interest in fashion or literature as a traitor. Friends, neighbors and even family members denounced each other and turned each other in, guilty or not. The Red Guard militia would recruit children to help do this dirty work.[59]

During this time of almost a decade, China plunged into a hell of murder, rape and torture. Horrifically, the party actually initiated a cannibalism drive. The purpose? To purge any trace of the bourgeoisie. At one school in the south, students beat their geography teacher to death, then forced another teacher to rip out his heart and liver, which the pupils then barbecued and ate. Such cannibalism was more frequent than one might imagine: as China expert Frank Dikotter explained: "It was about not just eliminating your class enemy, but devouring him."[60]

The purge was prolific and creative: executions included beheadings, boilings, live burials, stonings, drownings and disembowelings. In Dao County alone, the government eliminated thousands by driving people over cliffs to plunge to their deaths. They made sure to include children, since the children might seek to avenge their family's deaths later, so it was considered the better part of discretion to wipe out the family line. Soldiers also marched millions to the countryside after they finished school, some of whom were girls as young as fourteen. Thousands of young girls were left at the mercy of villagers, who then raped them.[61] All in, the Cultural Revolution alone killed 2 million more people.[62]

Mao and the Chinese communist party rejected all forms of religion, opting for the atheistic socialism of Marxism-Leninism, which viewed religion as the "opiate of the masses."[63] Still, Mao had no problem if people treated *him* as a god. With the help of the People's Liberation Army, Mao helped established just that. All Chinese were to read the Quotations of Chairman Mao (known as Mao's Little Red Book), and the government elevated Mao's writings to an infallible philosophical system called "Mao Zedong Thought."[64] Children and everyone else would chant a poem: "The East is red and the sun rises; in China there emerges Mao Tse-tung."

Even today, decades after his death, ordinary Chinese revere him as a god, even bigger than Jesus.[65] Even the present regime tries to temper the people's desire to view him as a deity.[66]

Fidel Castro

The world seems to view Fidel Castro like a kindly uncle; even a Santa Claus, *sans* the reindeer. It is unclear why; it might have been because of his apparent successful defiance of his much larger and far more powerful foe to the north, the United States. But both the media and history seem to have given a pass to this brutal dictator, more than the other ruthless (particularly communist) dictators. Many media outlets and American celebrities seem to revere this man.

After years as a political revolutionary, Castro and his forces mounted a series of successful military campaigns in 1958 to capture key areas throughout Cuba. Castro's efforts finally led to the collapse of Batista's government. A new government formed, which the United States recognized quickly, and Castro himself arrived in Havana to cheering crowds and assumed the post of commander-in-chief of the military. In February 1959, Castro became prime minister.[67]

Castro then implemented far-reaching reforms by nationalizing factories and plantations in an attempt to end U.S. economic dominance on the island.

Although Castro repeatedly denied being a communist, his policies looked like Soviet-style control of the economy and government. He soon limited the size of land holdings and forbade foreigners from owning property. By the end of 1959, Castro's revolution radicalized, with purges of military leaders and suppression of media critical of Castro's policies.[68]

Many supporters point to how Castro opened 10,000 new schools and increased literacy to 98 percent, and provided universal health-care system. But civil liberties whittled away, as the government took away labor unions' right to strike, shut down newspapers, and harassed religious institutions.[69]

Many others lost their lives fighting for and against Castro. Some drowned trying to leave Cuba. The exact body count is elusive, but credible estimates range from 35,000 to 141,000. But experts of Castro's revolution know this much: During his nearly five decades in power, the toll kept mounting.[70]

Castro did not believe in God and considered religion to be "backward."[71] One of his apparent non-backward policies in the 1960s involved extracting most of the blood from his firing squad victims before they were shot, which he would then sell to other communist countries for $50 a pint.[72]

After the Cuban Revolution, Fidel Castro decreed Cuba an atheist state. He also exiled priests or sent them to "reeducation camps."[73]

Che Guevara

Castro may have been the darling of the intellectual left, but almost everyone seemed to love his sidekick, Che Guevara (Robin to Castro's Batman, if you like). After all, he looked cool, what with his apparent youth and impish long hair. Pictures of him portrayed a man of seriousness and purpose, too. He was handsome and projected confidence and charisma. And he was one of those "bad boys" women just can't resist.

When I was in college, posters of him adorned dorm rooms and kiosks everywhere. That famous two-toned Jim Fitzpatrick lithograph elevated Guevara to almost romantic status. The poster had him looking vaguely yet with apparent determination to some better future—exactly where was never clear but that's not important right now.

Guevara first met Castro in the mid 1950s in Mexico with other radical exiles from Cuba. Guevara then was instrumental in helping Castro seize power from Cuban dictator Batista in 1959 and later served as Castro's right-hand man. Guevara advocated peasant-based revolutions to combat social injustice in Third World countries. Castro later described him as "an artist of revolutionary warfare."[74]

Guevara resigned in April 1965, possibly over differences with Castro about the nation's economic and foreign policies. Guevara then left Cuba, traveled to Africa and eventually came back to South America in Bolivia, where the government there captured and killed him. Following his death, Guevara garnered the status of hero around the world, mostly as a symbol of revolution.[75]

Guevara was a devout atheist.[76] Among other things, he was accused of ordering the deaths of hundreds of people in Cuban prisons during the revolution.[77] It is difficult to know how many others he may have killed outside of Cuba. His writings reflect numerous "might makes right" venomous barbs against due process, freedom, imperialism and Christ.[78]

You might be thinking at this point that Che's sprees were a far cry from those of Stalin, Hitler, or Mao. But the fact that Guevara killed far fewer than Stalin, Hitler, and Mao does not convert him into a beloved public servant. In fact, using that calculus, you could declare Charles Manson (who killed fewer than ten people) a saint.

Che Guevara was still a killer, and a prolific one at that. He was an idealistic atheist, believing in the highest principles of a godless communism.

Ceaușescu

Nicolae Ceaușescu was the dictator who intrigues me the most. For over thirty years, Ceaușescu and his wife Elena turned Romania into a laboratory for fear, misery and poverty. Assuming power in 1965 after the death of his predecessor, Ceaușescu quickly consolidated power by neutralizing his political rivals in the Romanian Communist Party, and by reorganizing the structure of Romania's dreaded secret police organization (the infamous Securitate) into a tool capable of completely suppressing public political expression and dissent. He was just getting started.[79]

North Korea's dictator Kim Il-sung once paid a visit to Ceaușescu. Ceaușescu was so impressed with all of Kim's delightfully brutal teachings that he wanted to model himself accordingly. Soon, Ceaușescu embarked on the creation of a "his and hers" dictatorship by creating a personality cult consisting of himself and his wife Elena. He also pursued a policy of economic collectivization that transformed an already economically fragile nation into a poorhouse.[80] In addition to ruthless tactics to suppress dissent, he amassed staggering wealth for himself and his wife, living in opulent palaces beyond the imagination of any wealthy society.[81]

The Ceaușescus had required the media to refer to them with names such as "The Source of Our Light," "The Celestial Body," and "The Treasure of Wisdom and Charisma." They in turn welcomed and believed the flattery they themselves had commanded the press to write about them. It never occurred to them that the whole nation feared and detested them.[82]

In 1989, after rising economic discontent led to a public demonstration and uprising in the city of Timișoara, Ceaușescu ordered the Securitate and Romanian army to disperse the crowds and brutally punish the leaders of the demonstration. However, after returning from a state visit to Iran, Nicolae and

Elena Ceauşescu found out the demonstrations had spread to Bucharest, and that in their two-day absence, the leadership of the Securitate and Romanian army decided to shift their loyalties and launched a *coup d'etat*.

The dictator and his wife tried to flee by helicopter, but the new anti-Ceauşescu military stopped them. Then they tried to flee by car, but civilian police stopped them. The police apparently detained them in the back seat while listening to the radio to see if the anti-Ceauşescu coup would succeed.[83]

It did. Soon the "King and Queen" of Romania were facing an impromptu trial, lasting only one hour. Moments later, they found themselves facing the wrong side of a firing squad. The firing squad consisted of soldiers who had drawn straws to hopefully *get* the chance to shoot the Ceauşescus.[84] Hundreds of other soldiers had clamored for the opportunity, but most had missed out: it was almost as hard as getting tickets to see *Hamilton*.

The firing squad began shooting as soon as the two were in position against a wall. In the end, 120 bullets were found in the couple's bodies.[85]

Most intriguing was that even at the moment before their deaths, Nicolae and Elena Ceauşescu were flabbergasted—outraged, really—that anyone had questioned their benevolence, let alone that anyone would actually seek to *execute* them. They perceived themselves to their very last moments as truly generous leaders whose people still loved them. "Shame, shame on you," Elena Ceauşescu said to her executioners. "I brought you up as a mother." It was as if they thought their executioners were just spoiled ingrates.[86]

Like Stalin and virtually every communist before him, Ceauşescu was an atheist who imposed his atheistic vision throughout his reign. While he at first worked with the church for purposes of maintaining and manipulating power, he soon moved to squelch religious observance, arresting religious dissenters and demolishing churches as part of a "modernization" program, among other hostile steps against the religious.[87] Historians estimate he killed 5,000 during the 1989 revolution that eventually ousted him. He was responsible for thousands of more deaths each year during the 1980s from deprivations his programs caused. He ruined tens of thousands more lives during his reign.[88]

Marshall Josip Broz Tito

During his long rule (1945–87) the world seemed to like Marshall Tito's seemingly nice, renegade style of communism. Here was a man who carved out his own brand of communism. And he wouldn't let those Russians push *him* around, no sir.

The *New York Times* spoke lovingly of him, claiming that Tito sought to improve life and that "Yugoslavia gradually became a bright spot amid the general grayness of Eastern Europe."[89]

Perhaps what made him so appealing was his apparent resistance to Soviet expansionism, and that he resisted Stalin in particular. Indeed, when Stalin died on March 5 in 1953, authorities found in his office a letter from Tito, asking Stalin to "stop sending people to kill me."[90] One theory suggests that Tito actually poisoned Stalin. Needless to say, "The two leaders were bitter enemies, after Tito had used World War II as an opportunity to spark a revolution and lead Yugoslavia to independence from Soviet influence."[91] All in all, Stalin ordered attempted assassinations upon Tito at least twenty-two times.

But put aside the love for Tito's resistance, and you find the ruthless killer underneath:

The Communist machinery realized very early that their policy of "Tito-ization" would not work on the Croatians. They pounced on any rebels and, on August 10, 1941, President Josip

Broz Tito ordered that "provocateurs and traitors" must be liquidated immediately.[92]

Tito's secret police effectuated surgical assassinations as well, all aimed to scare other dissidents and emigres both at home and abroad.[93] Not surprisingly, like many communist leaders before and after him, Tito lived like a monarch, all the while proclaiming his dream for utopian communism for Yugoslavia.[94] In the process, he managed to kill half a million people, mainly "collaborators," "anti-communists," rival guerrillas, Ustashi, and general critics.[95]

Tito was an avowed communist and had no interest in God.[96]

Ho Chi Minh

Many assert that Ho Chi Minh of Vietnam was a "reasonable" communist, a seeker for true justice for his people—a reputation Minh manipulated for himself. His birth name was Nguyen Sinh Cung but he went by many pseudonyms including "Ho Chi Minh," or "Bringer of Light," among fifty other names during his lifetime.[97]

Ho Chi Minh's terror began as soon as he consolidated his power in the North. More than a year before his 1954 victory over the French, he had launched a savage campaign against his own people. In virtually every North Vietnamese village, strong-arm squads assembled the populace to witness the "confessions" of landowners. As time went on, businessmen, intellectuals, school teachers, civic leaders—all who represented a potential source of future opposition—were also rounded up and forced to "confess" to "errors of thought."

There followed public "trials," conviction and execution. His henchmen shot, beheaded, and beat people to death. They tied people up, threw them into open graves and covered them with stones until the stones crushed them to death.

Historians believe that between 50,000 and 100,000 people died in these bloodbaths—in a coldly calculated effort to discipline the party and the masses.

During his power grab in the North, "Uncle Ho" revealed that he was "in reality...a 'fascist with a human face.'" Ho massacred his countrymen by the thousands in a Soviet-style "land reform" campaign. When peasants in his home province protested in November 1956, his men descended upon the province, killing 6,000.[98]

During the 1950s, his men suppressed political opposition groups and imprisoned those publicly opposing the government in hard labor camps. His regime would lure many middle-class, intellectual northerners into speaking out against him, only to imprison or execute them in gulags. Political scientist R. J. Rummel suggests a figure of 24,000 camp deaths during Ho's rule of North Vietnam between 1945 and 1956.[99]

The government launched "rent reduction" and "land reform" programs, mostly to exterminate class enemies. Declassified Politburo documents confirm that about 1 in 1,000 North Vietnamese (i.e., about 14,000 people) were the minimum quota targeted for execution during the earlier "rent reduction" campaign; the number killed during the multiple stages of the considerably more radical "land reform" was probably many times greater.[100]

Communist cadres gave estimates that land reform executions resulted in 120,000 to 200,000 deaths. The full death toll was even greater because victims' families starved to death under the "policy of isolation." As communist defector Le Xuan Giao explained: "They isolated the house, and the people who lived there would starve... They wanted to see the whole family dead."[101]

As many as 500,000 North Vietnamese may have died because of Ho's policies.[102] And yes: Ho Chi Minh was an atheist, leading an atheist regime, advancing an atheist ideology.[103]

Pol Pot

"Pol Pot" was born in 1925 as Saloth Sar. His father was a prosperous farmer, and his family had connections to the royal family. In 1949, Pol Pot won a scholarship to study radio electronics in Paris. He failed to obtain a degree but immersed himself in Marxism and revolutionary socialism, bonding with other like-minded young Cambodians studying in Paris.[104]

The members of this so-called "Paris student group" became the leaders of the Khmer Rouge. Pol Pot returned to Cambodia to work for the Kampuchean People's Revolutionary Party (KPRP), the Cambodian communist party.[105]

After some political maneuvering, Pol Pot assumed power of the Khmer Rouge, a communist guerilla group, and took over Phnom Penh on April 17, 1975. Pol Pot erased the traditional calendar, decided that all prior history was irrelevant and, like during the Reign of Terror before him, reset time itself to "Year Zero."

He immediately directed a ruthless program to "purify" Cambodian society of capitalism, Western culture, religion and all foreign influences. He wanted to create an isolated and totally self-sufficient Maoist agrarian state. He killed anyone who opposed his vision. His regime expelled foreigners, closed embassies, and abolished the currency. It prohibited markets, schools, newspapers, religious practices and private property. It identified and executed public servants, police, military officers, teachers, ethnic Vietnamese, Christian clergy, Muslim leaders, members of the middle-class and the educated.[106]

During the almost four years of Pol Pot's rule, Cambodia lost 2 million Cambodians, or 30 percent of the country's population. Starvation, torture or execution were the primary causes. Almost every Cambodian family has lost at least one relative during this gruesome holocaust.[107]

Pol Pot's regime forced the country's entire population to relocate to agricultural labor camps, the so-called "killing fields." Former city residents received unending political indoctrination and brainwashing. The regime encouraged children to spy on adults, including their parents. Crimes punishable by death included not working hard enough, complaining about living conditions, collecting or stealing food for personal consumption, wearing jewelry, engaging in sexual relations, grieving over the loss of relatives or friends and expressing religious sentiments.[108]

Some historians and critics claim it is unclear on whether Pol Pot was an outspoken atheist. But under Pol Pot, the Khmer Rouge had a policy of state atheism. It banned all religions, and repressed adherents of Islam, Christianity, and Buddhism. The regime massacred nearly 25,000 Buddhist monks alone.[109] Not surprisingly, research reveals no meaningful suggestion that Pol Pot followed or respected any religion.

Kim Il-sung

From 1948 through 1987 the Democratic People's Republic of Korea suffered at the hands of Kim Il-sung, an absolute communist dictator who turned his country into an Orwellian state. His control was so tight that we have little information about the regime's purges, executions, and concentration and forced labor camps. But through defectors, escapees, agents, Korean War refugees, and analyses of Korean publications and documents, we know there was systematic democide.[110]

Jung Il ruled without mercy. North Korean troops advanced into South Korea during the Korean War, systematically massacring South Korean government officials, anti-communists, and anyone the communists deemed hostile to them. In addition to forcing POWs into military service, the North also forced 400,000 South Koreans into their army.[111]

Aside from the war (1.5 million civilians killed), North Korean domestic democide has few estimates, but significant hard labor deaths are certain. The party would sometimes order tens of thousands of citizens to leave for months at a time to work on a remote dam, irrigation canal, bridge, or other project. With horrible conditions, many people would perish as a result; the party would execute a great deal more for laziness or anti-party behavior.[112]

North Korea has been responsible for killing about 1.3 million of its own men, women, and children. While Stalin and Mao managed the most killing of their own countrymen in their respective early years, the internal killing of North Koreans has continued since 1948 and if anything, has tended to increase in recent years.[113] His son and grandson, Kim Jong-il and Kim Jong-un, have kept Kim Il-sung's brutal traditions and beliefs alive and well.

Although Kim Il-sung attended church services during his teenage years,[114] he became an atheist shortly after, and stayed so the rest of his life. His son and grandson were atheists, too, ruling a state where atheism was and remains enforced among all its people.[115]

Benito Mussolini

God's disappearing act didn't stop with communism or socialism. Fascism and other totalitarian regimes showed God the door, too. The leader who first brought fascism into fashion and onto the world stage was Benito Mussolini.

From very early on in his formative years in the first decades of the twentieth century, Mussolini was an avid socialist, devouring seemingly everything he could about Nietzsche, Marx, Engles, and other socialists. By 1911, he had become one of Italy's most prominent socialists. Over the years, he would tustle with the party mostly for purposes of aggrandizing his power. He would reject classic egalitarian Marxism, or "orthodox socialism," on the one hand but embraced Nietzsche's philosophies on the other. He ultimately referred to himself as a "nationalist socialist," seeing nationalism as the best vehicle by which to implement socialism.[116] He was not alone: as historian Anthony James Gregor noted, all the original founders of fascism—in Italy, Germany, England and France—were socialists and leftists.[117]

Thus, fascism was born. And the real fascists knew that they were on the political left. You could call it whatever you pleased, but it was a thorny rose by any other name. Hitler, who modeled his fascist takeover of Germany after Mussolini, was so committed to socialism that he changed the name of the German Workers Party to the National Socialist German Workers Party.[118]

Mussolini soon consolidated power, crafting laws that gave him full dictatorial powers. Eventually, the quest for power led to horrific efforts to "pacify" Libya and Ethiopia. Italy used mustard gas and phosgene against its enemies. Under Mussolini, the Italians killed hundreds of thousands of Ethiopians between 1936-1941, then about 7% of Ethiopia's total population.[119] Mussolini ordered Marshal Rodolfo Graziani to initiate and systematically conduct a policy of terror and extermination against the rebels and anyone working with them. Mussolini also personally ordered Graziani to execute the entire male population over the age of 18 in one town and in one district ordered that "the prisoners, their accomplices and the uncertain will have to be executed" as part of the "gradual liquidation" of the population.[120] Believing the Eastern Orthodox Church was inspiring Ethiopians to resist, Mussolini ordered targeting Orthodox priests and monks in revenge for guerrilla attacks.[121]

Mussolini also enacted Degree Law 880, which made Italians marrying or even having sexual relations with the local population a crime punishable with five years in prison. The reason? It would make Italian soldiers less likely to kill the local population.[122] Mussolini favored a policy of brutality partly because he believed the Ethiopians were not a nation because black people were too stupid to have a sense of nationality. The other reason was that Mussolini was planning on bringing millions of Italian colonists into Ethiopia and he needed to kill off as many Ethiopians as possible to make room for the Italian colonists, as he had done in Libya.[123]

Mussolini's religious upbringing was a story of conflict: His mother was devoutly Catholic and his father was hostile to the Church.[124] His mother Rosa had him baptized into the Roman Catholic Church, and took her children to services every Sunday. His father never attended.[125] Mussolini regarded his time at a religious boarding school as punishment, and compared the experience to hell.[126]

Mussolini became anti-clerical like his father. As a young man, he proudly announced he was an atheist.[127] Several times he would try to shock audiences by calling on God to strike him dead.[128] He believed that science had proven there was no god, and taunted that the historical Jesus was ignorant and mad. He considered religion a "disease of the psyche," and accused Christianity of promoting resignation and cowardice.[129]

Mussolini idolized Friedrich Nietzsche. According to Denis Mack Smith, "In Nietzsche he found justification for his crusade against the Christian virtues of humility, resignation, charity, and goodness."[130] He lauded Nietzsche's *Ubermensch* ("Superman") concept: "The supreme egoist who defied both God and the masses, who despised egalitarianism and democracy, who believed in the weakest going to the wall and pushing them if they did not go fast enough."[131] For his 60th birthday, Hitler gave Mussolini a gift: the complete set of the works of Nietzsche.[132]

Mussolini made vitriolic and provocative attacks against Christianity and the Catholic Church. He denounced socialists who were tolerant of religion, or who baptized their children. In fact, he called for the expulsion from the party of any socialist who accepted religious marriage. He denounced the Catholic Church for "its authoritarianism and refusal to allow freedom of thought ..."[133]

Despite having made such attacks, Mussolini tried to win popular support by appeasing the Catholic majority in Italy. In 1924, Mussolini arranged for his children to receive communion. In 1925, he had a priest perform a religious marriage ceremony for himself and his wife Rachele, whom he had married in a civil ceremony 10 years earlier.[134] On February 11, 1929, he signed a concordat and treaty with the Roman Catholic Church.[135] Under the "Lateran Pact" or treaty, Vatican City was granted independent statehood and Church law would prevail—rather than Italian law—and Italy would recognize the Catholic religion as Italy's state religion. The Church also regained authority over marriage, all secondary schools could teach Catholicism, birth control and freemasonry were banned, and the clergy received subsidies from the state and was exempted from taxation.[136]

Mussolini's manipulations worked: After receiving all these goodies, Pope Pius XI praised Mussolini. The official Catholic newspaper even pronounced "Italy has been given back to God and God to Italy."[137]

But the reconciliation with the Church fizzled quickly. Mussolini soon declared the Church subordinate to the State, and even referred to Catholicism as a minor sect that had spread beyond Palestine only because it had grafted onto the Roman empire.[138] He soon confiscated Catholic newspapers, and the Church soon came close to excommunicating Mussolini.[139]

Despite a public reconciliation with the Pope in 1932, Mussolini still would make sure not to look subordinate to the Church. His party ordered that pronouns referring to him "had to be capitalized like those referring to God . . ."[140] By 1938, he would sometimes refer to himself as an "outright disbeliever," and once told his cabinet his appreciation that "Islam was perhaps a more effective religion than Christianity" and that the "papacy was a malignant tumor in the body of Italy and must 'be rooted out once and for all', because there was no room in Rome for both the Pope and himself."[141]

Like most of our other dictator friends, Mussolini openly expressed disdain for religion, while simultaneously demanding that his people regard him almost as a deity.

As the expression goes: *plus ça change, plus c'est la même chose:* The more things change, the more they stay the same.

Remember that now.

"Hitler, Hitler, Hitler!"

Adolph Hitler elevated himself to the Fuhrer ("the Leader"), and he demanded his people to direct all allegiance to him. Once Hitler had obtained total power, he never invoked God's or Jesus' name. Then he sought to eliminate God, and the people who gave the world His troublesome Ten Commandments. In all his quests for power, that was his core purpose.

The fact that Hitler played into the latent existing antisemitism of the day does not mean he supported Christianity. Far from it, and just like Mussolini before him, Hitler had contempt for Christianity (see below). But he was more than happy to exploit German contempt for Judaism—for the moment. But he dedicated himself to only one overall mission: destroy God and anyone who supported Him.

And destroy he did. Hitler killed 6 million Jews in the span of approximately five years. And Jews were only "one of four groups racially targeted for persecution in Nazi Germany and in German-controlled Europe"[142]; gypsies and Poles were targets too. All told, Hitler's Holocaust was responsible for the deaths of at least 11 million people.

But wait, what's this? On the Internet, you will find people constantly referring to Hitler as a devout Christian, and that Hitler had embraced Christianity as the very core of Nazism. So their argument becomes "Hitler was a Christian! Hitler was a Christian!" and that this reflects the evil nature of Christianity itself, or at least that the greatest mechanized slaughter of all time happened in the name of Christianity.

They're like Janice Brady from *The Brady Bunch* TV show, who's always complaining about her older sister, Marsha ("Marsha, Marsha, Marsha!"). You'll find references to Hitler's supposed love for Christianity, especially in his creed *Mein Kampf,* which he wrote in the 1920s while in prison, and in his early days before he attained complete power in 1933. But to believe Hitler was a Christian is like believing that the four guys from the music group the Village People were really a policeman, a cowboy, a sailor, and an Indian chief.

His seemingly pro-Christian fervor was just a ruse: he orchestrated it solely to get the Christians to either back him, or at least not to get in the way. And nothing he advanced or did was remotely Christian nor "for" Christianity.

It turns out that dictators manipulate, lie and deceive. Who knew? And Hitler had lied and deceived over and over again: he lied to the rest of the world when he said he wanted only peace. Then he lied that he wouldn't pursue any territory after acquiring Czechoslovakia. He lied to the Russians when he signed a treaty that he wouldn't go to war with them. He lied and deceived the world about his plan to annihilate the Jews and all other supposed "undesirables."

His specific lies were extensive: "We have no territorial demands to make in Europe"; "I do not desire anything further than that this German nation shall take its place and grow into the unity and co-operation of the European community" (March 1936); "We want nothing from France—nothing at all" (September 1938); "Germany does not conduct a war against small nations" (April 1940).[143]

Those who claim Hitler was a devout Christian understand that he was a ruthless, psychopathic liar who would say anything to accomplish his murderous scheme to wipe out all non-Aryan people from Europe and beyond. Except for his supposed deep faith in Christianity—*that* you can apparently take to the bank.

We know better now. As Historian Paul Johnson observed, Hitler *hated* Christianity with a passion. After assuming power in 1933, Hitler told Hermann Rauschning that he intended "to stamp out Christianity root and branch."[144]

And then this, from Hitler himself: "You see, it's been our misfortune to have the wrong religion. Why didn't we have the religion of the Japanese, who regard sacrifice for the Fatherland as the highest good? The Mohammedan religion too would have been much more compatible to us than Christianity. Why did it have to be Christianity with its meekness and flabbiness?"[145]

And then, in 1933, away from the public, Hitler explains his plans to *destroy* Christianity: "It is through the peasantry that we shall *really be able to destroy Christianity*, because there is in them a true religion rooted in nature and blood"[146] (emphasis added).

And his contempt for Christianity grows more with time. By 1940, he states, "The religions are all alike, no matter what they call themselves. They have no future—certainly none for the Germans. *Fascism, if it likes, may come to terms with the Church.*

So shall I. Why not? That will not prevent me from tearing up Christianity root and branch, and annihilating it in Germany"[147] (emphasis added).

And more contemptuously yet:

> Whether it's the Old Testament or the New, or simply the sayings of Jesus, according to Houston Stewart Chamberlain—it's all the same old Jewish swindle. It will not make us free. A German Church, a German Christianity, is distortion. One is either a German or a Christian. You cannot be both. You can throw the epileptic Paul out of Christianity—others have done so before us. ... It's no use, you cannot get rid of the mentality behind it. We don't want people who keep one eye on the life hereafter. We need free men who feel and know that God is in themselves.[148]

Indeed, his true and seemingly consistent belief appeared to be pantheistic, if anything, reaching back to a world that worshipped nature: "The old beliefs will be brought back to honor again . . . the whole secret knowledge of nature, of the divine, the demonic . . . We will wash off the Christian veneer and bring out a religion peculiar to our race."[149]

Yehuda Bauer, professor of Holocaust Studies at Hebrew University in Jerusalem, describes the real "god" of Hitler and the Nazis: "They wanted to go back to a pagan world, beautiful, naturalistic, where natural hierarchies based on the supremacy of the strong would be established, because strong equaled good, powerful equaled civilized. The world did have a kind of God, the merciless God of nature, the brutal God of races, the oppressive God of hierarchies."[150] In other words, not Christian.

As Hitler grew in power, he made many other anti-Christian statements. For example: "I'll make these damned parsons feel the power of the state in a way they would have never believed possible. For the moment, I am just keeping my eye upon them: if I ever have the slightest suspicion that they are getting dangerous, I will shoot the lot of them. This filthy reptile raises its head whenever there is a sign of weakness in the State, and therefore it must be stamped on. We have no sort of use for a fairy story invented by the Jews."[151]

It was political pandering, just like many of our past and current politicians who invoke God's name to gain support. Also, it seems probable that Hitler, being the great manipulator, knew that he couldn't fight the Christian churches and their members right off the bat. So he made statements to put the church at ease for the moment.

It was all a ruse. Hitler just wanted to bring the church into line so that it wouldn't interfere with his scheme. "He knew he dare not simply eradicate it: that would not have been possible with such an international organisation, and he would have lost many Christian supporters had he tried to. His principal aim was to unify the German Evangelical Church under a pro-Nazi banner, and to come to an accommodation with the Catholics."[152]

In other words, while he was certainly evil, he also knew which fights he could win (at least until 1941) and only fought those.[153]

Indeed, he understood all too well that Christianity, in the long run, *was his enemy*. As Hitler wrote: "Pure Christianity—the Christianity of the catacombs—is concerned with translating the Christian doctrine into fact. It leads simply to the annihilation of mankind. It is merely wholehearted Bolshevism, under a tinsel of metaphysics." Switch a few words around and you'd think you were listening to Joseph Stalin. And like Stalin, Hitler believed history was on his side: "Do you really believe the masses will ever be Christian again? Nonsense. Never again. The tale is finished . . . *but we can hasten matters. The parsons will be made to dig their own graves*"[154] (emphasis added).

Still not convinced? It is virtually impossible to find a speech, especially in his later years, whereby he spoke of love for God or Christ. By contrast, it is telling how he demanded the world to pledge allegiance to him, the *Fuhrer*—not to God, Jesus, or any other higher power.

The ultimate violation of the commandments is where one carry's God's name in vain, meaning doing evil and claiming to do so in the name of God. Why is this particular violation so contemptible? Because it inverts what is good, and uses it to do evil. This is why we hold priests who engage in child molesting with far greater contempt than someone doing so outside of a faith. It is committing evil under the *guise* of faith and goodness. It gives God a bad name.

This is the kind of evil Hitler mastered so well. Yet there are those who take his few references to Christianity seriously, merely because he made reference to it. The atheist particularly claims Hitler was a believer because he mentioned God a couple of times, and some SS posters read "*Gott mit un*s (God is with us)."

But just because someone invokes God or Jesus doesn't mean he believes in God or Jesus. It's what any smart con man would tell you do—know your audience, then exploit them into thinking you're one of them. Kill them later.

Hitler was just like his fellow killers Mao and Stalin. Each of them envisioned a Brave New World—one without God. He *appealed* to Christianity and to Christians' latent antisemitism, but only as a tool to aggrandize his power.[155] He ultimately wanted to destroy Christianity itself—after he destroyed Judaism. In this way, he viewed Christianity much like he viewed Stalin—a necessary ally whom he would turn against when he invaded Russia in 1942.

Hitler was no Christian and never acted as a Christian. Adolf Hitler was godless. And he did what all the other godless leaders had done: mass killings on an epic scale.

The above leaders are only some of the more famous godless leaders who destroyed, tortured, pillaged and killed on a mass scale. There are hundreds more,[156] all of whom had one thing in common: godlessness as a cornerstone of their governing ideology.

The stories of the atheist leaders should evoke the famous fable of the scorpion on the back of the frog who's carrying across the stream. He *must* kill the frog. After all, he can't help it: It's what scorpions do.

Now, let us take on the comparative numbers from the religious side.

The Religious Killings

Let's review the Christian and Jewish governments who ordered killings in the name of Christianity and Judaism:[157] Other than the Inquisitions, there are very few, and certainly not in any mass numbers. But the atheist will protest: there were the Inquisitions, the Crusades, the European religious wars, the Pograms of Russia and Eastern Europe, the Ku Klux Klan, and the Salem Witch Trials all killed vast numbers of people.

Let's put aside that few of these were killings which religious governments ordered, orchestrated, or even condoned. For example, a vast, papal-controlled, grand and singular inquisition never really existed in Europe.[158] The Salem Witch Trials were the product of momentary hysteria, which a few mischievous and opportunistic girls brought about to foment trouble, claiming certain individuals among them were witches who had possessed them.[159] Although there is debate as to whether the Crusades were defensive in nature, the purpose of the Crusades was not to wipe out a religion or people. It was designed to liberate Jerusalem, responding to (or in connection with) a spread of Islam in the Levant, and into Europe.[160]

While there was certainly violent anti-Semitism throughout European history, and governments turned a blind eye and even seemed to support the attacks upon Jewish communities in Germany during the medieval era, as well as later pogroms in Russia and Eastern Europe,[161] the Church did not condone, let alone order, such pogroms. If anything, the pogrom attacks upon Jews—often stemming from false accusations of Jewish diabolical conspiracies—represented an attack *upon* religion (i.e *against* Jews), rather than *by* religion (i.e. *by* Christians on behalf of Christianity).

Finally, the Church did not found the KKK; a bunch of racist jackasses did. Nor is there meaningful evidence that the Church supported or encouraged the KKK.

But let's assume that religious authorities had indeed instigated all the horrors the atheist claims, or that if it were not for Christian or Jewish faiths, these horrors would never have occurred. Then we'll compare numbers:

The Spanish Inquisitions

Catholic Monarchs Ferdinand II of Aragon and Isabella I of Castile established the Spanish Inquisition (*Inquisición española*) in 1478, primarily to maintain Catholic orthodoxy in their kingdoms. Royal decrees in 1492 and 1502 ordered Jews and Muslims to convert or leave Spain. It was the largest and most notable of the wider Christian Inquisition, along with the Roman Inquisition and Portuguese Inquisition.[162]

Various historians question earlier centuries' accounts of the scope and brutality of the Spanish Inquisition, much of which they now believe Protestants probably exaggerated during the waves of anti-Catholicism during those times. Records are incomplete, but it appears the Inquisition charged 150,000 persons with crimes. Only 3,000–5,000 people were executed.[163]

The Crusades

The papal and other campaigns to reclaim the Holy Land took place between the years 1095 and 1272. An accurate count of the death toll during the entirety of the crusades does not exist. The common guess brings the body count to around one million. But this number includes Christian crusaders, Muslims and Jews, together (Crusaders killed approximately 5,000 Jews in the Rhineland on their way to one of the Crusades). This estimate also includes those who died from disease, those who were sold into slavery and many who died before they made it to the Holy Land.[164]

The Crusades lasted about 177 years. Assuming a total death toll of one million, this adds up to less than 6,000 a year.[165]

Salem Witch Trials

Accurate records exist regarding the Salem witch trials. The trials began during the spring of 1692, and quickly created a wave of hysteria throughout colonial Massachusetts. A special court convened in Salem to hear cases. Bridget Bishop, the first "witch," was hanged that June. While some 150 more men, women and children were accused over the next several months, only eighteen others followed Bishop to Salem's Gallows Hill.

By September 1692, only four or so months later, the hysteria ended.

Total killed: Nineteen.[166]

Christian Anti-Semitism and Pogroms

It is true that the Catholic Church instigated large discriminatory and marginalizing measures against the Jews for much of its history, preferring to cloister Jews in ghettos. Further, when Martin Luther could not convert the Jews to Protestantism, then he, too, condemned them.[167] Worse, in Luther's book *On the Jews and their Lies*, Luther excoriates Jews as "vipers, disgusting scum, canders, devils incarnate." In the treatise, Luther describes Jews as a "base, whoring people." Luther further expounds: they are "full of the devil's feces . . . which they wallow in like swine."[168]

Apparently, he was just getting started: he provided a list of recommendations against Jews: "Their private houses must be destroyed and devastated . . . Let the magistrates burn their synagogues and let whatever escapes be covered with sand and mud. Let them be forced to work, and if this avails nothing, we will . . . expel them like dogs." He even wrote: ". . . we are at fault in not slaying them . . ." a passage that may have served as a "giant step forward on the road to the Holocaust."[169] Whole Jewish towns in Germany suffered complete destruction during Medieval times, and suffered even more in the way of harassment and marginalizing.[170]

But there are differences: First, neither the Catholic nor the Protestant Churches actually participated or ordered the destruction of Jews. It was local government or peasant mobs that did that. This is not to excuse the rampant anti-Semitism that existed throughout Russia and Europe, but it is necessary to differentiate.

Second, it wasn't "religion" which fostered or perpetuated anti-Semitism. Anti-Semitism has been even *more* rampant among the atheists than among the Christians, as we discussed above regarding fascism and communism. It existed among secularists during the Enlightenment, and exists among leftists and those who are anti-Israel even today. Likewise, it is rampant within Islam.[171] It even exists in modern Japan, which has had very little experience with Jews or Christians.[172]

It was the *religiosity* of the Jews—their unique faith in Torah, their sense of chosenness, and their quest to hold the world to a God-based moral standard—that frenzied uninformed Catholics, Protestants, the godless, conspiratorialists, and all other Anti-Semites alike, and that made them seek to marginalize the Jews and even call out for their destruction.

In any event, even if one were to view the Russian Pogroms as "evidence" of religious killings (which he should not), the numbers are marginal when one compares them even to just the short stretch of the French "Reign of Terror." The most liberal of estimates of Russian Pogroms appear to place the total number killed at no greater than 7,500 since the first Pogrom of 1821 in Odessa.[173]

The Ku Klux Klan

It is a fallacy to argue that the Ku Klux Klan (KKK) engaged in its mayhem *because* of Christianity. As we discuss below, the primary social movement that the Christian faith developed before the Civil War was the anti-slavery *Abolitionist* movement—which some may argue would be inconsistent with the KKK platform.

Abolitionism started with Christian agitators who based their opposition to slavery on the specific teachings of Christianity. They were similarly on the front lines for the end of Jim

Crow laws and for the advancement of civil rights, and the fight against eugenics.

But the atheist ignores these facts, and asserts nevertheless that the KKK was some Christian movement, which would (presumably) not exist nor be able to effectuate its mayhem without its Christian roots. What's their argument, you may ask? The KKK burned Christian crosses in their meetings and as a form of intimidation on many of their victims' front lawns.[174] So, there you go.

In other words, Christianity teaches that slavery and racism is both evil and immoral and contrary to all of the Bible's teachings, on the one hand; and that slavery and racism are proper, moral, and based solidly on the Bible's teachings, on the other.

Just so that we're clear.

What explains this supposed conundrum? How about the possibility that the KKK never behaved in a Christian way, but harkened to Christianity as a means to justify its evil and perhaps to attract other members (say, like Hitler and Mussolini did)? How about that they were just white-supremacist racists, who happened to be *born* Christians?

Merely calling yourself a "Christian" organization does not make it so, nor what you do "Christian." The atheist will also have a tough time finding a minister, reverend or priest who advocated that what the KKK did was Christian. For that matter, he'll have a tough time showing anywhere in the Bible or New Testament where it advocated for slavery, racial discrimination or killing on racial grounds.

But let's assume, again for the sake of discussion, that the blood of the KKK somehow should lay at the feet of Christianity. How many people died because of what the KKK did?

During the height of its horrific reign from 1882 to 1968— eighty-six years—the Ku Klux Klan lynched a combination of 3,446 blacks and a handful of white supporters.[175]

Religious Wars

During the Reformation, Catholics and Protestants warred with each other for decades. Further infighting continued sporadically over centuries. The French Wars of Religion of the 16th century, also known as the Huguenot Wars, led to the deaths of approximately 3 million people as a result of violence, famine and disease. The Thirty Years' War in what is now Germany (1618–48) took approximately 8 million lives.[176] The St. Bartholomew's Day massacre was actually a series of massacres lasting several weeks in which Catholic mobs killed between 5,000 and 30,000 Protestants throughout the entire kingdom.[177] Certainly, there is no denying that religion was the primary basis for such deaths.

The Godless v. the Religious: The Tally

There is no comparison: In terms of killings (and for that matter, mayhem, rape and torture), atheism has got religion beat. Even if one could consider all the killings in the "religious" column name to be actual killings in the actual name of Christianity or Judaism (it is not), such killings are wildly less than those killed from atheism. Further, atheism killed hundreds of millions in the span of only thirty years—Hitler alone killed approximately 11 million in only five years. The number of killings on (the alleged) behalf of Christianity ranged were minor in comparison, and ranged over approximately 800 years.

Keep in mind also the puzzling fact that the alleged killing sprees in the name of Christianity or Judaism haven't occurred for more than 300 years. To complain about what the Church had done that long ago (even if you could blame it on the belief in God) violates any sense of a statute of limitations. What slaughters have Christians done in the past 300 years? Or, to twist the lyrics of the famous Janet Jackson song: "What have you *not* done to me lately?" By contrast, the vicious killings, tortures and persecutions in godless regimes (China, Cuba, Russia, Vietnam, Cambodia, etc.) have been relatively recent and continue today.

Then consider all the substantial *good* which Christianity and Judaism has bestowed (see discussion below) in the past, say, four thousand years. Then consider godlessness; godlessness as an ideology has contributed *nothing* to advance civilization: no hospitals, no art, no music, no architecture, no schools, and no universities. It didn't even create a YMCA.

Does godlessness create monsters? Does atheism kill? It should be clear: wherever there was godless rule, devastation on a horrific scale followed. There was no one to answer to, except to the dictators themselves and their own vision of a just order—always with themselves at the helm of some imaginary ship for which only they knew how to set course.

As the famous Soviet dissident Alexander Solzhenitsyn stated in his famous Templeton Address of 1983: "Men have forgotten God. That's why all this has happened."

Atheism and the Birth of the Abortion Culture

There is a lot of political charge to the issue of abortion, so I have not included the unborn in the numbers of atheism's slaughters. But godlessness indeed resulted in an explosion of abortions–both voluntary and involuntary. Its impact upon culture echoes even today.

In Nazi Germany, the law allowed abortion for "racial hygiene" purposes, or where the Nazis didn't approve of the race of the parents.[178] For non-Aryans, abortion was often compulsory, while providing abortion for pure "Aryans" was not only prohibited but a capital offense.[179] It followed the Communist policy (see below) that abortions were proper—if they served a state purpose. Morality was not a part of the discussion.

In 1920, Communist Russia became the first country to legalize abortion *up to birth without restrictions*. Lenin and his political faction saw abortion as an effective means to help destroy the family unit and to get more women into the workforce.[180] The Bolsheviks even designed a machine for suction abortions which abortion clinics in America still use today.[181]

This "abortion culture" became deep-rooted and almost integral to Russian society, even today.[182] The practice has become so normalized—abortions are actually cheaper than any other forms of birth control—that it has become the primary birth control method, and women report not trusting any form of contraception.[183] Until recently, Russian women reportedly had an average of seven abortions over their lifetime.[184] In 2003, according to the BBC there were 13 abortions in Russia for every 10 live births; Reuters reported in 2009 that there were 73 abortions per 100 births in Russia.[185] Contrast that to the United States, where the ratio peaked at 36 abortions per 100 lives birth in 1984 and has steadily declined since then.[186]

The abortion culture pervaded most of communist eastern Europe, most strikingly in Romania.[187] In China, the situation has been even more dire: according to official statistics, authorities forced 6.7 million women in China to have abortions under the "one-child" policy in 2012 alone, and previous decades' numbers often topped 10 million annually.[188]

In the past four decades, the Chinese government forcibly sterilized men, and had intrauterine devices inserted into hundreds of millions of women, per Chinese family-planning policies. . . . "Many women who were seven or eight months pregnant were forced to have abortions," a former family-planning team member said. "Hospitals never refused, despite the risks. Because it was a government order, no one dared say no."[189]

The Atlantic magazine sees the distinction between America's approach to abortion and most of the rest of the world's approach as follows: America sees abortion as a moral issue, whereas much of the rest of the world sees it as a matter of the "common good."[190] That might be a good assessment of the distinction, but read that again: for the *common good*—whatever that might mean. The government would decide the fate of thousands and millions of lives depending on what *it* would determine was the "common good"—or more aptly, the government's *goal*—for the moment: like how you might adjust your automatic sprinklers based on how much rain your lawn has been getting.

For Lenin during the early years of Russian communism, abortion served the goal of breaking up the family and getting women to work (expand abortion). For fascist Italy and later Romania, the goal was to *increase* the population (restrict abortion). For China, the goal was to *decrease* the population (expand abortion). But the consideration of right or wrong about ending the life of an unborn child? You might as well fret about the feelings of your toenail clippings.

There is scant reliable information other than the Chinese statistics referenced above as to how many abortions godless governments urged or forced upon its citizens. But with this "common good" approach and the ratio of abortions to live births referenced above, the numbers likely match all who were killed in both World Wars.

Whatever one might believe about abortion, most Americans will agree: they prefer living in a country where people at least debate the *morality* of abortion. For in their hearts, they must know that a nation that does not have at least some squeamishness about the taking of *pre*-birth lives is a nation that might not be so squeamish about the treatment of *post*-birth lives.

Why? Because one day the authorities may just not view your life to be part of the common good.

Guilt by Association?

The atheist will take offense to these associations of killings and indifference to life. He will argue that being an atheist doesn't automatically make one a killer. This argument is called the "guilt by association" argument. Notably, he'll make that same "guilt by association" argument when he maligns all Christianity on account of the Inquisitions, the Crusades, and the pedophilia scandals. But I digress.

The atheist is partially correct: not all ruthless dictators are atheists. And of course, he's right: being an atheist alone doesn't make you a killer. Being an atheist alone doesn't even make you a bad or mean person. But being an atheist dictator advancing an atheist doctrine has *always* led to brutality and killings. In other words, give *power* to the atheist doctrine and horrible things seem to happen.

The reason, as we can see from the one commonality of all the atheists we've described above, is that a doctrine which roots itself on the rejection of the Judeo-Christian God (whether it is fascism, communism, or Nazism) requires that all be on board with the program. Everyone. If you are not with the program, you disappear. And it is all the more easy when you view humans as soulless blobs of clay you can manipulate and dispose of as you please.

But as I'll discuss later, there's something within us all that *demands* a higher being. It's an instinct even most atheists seem to acknowledge. And if that higher being is not God, then it will be a man. You'll see that man on posters throughout the country, demanding allegiance and money from his subjects—whether that's Stalin, Hitler, Kim Jong-un and his father before him, Saddam Hussein, Ho-chi Min, Mao, Ceauşescu, or Castro. That man cannot allow different visions from his own because to do so would mean others had equal rights, any of whom could knock him down from his godly perch. And the dictator will do anything to protect his vision.

The atheist will respond that this isn't fair: There were many dictators who believed in a higher being, and they imposed their will as well. Yes, that is correct, but dictators who *truly* ruled with a sense that they ultimately had to answer to a higher being (the various kings, queens, and emperors of Europe, for example) understood that God imposed *some* responsibilities and boundaries upon them. And so, while wars raged with neighboring countries for territory, you rarely saw such kings, queens, or emperors embark on a systematic extermination of their enemies via gulags, concentration camps, or otherwise. On the contrary, kings and queens even married their sons and daughters off to other countries to cement alliances.

The atheist may argue at this point that the Spanish Inquisition involved a "systematic" attempt to exterminate Jews and other "undesirables" from Spain starting in 1478. And there were the Crusades, which began in 1095.

Here's the fallacy in both these events: (1) They are mere outliers in Christian history; (2) They occurred several hundreds of years ago and a thousand years ago, respectively; (3) They suffer from overzealous re-interpretation in the history books, particularly the Crusades (the point of the Crusades was not to kill the Jews along the way but to liberate Jerusalem from the Muslims; further the Crusades were arguably in response to the Muslim effort to conquer Europe); and (4), They in no way compare in numbers to the horrors of the godless dictators of the French Reign of Terror and the twentieth century.

Even with the horrors of Radical Islam today, there is no comparison to the murder and mayhem which godless regimes effectuated *as their primary goal.* In other words, where the Judeo-Christian God is present and bad things happen, they are *exceptions* to what Christianity and Judaism urges. By contrast, murder, mayhem and abject brutality are the *rule* in godless regimes, and always have been.

But even if people acting in the name of religion have done some bad to the world—and surely some have—here's how I respond:

What's your point?

Is religion supposed to be perfect? Are you willing to accept God only if there are positively no blemishes in a religion's history? That's a standard even the atheist doesn't expect of himself, his friends, his spouse, his profession, his country, his kid's school, his gardener, his doctor, accountant, or of anyone or anything else whatsoever. But religious authorities? That's apparently a different story.

The atheist's perception of God is that He must be about perfection—whatever "perfection" might mean. In their eyes, because *God* is perfect, then every human religion that honors Him must be perfect, too. Otherwise the whole notion of religion must fall apart. That is why they point to Radical Islam, the Crusades, the Inquisition, the pedophilia scandals and announce the discussion is over.

Their logic is unsound. Religion is merely a vehicle by which to know God, just as a car is a vehicle to get from point A to point B. You can abuse cars, airplanes, money, morphine, the law and just about anything else. But few would push the abolishment of any of those things just because others might have used them for evil purposes in the past.

Under the atheist's theory, we should ban parenthood. After all, there have been many abusive parents. Likewise, there have always been corrupt judges and judicial administrators. The police, the military, school systems, hospitals, and the penitentiary system have all had their share of abusive agents. They've taken bribes; concealed incriminating evidence; blackmailed; engaged in nepotism; embezzled; had inappropriate sexual liaisons;

wrongfully incarcerated people out of spite, revenge, or fear; raped people in custody, abused women and other minorities, selectively enforced laws, and defrauded the public. For that matter, governments in general have also been guilty of all such things.

And guess what? We all know that these evils will continue in the future.

Yet we would never think of dismantling the judiciary because of one or even several corrupt judges. We would never eradicate the police force because some cops sometimes mistreat some criminal suspects. We would never outlaw hospitals because some doctors overbill for procedures or engage in insurance fraud. We would never rid ourselves of government because some politicians exploit their position for personal gain or sexual favors.

Why wouldn't we? Because we understand that these institutions are fundamental to our social infrastructure. These institutions suffer from these imperfections *because human beings run them*. The imperfections of human beings infect these systems.

As absurd as the atheist's arguments are, many atheists premise their argument that we should do away with the notion of God (or that God doesn't even exist) on precisely this line of logic: In short, the atheist expects and allows for imperfection and abuse in all institutions and in all things—except for the institutions of religion. *Those* institutions must be perfect. If there is any abuse of any kind in *those*, there must be no God. But human beings can and have distorted and abused just about everything—even God. That distortion does not make God Himself evil.[191]

A hospital is only a building; it is the quality of the doctors that make it something more. A country is only a land with borders; it is the quality of its governance that makes it more. A computer is only as good as the software that runs it. But no hospital has diagnosed and treated all its patients perfectly; no country has not had blemishes in its history. And no computer has not generated that annoying spinning circle from time to time.

Humans run religious institutions. The atheist's fallacy is that he confuses religious institutions, which imperfect *humans* operate, as though *God* Himself operates them. Indeed, by using the word *"mis-*use" we implicitly acknowledge that what such abusers do (like the Islamists) is *outside* the proper pursuit of God. To view otherwise is like refusing to acknowledge the beauty of the Sistine Chapel because there is a crack there in the ceiling.

Remember: The question is what the *core* offering of any ideology is, and whether that core offering leads to more harm than good.

But I'm sympathetic: When I see that spinning circle on my computer, I want to throw it out the window, too.

Then I remember: it's just the software.

Progressivism

Progressivism as a concept was simple: humankind need not look to the past for wisdom, nor up to the heavens for humility, but rather to itself only. Adherents embraced collectivism, and many of them looked to the strongman Mussolini as a great example, especially in the 1920s. Yes, he ruled with a strong fist, but dammit, he got the job done. And as we noted above, Mussolini himself was a man of the Left, a point history often overlooks.

Although Theodore Roosevelt originally served as a Republican, the trend of the progressive era and its agenda swept him off his feet. He quickly adopted all things progressive. He now believed in extensive government involvement in business affairs. He rejected outright the "old thinking" of the Founding Fathers. When he lost his party's nomination in 1912, he pursued the presidency a second time through his progressive third-party (nicknamed the "Bull Moose Party").

As Theodore Roosevelt acknowledged in a private letter near the end of his life:

> "I do not for one moment believe that the Americanism of today should be a mere submission to the American ideals of the period of the Declaration of Independence. . . Such action would be not only to stand still, but to go back . . . But I will go further . . . I have actively fought in favor of grafting on our social life, no less than our industrial life, many of the German ideals."[192]

The Progressives pursued reform through a new conception of government or, more precisely, "the State." This "German idea of the State," moved away from the American Founders' understanding of government in two key respects, both of which help explain the Progressives' later enthusiasm for eugenics (see discussion below).[193]

First, the power of government for Progressives was not just to secure the natural or "inalienable" rights of man, as the Declaration of Independence contemplated. As the German-trained progressive political scientist and future New Dealer Charles Merriam concludes in a 1903 survey of progressive thinking, "The question is now one of expediency rather than of principle . . . each specific question must be decided on its own merits, and each action of the state justified, if at all, by the relative advantages of the proposed line of conduct."[194] In other words: government gets to do whatever it thinks is right.

As the German-trained progressive economist Richard T. Ely likewise echoed: "there [should be] no limit to the right of the State, the sovereign power, save its ability to do good." The first step toward bold reform was to "untie" the hands of government.[195]

But the Progressives did not advocate an indiscriminate exercise of power; they based their ultimate aim of "the State," the "good" objective on a notion of human excellence or "perfection."[196] For Progressives, this gave them a sense of entitlement, even a sense of obligation, to treat different races (whom they believed were at varying stages of development), differently in both law and policy.[197]

This thinking continued and even strengthened over the decades. Before World War II, many liberals in Europe and the United States viewed fascism as a progressive social movement.[198] Ultimately, in some respects American Progressivism itself became the major source of the fascist ideas which Mussolini and Hitler eventually applied in Europe.[199]

Franklin Delano Roosevelt (FDR) and other Democrats became admirers of Fascism and Mussolini and drew inspiration from fascist uprisings before WWII. Roosevelt himself once called Mussolini "admirable," adding that he was "deeply impressed by what he has accomplished."[200] Mussolini returned the compliment: he likened Roosevelt's many proposed reforms to the Fascist principle that the state no longer leaves the economy to its own devices. "Without question, the mood accompanying this sea change resembles that of Fascism."[201]

The universities, the media, and Roosevelt's own administration were among those rallying around the bold new fascist approach.[202] FDR's adviser Rexford Guy Tugwell said this of fascism: "It's the cleanest, neatest, most efficiently operating piece of social machinery I've ever seen. It makes me envious ... I find Italy doing many of the things which seem to me necessary ... Mussolini certainly has the same people opposed to him as FDR has."[203]

Even NAACP co-founder W. E. B. DuBois viewed the Nazi rise positively, saying that Hitler's dictatorship had been "absolutely necessary to get the state in order." [204] New Republic editor

George Soule noted approvingly that the Roosevelt administration was "trying out the economics of fascism."[205]

Other media progressives gushed, too: after Roosevelt's inauguration, New York Times reporter Anne O'Hare McCormick wrote favorably that Washington, D.C., has become "reminiscent of Rome in the first weeks after the march of the Blackshirts, of Moscow at the beginning of the Five-Year Plan ... America today literally asks for orders." The Roosevelt administration, she added, "envisages a federation of industry, labor and government after the fashion of the corporative State as it exists in Italy."[206] The National Recovery Administration (NRA), a New Deal agency, published a report stating boldly, "The Fascist Principles are very similar to those we have been evolving here in America." [207]

The Progressives believed that America needed to unshackle themselves from the once meaningful but now quaint notion of individual freedom. The world had grown up, after all, and the modern age demanded bold, persistent change if anyone expected *real* progress to happen. And the grass sure was looking a lot greener on the European side.

In the end, after the world saw the horrible consequences of fascism and its even more evil cousin, Nazism, the progressives moved very quickly to disown their earlier crush on fascism. It was like a wife who catches her husband cheating, but the mistress she catches him with turns out to be quite ugly. He's embarrassed more about that than the actual cheating, and the wife is insulted to think he would cheat on her for someone so ugly. In the end, both the wife and husband conclude that it's better to just pretend nothing ever happened.

But you know something? They *did* love fascism. The progressives and the godless can't escape it. They just never stopped to think of the inevitable consequences of a world without God and freedom. And that was what was truly ugly.

Eugenics

Perhaps the most stark example of the Progressives' willingness to disregard individual liberty was in their support for eugenics. Eugenics was the "science" of improving a human population through controlled breeding to improve desirable heritable characteristics.

Eugenics was the brain child of Francis Galton, who was born into a Quaker family in Birmingham, England, in 1822. Interestingly, he was a cousin of Charles Darwin, and "he shared the Darwinian agnosticism and antagonism to Christianity for most of his adult life."[208]

Galton was an amateur scientist and wrote prolifically. He invented multiple contraptions and concepts.[209] But the publication of Darwin's *Origin of Species* in 1859 was a turning point in Galton's life. As he wrote to Darwin directly, "[T]he appearance of your *Origin of Species* formed a real crisis in my life; your book drove away the constraint of my old superstition [i.e. religious arguments based on design] as if it had been a nightmare and was the first to give me freedom of thought."[210]

Galton was among the first to realize the implications which Darwin's theory of evolution posed: We each inherit our talents and gifts from our ancestors, and conversely, we inherit the *lack* of such talents or gifts. So, as Galton saw it, paupers were paupers because they were biologically inferior, not because of environmental circumstances.[211]

Galton thus believed that society should breed humans selectively, like animals. To summarize this concept, he coined the term "eugenics" in 1883 [Greek: εὐ (*eu*) meaning "well" and γένος (*genos*) meaning "kind" or "offspring"] for the study of ways of improving the physical and mental traits of humans.[212]

The possibility of the existence of a human soul, a Designer of the universe (let alone God), dignity or free will were not part of

Galton's program. In his first published article on this subject in 1865, he viewed religious sentiments as "nothing more than evolutionary devices to insure the survival of the human species."[213]

In short, godlessness and antagonism to religion were at the heart of the eugenics movement, from its very birth.

Years later, Edward A. Ross, who had pursued graduate study at the University of Berlin and at Johns Hopkins University, was one of the main advocates of eugenics in America. Ross eventually joined several other prominent supporters of eugenics at the University of Wisconsin, including President Charles Van Hise and Ely himself. In his *Conservation of Natural Resources in the United States*, Van Hise expresses dismay that "even in civilized countries . . . defectives of various classes are allowed to propagate the race." The solution for this problem, he urges, is "eugenics." Whatever the method chosen, he wrote, "it should be thoroughgoing. *Human defectives should no longer be allowed to propagate the race*"[214] (emphasis added).

Van Hise noted that adopting eugenics "will require a 'transformation of the ideals of the individual, who has felt himself free to do with what he has as he pleases, to social responsibility.' Such a transformation would entail 'as great a change of heart as has ever been demanded by seer or by prophet.'" He insisted that "each man [should] *surrender his individualism so far as is necessary for the good of the race*. He who thinks not of himself primarily, but of his race, and of its future, is the new patriot" (emphasis added).[215]

In a chapter entitled "Race Improvement," he encourages putting "paupers and feeble-minded" persons in custodial institutions ". . . [to deny them] opportunities to become the parents of a vicious progeny," or to marry.[216]

How could Americans have adopted this, you may wonder. Wasn't America founded to preserve and promote individualism and the sanctity of the individual?

Well, sure, but the times were changing. The Progressive economists saw social science as a guide to social management. The new broad acceptance of Darwinism in the late nineteenth century, combined with a new sense that America should approach its social problems scientifically, led to a wholehearted embrace of eugenics. Public policy could ensure the "survival of the fittest" and the purity and strength of the human race. . . . Eugenics "clubs" grew rapidly, and many leading intellectuals of the early twentieth century, including economists John Maynard Keynes and Irving Fisher, saw their work through the "lens" of eugenics.[217]

Observant Jews and Christians fought against the new eugenics trend.[218] But the godless? Not so much. In fact, it is difficult to find any notable atheist, agnostic, or secular individual or organization who stood against the eugenics movement at the time.

And why *would* any atheist fight it? Morality was irrelevant to atheism as a belief system. And so, godlessness was at the very core of eugenics. Without God and morals, progressivism could now unmoor itself from the thousands of years of a moral code that would otherwise have stopped eugenics in its tracks. To the new progressives, the religious moral code of the ancients was antiquated and contrary to the new scientific vision of how to better mankind. And godlessness was growing, rapidly.

In doing the bidding of eugenics, progressivism unmasked itself: It was cruel, cold, cunning, and calculating. Any notion of mercy or humanity was entirely absent. To the progressive, it wasn't so much "killing" of "less fit" undesirables as it was making the lives for the remaining "more fit" more pleasant and productive. At least this is what they told themselves as they sterilized more than 60,000 victims through the 1970s, including criminals, the mentally disabled, drug addicts, paupers, the blind and deaf, and people with epilepsy and syphilis.

In 1923, Fritz Lenz, a German physician and geneticist advocate of forced sterilization, criticized his countrymen for lagging behind the United States in the enactment of sterilization laws.[219] He supported the German "racial hygiene" program, and shortly after Hitler became Chancellor of the Third Reich in 1933, the Nazis began to catch up in earnest.[220] Soon Nazi Germany's first sterilization law was born, mandating sterilization for all persons they believed had congenital feeblemindedness, schizophrenia, manic depression, and other undesirable characteristics. The purpose of this law was "to prevent ...poisoning the entire bloodstream of the race."[221]

The Nazi sterilization law went well beyond existing American precedents. Still, as historian Jonathan Spiro notes, the Nazi statute was "quite consciously based on the model sterilization law of Harry H. Laughlin and the American Eugenics Society."[222] The *Eugenical News*, a publication closely tied to Laughlin's, was proud of its paternity. There was even scholarly exchange between leading American eugenicists and the men who became the leading advocates, architects and administrators of the Nazis' "racial hygiene" program.[223]

The Nazis adopted much of their horrific racial purity laws from their like-minded American friends, and Hitler himself happily gave the Americans credit.[224] Similarly, the American founders of the eugenics movement applauded the Nazis for their eager implementation of eugenics.[225] It was a mutual admiration society.

When and why did the eugenics movement finally fall out of favor? The general consensus is that, following World War II, the world saw the horrendous consequences of an ideology that advanced the notion of a "superior" race.[226] The mirror to our darkest, godless side was far too revealing and painful.

But unlike the end of World War II itself, eugenics did not suddenly leave the world on a formal date of surrender, following some momentous ceremony on a battleship. It faded out of public discussion, ever so slowly, like when you realize one day that that child molester on your street no longer lives there. There's a bit of embarrassment, too: He had been that "great" local babysitter you and others had recommended to everyone else. But now no one knows quite what he might have done to the children, and frankly a part of you would rather not think of it.

But the godless monster of eugenics did live, right here in America. Its henchmen carried out its horrors, and its ideology spread throughout the world to justify the destruction not only of the "unfit," but also of whole peoples. It also eventually ushered in a culture of unapologetic and righteous callousness to the unborn.[227]

Like with the child molester who lived among us in the neighborhood, eugenics and its consequences still haunt us. They will continue to do so until we openly acknowledge eugenics' evil past and its godless roots.

CHAPTER II

THE BATTLEGROUND

Now that we've seen how destructive and cruel godlessness can be, it's worthwhile asking *why* it is so. After all, it could be a series of coincidences. You could argue that, yes, those dictators were godless, but that is just a *correlation*, not causation. Correlations alone don't prove anything. For example, traffic and sunsets often go together, but one doesn't necessarily *cause* the other.

The atheist may argue that perhaps each of the godless dictators merely happened to be godless, or the world was godless anyway, and they were merely players in an already-godless world.

But the godless ideology of these dictators was *instrumental* to the way they ruled, central to each of their destructive paths. Further, if it was mere correlation, you would expect at least *some* country's leaders who *did* believe in God (or were at least not godless), to engage in similar murder sprees. But that seems not to happen.

Here's my personal journey: I rejected God when I was eleven, and it was only in the middle of college when I found Him again. And I remember how the moment felt. It was as though my brain caught fire. It was as if I broke the ceiling I had imposed upon myself. Because ever since then, I have been able to see different facets of life and science I never allowed myself to see before. I discovered that when you avail yourself to the notion of God, you constantly ask yourself: *Why?* Or better yet: *Why is it so?*

For example: Why do we love and even seem to need music? Why do we have free will and animals do not? Why do we aspire to anything? Why do we even have a sense of purpose at all? (Or, if you like, what is the purpose of having a purpose?) Why do we appreciate beauty? Why do we have a love for learning and for science? Why do we yearn for truth and justice?

As an atheist, I just didn't ask such questions: I accepted the world and the universe as it was because the answer was that everything happened randomly. Survival of the fittest explained everything. What you see is what you get. There was no "why is it so?" There was only "it is what it is." When you probe an atheist with such questions, they'll shrug. You might as well have asked them what the color yellow smells like.

But take survival of the fittest as a simple example. When you're an atheist, you think everything is the result of mutations that survived over others. Why? Because they adapted to the environment better. That's why we have a nose, for example—so we can smell. A creature without a nose presumably can't smell a predator, and the predator could catch and eat him.

It's concise, orderly, clean. You don't have to think much because one concept and one concept only—natural selection—provides an answer for absolutely everything.

But you ask a follow-up question: does this really explain *everything*? Aren't there some things for which natural selection makes no sense as an explanation?

What about humor, free will, and a sense of beauty or purpose? It is difficult to understand how any of those came to us from natural selection (I'll discuss this more later). And, in any event, another question arises with explaining the ordinary mutations: why do we not see any fossil record showing these numerous mutations? If there were such mutations in a nice, orderly fashion, wouldn't we expect the fossil record to show gradations of ever-evolving life?

Unfortunately for the atheist, the fossil record instead shows a veritable "explosion" of varied species, all seemingly arriving at the same time (often referred to as the "Cambrian Explosion"). That doesn't jibe well with the notion of orderly evolution slowly taking place over millions and billions of years.

Or how about the eye? The complexity of the eye seems to have evolved quite *similarly* among many different mammals. But the odds that each mammal evolved the *same kind of eye* in its own *separate* "tree of evolution" is infinitesimally small (actually, to say "infinitesimal" does not even approach the true degree of improbability. It is more like "infinitesimally infinitesimal"). Also, there is no meaningful evidence of anything "pre"-eye; it just seems to have appeared. And there is scant evidence of the evolution of the eye itself.[1]

My new favorite brain-twister: our brain's capacity for information is astounding. It turns out that neurons combine so ingeniously that each one helps with many memories at a time, exponentially increasing the brain's memory storage capacity to close to 2.5 petabytes (or a million gigabytes). For comparison, if your brain worked like a digital video recorder in a television, 2.5 petabytes would be enough to hold three million hours of TV shows. You would need to leave the recorder on for *more than 300 years* to use up all that storage.[2]

Why would we have so much capacity? If everything is the product of survival of the fittest, why do we need such gigantic information storage in our brains? Did we ever have a time where we used all that capacity? If not, then how could evolution have created it—since we weren't ever using it, let alone using it for our survival? Did someone with capacity for, say, only 1 million hours of TV shows have more of a difficult time surviving in the wild? How did all that capacity become important? Was that memory really necessary to *survive*? Why wouldn't we just have the amount of capacity sufficient to know when danger is near and sense where the best food locales are? Do we really need knowledge of advance physics, chemistry, or even algebra to *survive*? In fact, to survive in the wild, do we truly need memories or need for information storage at all, at least the intensely detailed kind we have about some nasty thing our first-grade teacher said to us? And if it's a question of survival, why don't animals have anything remotely similar in size to the human brains' capacity?

Survival and natural selection *could not have produced this.* And yet there it is: A vast amount of brain capacity sitting idle, doing nothing; twiddling its proverbial thumbs.

I came to discover that atheism and evolution are codependent; they go hand in hand with each other, like an electron must have its proton, yin must have its yang, and Abbott must have his Costello. Atheism makes no sense without evolution to explain our universe and our existence, and evolution—as most scientists today present it—makes no sense unless there is no creator controlling or manipulating anything.

And if you do believe in God, it would be difficult to incorporate why God would just leave all creation and the development of humankind to complete chance. How would that work? Evolution creates humans, and then at some point God notices and says to Himself, "Well, now that you're here, I guess I should get involved"?

It is binary. Either God created the universe and all within it, or He did not. Once I realized this philosophical reality, while at the same time realizing free will, beauty, humor, and so forth could not possibly arise out of evolution's proposed "survival of the fittest" approach, God became a scientific deduction.

And I was on my way.

That was part of my personal journey. But an equally and perhaps more important part of that journey was the realization that atheism kills. It is a destructive hurricane that kills consistently, and kills a lot. While we may not know exactly how the hurricane will twist and turn, we do know there will *only* be massive damage in its wake. And as far as we know, no hurricane has ever taken a side-excursion to build anything.

For reasons that I'll explain in this book, the very nature of atheism actually *demands* destruction and oppression. Indeed, contrary to the cute epithet of the religiously disaffected—that God is responsible for more death and destruction than anything else in history—the reverse is true. Remember: in atheism, mayhem is the rule; goodness the exception.

What This Book Is *Not* About

This book is *not* about proving the existence of God. This book is also not about proving that atheists are wrong. Plenty of books and discussions are available about both of those topics. While I will touch upon these, the thrust of this book is to show the natural devastating impact of atheism, particularly when a government adopts it as policy.

All the same, it's important to know what the atheist thinks, because it helps reveal the destruction that godlessness brings. And having been an atheist myself, let's get it all out in the open and make the best argument possible.

That's right: the argument *for* atheism. Here it is:

The Argument *for* Atheism

At the mature age of eleven, I had figured it all out: because you cannot feel, hear, see, touch, or smell God, it is highly unlikely that He exists. My brother and I had some debate over this. He insisted that God exists and refused to acknowledge my arguments, but I always pressed on with him.

Here's the argument:

God is only a social safety net, which makes us feel secure, given that we live in a cold, nasty universe. Evolution demonstrates that things developed randomly, and we slowly mutated over millions and billions of years to be the intelligent species we are today.

God is a primitive notion. From the days of the cavemen, we humans have sought solace in the stars and nature, desperately hoping that someone was out there, directing our lives. This gave those lives a sense of structure, purpose, and hope. In such times, we understandably needed that hope just to survive. In fact, when we did not understand something, we simply assigned a "god" to it.

For example, although we certainly understood the sun's power to provide heat, to grow plants, and otherwise to sustain our lives, we didn't understand the sun itself. So we created a "god of the sun." We did likewise for the oceans, the sky, the air, and so forth. We even assigned gods later on (through the Greeks and Romans) for more abstract concepts such as war, love, and just about everything else we could not readily explain.

We moved forward in our civilization and slowly began to understand the true nature of things: the earth revolves around the sun, not vice versa; hurricanes are the product of wind patterns and temperature fluctuations as opposed to the wrath of any god. So we started abandoning those gods.

Of course, that did not mean we evolved to the point where we could explain *everything*. On the contrary, we still have a vast amount of information we do not know regarding space, science, biology, and even physics. We still cling to our God to explain all of those things we still don't understand. He's the last of the gods, if you like.

But we still fill in those gaps: that is obvious from the march of science. We will obviously know more about science in the future than we do today, just as we now know so much more than we did thousands of years ago. It does not, therefore, take much brainpower to figure out that science *will* likewise provide more answers, and the need for our present-day God will diminish and wither away.

What brought civilization to where we are is the scientific method—trial and error and peer-review through other experts in the field—which ultimately seeks truth above all else. That is wholly opposite to the approach of faith, which asks you merely to believe and motivates you through fear of the unknown and a promise of better things to come in some fantastical place they call "heaven." It is in fact Science that seeks—and gets—*real* answers to the unknown. Faith is also a ruse to control people, masquerading as a tool for morality and growth. But it is no different than telling your kids that Santa Claus will give them toys, if only they behave.

And then there are the horrors that religion has unleashed, at least organized religion. After all, it was the Catholic church that slaughtered so many in the name of God during the Inquisition. Didn't the Christians kill hundreds of thousands of Jews and Muslims during the notorious Crusades? The pedophilia scandal, which exposed a decades long practice of priests and other clergy abusing young children, is an unforgivable mark on the Church—a scandal which grew bigger and bigger precisely because it enjoyed the protection of the Church, while terrifying its victims with threats of hell-fire if they told anyone. Or worse yet: that this was God's will.

This is to say nothing of all the horrors of the Reformation and Counter-Reformation, where Protestants and Catholics tortured and killed one another with unimaginable cruelty—again believing they were doing "God's" work. Even after that, leaders repeatedly used God and Jesus as an excuse for the brutal take-over of land in Africa, Australia and the Americas. People used religion to justify slavery, and institutional racism after that.

Organized religion either enabled and encouraged all these horrible things to happen. The Muslim world even today engages in routine "honor" killings, and systematic rape; they behead and set those they capture on fire. They engage in unspeakable cruelty to little children.[3] Other have committed numerous terrorist attacks, including the infamous attacks of September 11, 2001, and continue to do so.

If God existed, and if he were truly so good and powerful, He would not have let such horrors occur at all, let alone in His name. For that matter, God would also refuse to allow general cruelty or evil to exist in the first place. In the words of Ivan Karamazov, in Dostoevsky's *The Brothers Karamazov*: "What about the children?" Even if you believe that bad things happen to people as punishment for some wrong in their past (a questionable theory), how can you apply this to a child who is dealing with inoperable bone cancer? How can you apply this to a child who is the victim of pedophilia, whom some monster abducted and sold into slavery or forced into child porn? No just god would allow such evil upon innocents.

A believer will talk about "free will" as the reason we have such evil. But this is nothing more than a mental contortion that sidesteps the issue, which is the horrible reality of evil. It goes nowhere to proving God's existence and still doesn't explain why God would allow an innocent small child to suffer cancer. The child didn't exercise his free will and "choose" cancer.

Finally, regarding the Torah, the New Testament, the Book of Mormon, the Quran, and so forth: it defies all credibility to suggest that God wrote any of these books. Clearly, men ("inspired" or not) wrote these books. They are at best fables and legends men have cobbled together and repackaged from local lore. Much of it was no doubt political, expedient and derivative. Above all, men crafted them for the ultimate purpose of controlling and manipulating what would otherwise be a volatile and fickle mob.

To believe any of the specific stories of the Bible is silly: It's literally incredible—and defies all science—to suggest that God created the world in six days (and the universe, no less) or that the earth is only five thousand-plus years old. We now know better: Earth is approximately 4 billion years old, and the universe is 15-or-so billion years old. It was nice to give comfort to those uninformed people two thousand years ago, but let's grow up and yield to science already.

Also, no evidence exists for the flood of Noah's time, and it is equally preposterous to suggest that Adam and Eve were the first human beings, not only because science shows we evolved from the apes, but we know that Cro-Magnon man existed way before Adam and Eve supposedly made their grand entrance. P.S.: how could Adam and Eve be the first humans when they only had two sons, Cain and Abel? Doesn't that violate basic biology?

It is also silly to talk about the subsequent miracles in the Bible (the burning bush; the parting of the Red Sea; Jesus' walking on water, raising people from the dead, and his own resurrection); or any conversations with God; interference by God; or struggles with God. It only insults the intelligence to suggest such "miracles" happened, when they clearly defy all laws of physics (miracles we incidentally don't seem to see any more in the modern age). Not only that, but there is scant evidence of any of the characters of the Bible, let alone miracles.

In short, the burden should be with the *believer* that a "creator" or the God we read about in the Bible, is real. The atheist need not prove that there is no God. That is asking him to prove a negative, like expecting someone to prove aliens do *not* secretly control our world.

And religion has impeded learning and science. What more evidence do we need than how the Catholic church put Galileo on trial for heresy after he had published *Dialogue Concerning the Two Chief World Systems,* which merely presented a debate between a heliocentrist and a geocentrist?[4] The institutions of God have always had a historical self-preserving tendency to suppress science. While that suppression is less intense today in America and the West, it is because secularization has finally allowed science to flourish, and the Church's all-encompassing political power has waned. In fact, the church only revoked its excommunication of Galileo in 1965.

Religious suppression and intimidation still thrive today, as we see in the Muslim world. Religion's efforts to suppress science and progress remain, too. Why? Because science is a *threat* to religion: people might find out the truth and revolt. Religion is necessary to keep a perceived structure, but it is only to maintain a status quo in favor of the rich and powerful—many of whom are the religious ones themselves.

We ignore the harsh realities of our world by pretending there is some scowling master watching our every misstep and thought. It may somehow give us comfort to believe that someone is in charge, but it is a false comfort—and a dangerous one at that. It makes us believe fantasies and untruths, which can only lead to irresponsible, and even evil, behavior.

Instead, we must assume responsibility for our imperfect world as it is, and roll up our sleeves and seek answers from the wonderful worlds of science and psychology, no matter how painful those answers might be. Only by doing that will we truly explain the realities of our world and universe and to make our world safer, kinder, and more productive.

We alone are our own caretakers. There is no one else out there. The sooner we realize this, the sooner we can accomplish great things. Karl Marx understood that well when he claimed religion is an opiate of the people. Drugs can only hurt, not build. And only *we* can do this building, not some invisible "God" in the sky.

While God may have served as a psychological "crutch" once upon a time when we needed it, we must now abandon Him—much like a butterfly should abandon the cocoon that played a part in its creation. The cocoon no longer serves any purpose.

And please don't tell me you have to believe in God to be moral or good. Animals live without God and we see several instances of animals rescuing each other in the wild, even if they are from different species. And there are many wonderful atheists who are law-abiding and moral to a fault. Likewise, there are many horrific religious people. Goodness ultimately comes from the heart, and we have evolved into a caretaking society over time, through logic and a sense of what is right for the community. The best code of conduct is not to do anything that would hurt others. You do not need God for that; just logic.

That is what will move us forward, not wasting time in church. We need to focus on the today, not some fantasy reward in an afterlife that no one can possibly know. There's a lot of work to do.

So, tell me: Have I gotten that about right?

The Argument *Against* Atheism

Here's a thought experiment: imagine a video of a leaf trickling down some rapids. We know it moves because of the force of wind above it and the force of water below it. Depending on the current, the interceding rocks and other things, that leaf will go this way and then that. But if you somehow could make the water, the wind, and the rocks disappear from the video, the leaf would appear to move by itself. It would be the same for a kite in the wind, or the swaying of a tree in a strong gust. They would all appear to be moving—acting—on their own.

Free will is the notion that we independently undertake our actions and choices, and therefore are responsible for them. But at some point during our stay on the planet, we come upon the question of whether we are the true authors of our own actions. Is free will only an illusion? Are we unwitting pawns in a world of "determinism"—a world where we take action not because of our own volition but because of all of the circumstances that led to that moment?

In short, are we just like the leaf floating down the river? Do we *perceive* ourselves to act independently, or are our actions (where we go, so to speak) merely the product of thousands of different forces that push us this way and then that?

One bottom line in philosophy classes is that true free will can only come from some outside force, a force that "gives" free will to its recipient. Another bottom line is that prior actions and statements "determine" our present actions, like the balls of a billiard table. For those who reject free will, *nothing* we do comes really from our own volition. Free will is merely an illusion. Further, it would mean we are not responsible for our actions, and of course, we have no need for a God—certainly not a God who judges.

After all, if we are not responsible for our actions and words, then why should we be accountable to God, or any higher being for that matter? In fact, it would be downright illogical and unfair. You might as well be angry at a tree when a branch breaks and falls on your car.

But this is where I started questioning my atheism. Eventually it struck me that determinism failed to explain our *humanness*, that we are *not* like the leaf floating down the river. No doubt we undertake certain actions because of outside forces, such as when I look for water when I am thirsty. But I still feel that I have a sense of morality—a simple sense of what is right and what is wrong, and that those should be guiding forces in life.

It also struck me as implausible that I did not have free will. I just could not accept this. I don't think anyone can meaningfully deny he has free will, assuming the alternative is that we have no real volition in our day to day matters. People can disagree philosophically, but the way each of us actually live our lives says otherwise.

I'll prove my point: suppose you're with a friend at a movie. You ask your friend to buy popcorn. But when he comes back with the bag, the popcorn is too salty. You don't like salt.

So, you punch him really hard in the face. And then you spit on him.

"What the—?" He moans out to you, reeling from pain and the blood that's now oozing out of his nose and mouth. "What the hell did you do *that* for?"

"I don't like salt," you explain, as you turn your attention back to the movie.

A reasonable response? After all, if there is no free will, and I can explain everything as merely the result of all the complicated and nuanced events in my life before that moment, then punching my friend is something I couldn't help myself from doing. So why should he be upset?

Free will and determinism are mutually exclusive. Either you have free will, or you don't. You don't have to believe in free will, but you must acknowledge that the alternative is determinism, one where every action and decision is merely a reaction to something else. It can be very sophisticated, like those elaborate mousetrap mazes, where each event creates a chain reaction leading to another. It's as if we live in a movie, where the beginning, middle, and end are all set in chapters. The movie characters *appear* to act as though they're making their own choices, but the screenwriter, the director, and just about everyone else involved in the making of the movie know better. There's a script here, after all.

But I sense that I have free will. I sense I am ultimately responsible for my actions. I sense that somehow I will face judgement for my actions, and that the ultimate arbiter of my actions will not be a man but something above man. I believe even the atheist has this sense in him, although he often fights it.

I like to think about stories, and why we even tell them. There's almost always a bad guy in every story, an antagonist. And if the story is worth anything, we truly dislike the bad guy, right? When we are angry at Darth Vader from *Star Wars*, we are not angry at him because he is mentally ill or because he had a poor upbringing. We are angry at him because he has *chosen* to do something we consider wrong or evil. We resent him for his *choices*. He has defied a norm that we expect all decent individuals in our society to live by.

But if they can't help themselves, isn't *any* punishment unfair? Without free will, we would need no prisons. We send people to prison not just because they might be dangerous to society (and that would apply only to some convicts, anyway), but because we are holding them accountable for the wrong they have committed.

The atheist's response to all this is: Don't fool yourself. The only reason you decide to choose what you consider "right" is that it is *logical* to do so. After all, would you want to live in a world where everyone can kill everyone else, rape everyone else, steal from everyone else, and so on? To them, we live in a world where everyone is in a perpetual "Mexican standoff" with one another, and that's what keeps us from killing, raping, and stealing from each other.

This argument fails because it assumes the individual first thinks on behalf of some "collective whole" whenever he does anything. But individuals act with very little regard to how their actions might affect the society at large. Most thieves and even murderers believe there should be laws against stealing and murder, yet they still steal and murder. History is replete with stories of how people act with no concern for anyone else at all, let alone a "collective."

And we *know* why we do not murder or steal. It is not *only* because we worry that other people might do it to us. We don't because we have a sense that doing such things violates a *code*. We learned from our parents, our clergy, and hopefully our schools, that there is a higher standard out there by which we must all live.

Ironically, the "logic" argument is illogical. If anything, logic suggests that we choose the most *ungodly* of actions. What do I mean by this? If we live in a truly deterministic world, and there is no one "watching" over me, then why not kill anyone that gets in my way?

Example: Say I fear that my boss might promote my co-worker, Mr. Brown, instead of me. But passing me over for promotion at my age means not only an end to my career advancement, but the end to the big raise that I expected—or at least that I was counting on. I also really need that raise to pay off my enormous gambling losses and to make sure Guido doesn't break my legs.

If logic is the basis for everything, why not *kill* Mr. Brown? Assuming I could get away with it, wouldn't this be exactly the "logical" thing to do? Remember, Guido will maim me if I don't pay him back with money from that raise. My family will all be out on the streets. By contrast, Mr. Brown is a younger, single man, with no kids. Don't the lives of my family members outweigh Mr. Brown's? Why should my kids and I suffer because of Mr. Brown?

Let's say I don't go the murder route. Why not instead go on a smear campaign about Mr. Brown? Perhaps I can digitally alter a photograph and show Mr. Brown in compromising photos with young boys. That would do the trick and get the boss to fire Brown. And, by the way, Mr. Brown probably was doing just fine financially. At least that's what I assume. Either way, I'm sure he'll land on his feet just fine. Why wouldn't that be logical?[5]

There are many other examples: why not cheat on your spouse, so long as he or she doesn't know about it. Why not lie about your background to get a job? Why not lie about your racial minority status to benefit from affirmative action preferential treatment? Why not secure a handicap placard for better parking everywhere, even if you're not handicapped?

Why say anything when you know your boss—say a movie mogul—routinely abuses and even rapes women? After all, he's helping you advance in the business. Why rock that boat?

As a lawyer, I have seen countless parties try to justify illicit behavior. This one was a caretaker of an old lady, but she didn't leave anything for him in her will as she promised, so it's okay if he forges the old lady's will to reflect a "reasonable" payment to him. An employee didn't yet receive the raise he thinks he should get, so he'll just pad his overtime or fake expenses.

One of the best illustrations of this was from the old English film, *Kind Hearts and Coronets*, where the protagonist has fallen on hard times, a victim of many misfortunes. But he is thirteenth in line to become a duke. Desperate, he embarks upon a plan to kill everyone ahead of him. What emboldens him is that he feels that the royal line has snubbed and mistreated him. In his mind, he *deserves* this dukedom, and it is *reasonable* for him to kill those in his way.

As wrong as these scenarios seem, people engage in them. And it happens on a larger level, too: slave owners used "logic" to justify slavery. The eugenics movement premised its sterilization programs on logic: why should the government drain its resources for the feeble-minded and criminally deranged among us? Wasn't it logical to rid society of such burdens? The United States Supreme Court approved the forced sterilizations of the mentally inferior on the supposedly logical grounds that "three generations of idiots are enough."[6] People have used logic to say it's okay to kill children up to the age of two if you regret having that child.[7] The Nazis took this logic to the next level to justify killing all those it considered undesirable. Stalin and other communist and fascist leaders despots killed anyone who opposed them. Sure, they'd rather not, but the Utopia of world socialism was waiting. So you gotta do what you gotta do.

This is where logic alone gets you. Logic alone is subjective. One man's logic is another man's madness. Do not fool yourself into thinking that *morality* is the same as *logic*. And do not think that logic will *lead* to morality. Just like a car you can use for good or bad, you can use logic for any purpose you like. Logic alone leads to nothing—or anything you like.

But murder is *inherently* wrong, atheists will counter. That may seem so now, but only after centuries of Christianity and Judaism made it part of our collective mother's milk. The Germanic tribes in the earlier part of the second millennium believed that murder was perfectly fine. There was no inherent punishment for it—no more than there would be for a crow who killed a small rodent for food. Even before then, the Greek Spartans (those lovable heroes of the Greco-Persian Wars of the fifth century B.C.) killed their children, particularly their boys, at infancy, if they deemed them too sickly or too small to be of value to the defense of the city. It was all very reasonable and logical to them.

And then we can look at much of history as quite illogical, yet very "right" to do: It wasn't logical that the Americans entered into World War I, and then into World War II. America might have been just fine without getting involved. Why risk our boys' lives? For that matter, why do we bother retrieving our wounded from the battlefield? Doesn't that increase the odds of the remaining soldiers being killed or wounded? Why help the Muslims in Kosovo, or fight in any of their places in the world? Why devote and risk our money, resources, and manpower to respond to catastrophes in Thailand, Haiti, or otherwise?

Between 1941 and 1944, the inhabitants of Le Chambon-sur-Lignon village, a Protestant village in southern France, helped five thousand refugees—including several thousand Jews—escape Nazi persecution. The village's pastor, André Trocmé, and his wife, Magda Trocmé, led the rescue effort. Villagers hid the refugees in private homes, farms, and boarding houses. They hid many Jewish youngsters in the local school, at which Andre Trocmé's cousin, Daniel Trocmé, taught. Nearby Roman Catholic convents and monasteries also provided shelter. Beginning in 1943, the villagers helped smuggle refugees to safety across the Swiss border. German police arrested Daniel, who died later in a concentration camp in April 1944.[8]

Despite the grave danger, the villagers of Le Chambon never hesitated. Years later, the villagers of Le Chambon refused praise for their deeds. One villager asked, "How can you call us 'good'? We did what had to be done."[9]

During Hitler's reign, there were many such stories. There was *nothing* logical about them. The logical thing for these rescuers would have been *not* to hide these Jews, *not* insert themselves, and just cooperate with the Nazis. Who could blame them? After all, world events had placed them in a position of tremendous risk. But these Christians saved the Jews anyway.

Similarly, during the days of slavery, Harriet Tubman risked her life and freedom to rescue hundreds of slaves. Was that logical? She had escaped slavery; why would she go back?

Most of us like to think we would also have helped the Jews and the slaves, had we lived during those times. But would we?

Without a core belief in God and an appreciation of the existence of good and evil, it's difficult to resist real evil. It's even harder when you think that evil doesn't even exist, or that everything is a matter of "nuance" or morally relative.

Many will argue that "in the long run," society will think in a collective sense. That's where good for the overall community will ultimately come together. First, let's put aside the obvious response that different people have a different view of what might work best for the larger community. We will always have disagreements about socialized medicine, regulations, tax rates, and whether we need bullet trains or bike lanes. Come to think of it, people seem to disagree on *everything*. That alone means we will rarely reach the same *logic* about anything.

Second, we humans are, and always will be, a collection of individuals all living together. We will never be individuals only working for, or even thinking of, some "collective." It is naive to think that any individual will ever completely toss away his own individual and logical self-interest in favor of the collective's "greater" interest.

It is difficult to see where individuals completely disavow their personal interests for the good of a community. People tend not to give up most of their property willingly to their neighbors. People tend not to willingly drain most of their own bank accounts to alleviate others' poverty. Businesses tend not to like competition, even though competition is good for society.

Here's a thought experiment: A large bag with a big dollar sign drops from a helicopter into a densely populated urban area—or for that matter *any* area in the world. Many people see it fall from the sky, and it's clear there's a lot of money in it. Someone with a megaphone in the helicopter yells, "Enjoy!" and the helicopter flies away.

Do all the people calmly walk toward the big bag of money, make a big circle around it, and appoint a trusted individual among them to then say: "All right. Let's do what's fair here and divvy up the money among us equally"?

No, we know what will occur: the person who gets to the bag first will "win" the bag. And then everyone else will fight him for it.

The day that people can think like the first scenario and not the second is the day we are (1) no longer humans and have become robots, or (2) well, I can't think of anything else.

The atheist places far too much faith in logic. Logic cannot alone be the answer to morality or making good decisions. The only place logic—by itself—gets you is self-preservation and self-interest. That kind of logic can always change depending on who is in power and what your needs are for any given moment. That is hardly a recipe for any consistent and reliable code of conduct for ourselves.

Logic is a tool that can lead to great geopolitical, business, and military decisions and even to great discoveries and innovations. But, like nuclear power, its use only makes sense if we also understand its potential for great harm.

God has imbued us with this very logic—in large part so that we can find Him. It is a gift that is wildly beyond the abilities of any other living creature on the planet. However, if we do not appreciate the *moral* limitations on logic, we risk the destruction of civilization.

Finally, here's a strange conundrum for the atheist: he believes in survival of the fittest as the source of morality. It may be logical or predictable that the strongest survive, but that has nothing to do with morality. After all, there is no "murder," "rape," or "theft" in the jungle.

On the other hand, the atheist is against murder, rape and theft—somehow on logical grounds. But we've shown above that logic alone won't prevent murder, rape or theft. Using just logic alone can even lead to them.

So pick your poison. Because you don't want to live under either theory.

The inherent flaw in the atheist's argument is that he must ultimately acknowledge that without God—or some other creator who judges us—morality must be relative. But the atheist rejects this and instead believes that *logic* is universal, and that there is only one logical answer to every circumstance. But we know that is not so. Logic without anything guiding will always bend relative to culture, time, and situation.

By contrast, morality from God provides consistent standards of behavior under all circumstances. We should use logic only with those standards of behavior in mind, and to *reach* those standards.

The Great Internal Irony of Atheism

Let's address the atheist's argument that he need not believe in God to be moral; that morality comes from his heart; and that he doesn't need a religion as a guidepost to tell him what is right and wrong. I always found this argument puzzling.

We understand that a healthy body temp should be about 98.6 Fahrenheit. Higher or lower than that means you are sick. Likewise, your blood pressure above or below certain ranges indicate you are unhealthy. We also have objective measures for what pleasant weather is (say about 72 Fahrenheit, and so much humidity); above that gets to be on the hot side, below on the cold. We say 18 is old enough for sexual consent, younger than that is statutory rape or even pedophilia. Nor can you contract or vote younger than 18. We say that if you drive above 65 miles per hour, you are violating the speeding laws.

You get the idea. There are many other standards that we apply in life, not just in health and in safety, but in math (we've all agreed to work with Arabic numbers, using base 10) and specific words to communicate, as well as grammar (verb agreement, tenses, conjugation and pronouns).

The atheist understands the need for standards, too. After all, how can one advance "science" without numbers and agreements on units?

But when it comes to what one might consider the most important aspect of our society—how we act with each other—it's something you just *know*. You know what I mean?

Atheists of all people should understand the flaw in their own argument; after all, they think that everything is relative, because there is no absolute "right" or "wrong." Their own argument that logic should lead to "good" or "right" decisions presumes there *is* an "absolute" standard in the first place. Otherwise, a decision or action can be "right" while any other decisions or action—even the opposite—can *also* be "right."

Some may call that confusing.

Either an absolute standard exists, or it does not. If you do not believe in God, then you must believe there are no absolute, universal standards; only *relative* standards. That is the intellectually consistent argument. But if you believe that pursuing a correct path is important, then that assumes there are indeed absolute, universal standards. Above or below that "standard" should indicate to us that we are morally unhealthy. It's objective.

For the believer, the Bible is humanity's guidepost for morality. But to be a "true" atheist, your attitude *must* be: "Whatever anyone does to me, that's what he does to me. It is not good or bad. It's just survival, and likewise *I* will protect myself in the interests of my survival. I don't mind if you do well, so long as it doesn't interfere with me. But if you do interfere, watch out."

Do you see the atheist's conundrum here? He cannot be a "moral" person because there are no real objective "morals." He may *individually act* morally because he knows a world without morals would be both devastating and terrifying. But that does not mean his atheism *leads* to moral behavior. He might choose to act moral *in spite of* his atheism, not *because* of it.

Atheism offers only emptiness and, ultimately, nihilism. To say an atheist can be or is moral *because* of his atheism is like saying George Washington was a great man *because* he had slaves. You cannot both subscribe to an ideology that by definition offers no morals and at the same time argue it is a moral system. While an individual atheist can himself be moral and caring, atheism itself can *only* be *amoral*—that is, without morals.

It's a contradiction that an atheist cannot truly square for himself. Even during my most intense atheism, I never argued that there could be morals without God. On the contrary, I proudly acknowledged the contrary: I knew morals had *nothing* to do with atheism. To argue otherwise would be like arguing a cheetah is a vegetarian. It's just not a part of what he is.

In the same way that today's social agitators and revisionists wrongly try to re-cast killers such as Mao, Castro, Ho Chi Minh and Che Guevara into selfless fighters for the common man, the atheist cannot fashion atheism into some righteous moral enterprise. It is not.

And the world seems to agree: a recent study of 3,000 people in thirteen countries over five continents presented a scenario of a fictional evildoer who tortured animals as a child, then grows up to murder and mutilate five homeless people. The study asked half of the group how likely it was that the perpetrator was a religious believer, and the other half how likely that he was an atheist. The study found that people were about twice as likely to assume that the killer was an atheist.[10] Remarkably, even *atheists* assume it.[11] The study showed not only that people consider atheism a doctrine without morals, but that they generally fear atheism as dangerous and "morally depraved."[12]

And here's the predictable, "no surprise" ending to this chapter: nothing "moral" has ever come out of atheism. Ever. Because there is nothing in atheism's business plan that calls for morality. You might as well expect an ice cream store to start delivering babies.

Morality? It's just not what atheism does.

The Unbearable Impossibility of Being

As we've shown above, morality cannot come about randomly through evolution. Other things are difficult to explain through evolution, or without the benefit of a "Giver:" our notions of beauty, music, self-awareness, love, humor and so much more. At some point, I had to accept the fact that evolution could not meaningfully explain the existence of any of these things. Most animals do not love and have relationships the way humans do, and yet they seem to survive.

Animals do not appreciate music the way we do (except for the appreciation some animals may have once in a while when humans play music for them). Humans *create* music. They gather together to hear it and even pay a lot of money for the honor. This is no evolutionary thing, and certainly not a matter of survival of the fittest. Yet people make careers out of music, and people feel that music soothes their spirits. Music somehow "speaks" to them in a way regular conversation does not. Music seems to summon the soul. It even creates that "tingly" feeling that seems to wrap around us, even lift us, like a temporary whirlwind. We can't explain it, but we do know you cannot truly explain it with evolution.

Evolution cannot explain humor or beauty, either. As far as I can tell, Bill Gates, founder of Microsoft, appears never to have made a joke in his life. Yet he seems to be surviving quite well.

The point is, humor is certainly not necessary for our survival, but it does seem to lift us up.

The same applies to beauty. While animals may prefer a stronger animal as a mate, that is a far cry from appreciating a sunset or the beauty of the Mona Lisa, the Beatles' *Hey Jude* or Shakespeare's sonnets.

Animals also don't seem to have a sense of an afterlife, or any continuation or sense from whence they came. There is only the "now" for them. For that matter, there is no sense of some better tomorrow for them (despite what the great Disney movie *The Lion King* may have suggested). Yet we humans feel it in our bones. Even when we don't believe in God, we contemplate our future.

In short, survival of the fittest appears to apply to animals, at best. We humans seem to need something more: elevation, meaning, and purpose. We always seem to be *reaching* for something more.

I Do Not Think That Book Says What You Think It Says

Next let's respond to the argument of the atheist—and Karl Marx—that the Bible manipulates people to keep them down, using tactics like fear of eternal damnation on the one hand, and false promises of rewards of an after-life on the other.

This argument evokes a wonderful moment from the movie *The Princess Bride.* There, a bumbling schemer named Vizzini has kidnapped a princess for ransom and is now transporting her to an evil king. The hero, the Dread Pirate Roberts, seeks to rescue her and chases Vizzini and his thugs through land, sea and cliffs. But despite Vizzini's consistent efforts to foil Roberts' advance (which include trying to sail much faster than Roberts, cutting a rope on a cliff Roberts was climbing to chase him, a sword fight with Vizzini's swordsman [Inigo Montoya] and a wrestling match with Vizzini's hired giant), Roberts easily overcomes them all.

Each time Vizzini learns of his team's latest failure to stop Roberts, he responds the same way: "Inconceivable!"

Finally, after hearing Vizzini say this word multiple times, his assistant Inigo pauses to tell him: "You keep using that word. I do not think that word means what you think it means."

And that might be the same retort to the atheist: I do not think the Bible says what you think it says.

Most atheists have not read the Bible, let alone meaningfully studied it. They know only of the "ridiculous" features, such as the six days of creation, Noah and the Flood, Adam and Eve, the parting of the Red Sea, the Ten Plagues and so on. So they dismiss it. They assume in all other respects that the Bible is chock full of guilting, scolding, and dire threats of destruction and hell if you don't do what the Masters say—whoever those Masters may be.

But not quite: here's a unique book that not only asks each of us to be responsible for his actions, but conveys repeatedly that God's highest desire for us is *to create, to be free, and be good to each other.*

And if it was indeed a book that conniving men had fabricated to "control" the masses, then just who are the master "control-lers?" There is no reference to the human "controllers," let alone a suggestion that some self-anointed men are to be in charge, other than God. Indeed, there is no aspiration to any ruling human authority at all.

Oops.

There's more: In the Bible, God repeatedly disapproves the notion of kings, at least the autocratic kind. He prefers for the people to govern themselves. Still, the Jews wanted their king, to feel on par with the other nations of kings around them. God repeatedly expresses his disdain for dictatorship, and warns the Jews—in so many words— to be careful what they wanted. Sure enough, over only a few generations, David's once formidable kingdom descends and splits into warring kingdoms, which in turn abandon God. The Israelites soon suffer conquest, destruction of the First Temple, and enslavement and dispersion by Babylonians who conquer them easily.

One would expect such a manipulative treatise to name preferred rulers, and demand that the masses give these rulers most of their wealth, and for that matter, all their women for their personal gratifications. But no such demands appear.

There would be calls for sacrifices and other rituals of intimidation. Somewhere in this cunning document, it would admonish the ordinary man and women never to speak up for themselves. It would tell them that they should be grateful for the miserable scraps their "masters" might dole out to them from time to time. There are no such words.

You would also expect the Bible to encourage racism, or at least some "caste" type system, to enable the "haves" to maintain their power. It does not.

Far from this, the Bible makes clear that God detests slavery, human sacrifice, polygamy, distinctions between rich and poor, adultery and incest[13]—institutions and attitudes you would not expect any "controllers" who want to maintain their power to easily forego. It focuses on the primacy of family and community. The Bible actively encourages personal growth, honesty, freedom, creativity, and goodness toward each other, to give charity and to otherwise help the poor and the sick. It advances cleanliness and the notion of justice. It celebrates the notion that everyone is equal in the eyes of God, and that notions of nobility, the first-born, or bloodline mean *nothing* (God chooses Abraham, Joseph, Moses and David as leaders or prophets. None of them descend from royalty; none are first-borns).

Perhaps most importantly—and most inconsistent with the "controller" mantra—the Bible *encourages and celebrates* resistance to tyranny, idolatry and human sacrifice.

In short, to believe that some devious men created the Bible in a disingenuous bid to manipulate and control people, there would be a curtain, and men behind that curtain controlling all that we see and believe, à la *The Wizard of Oz*. There are not.

So we return to Marx's quip about religion being an "opiate of the people" to control them. It begs the question: How so? The Judeo-Christian mindset fosters freedom and responsibility, self-betterment and education, justice and accountability, creativity and the delay of self-gratification. Far from "drugging" us, all of it sounds more like a whole lot of rolling up of sleeves and getting to work.

Ironically it is *Marx's* world of godlessness that was the true "opiate:" it promised a "one-size fits all," comprehensive caretaker government where no one would want for anything, which would simultaneously improve the lives of everyone.

And to believe *that*, you'd need a whole lot of opiates.

God's Hostility to Science?

Man only likes to count his troubles, but he does not count his joys.
— *Fyodor Dostoevsky*

As to the argument that religion has been hostile to science, it is hard for the atheist to meaningfully point to anything other than the Galileo inquisition (which, as it turns out, was hardly as despotic or suppressive of science as anti-religionists assert[14]). They cite Galileo as an "example," but citing an "example" suggests there are many other instances where religion suppressed scientific inquiry. You might as well say Ted Bundy was an American; therefore, all Americans are psychopathic serial murderers.

The claim that the church somehow opposed science does not fly: On the contrary, Catholics gave us some of the most important scientists *of all time,* including:

> ...Rene Descartes, who discovered analytic geometry and the laws of refraction; Blaise Pascal, inventor of the adding machine, hydraulic press, and the mathematical theory of probabilities; Augustinian priest Gregor Mendel, who founded modern genetics; Louis Pasteur, founder of microbiology and creator of the first vaccine for rabies and anthrax; and cleric Nicolaus Copernicus, who first developed scientifically the view that the earth rotated around the sun. Jesuit priests in particular have a long history of scientific achievement; they contributed to the development of pendulum clocks, pantographs, barometers, reflecting telescopes and microscopes, to scientific fields as various as magnetism, optics and electricity. They observed, in some cases before anyone else, the colored bands on Jupiter's surface, the Andromeda nebula and Saturn's rings. They theorized about the circulation of the blood (independently of Harvey), the theoretical possibility of flight, the way the moon affected the tides, and the wave-like nature of light. Star maps of the southern hemisphere, symbolic logic, flood-control measures on the Po and Adige rivers, introducing plus and minus signs into Italian mathematics—all were typical Jesuit achievements, and scientists as influential as Fermat, Huygens, Leibniz and New-

ton were not alone in counting Jesuits among their most prized correspondents."[15]

Who proposed what came to be known as the "Big Bang theory" of the origin of the universe? Georges Lemaitre, a Belgian physicist and classically trained Roman Catholic priest. The scientific community now fully accepts the Big Bang as "settled science." Lemaitre not only proposed the theory; he developed Hubble's law and constant before Hubble. (Fascinatingly, Einstein dismissed his theory, famously retorting, "Your calculations are correct, but your physics is atrocious".)[16] Alexander Fleming, who invented penicillin, was a man of faith who pursued his invention largely as part of his faith. Jean-Baptiste Lamarck (1744–1829) prefigured the theory of evolution with Lamarckism. More recently, many devout Catholics were Nobel Laureates in Physics, Medicine, and Physiology, including Erwin Schrodinger, John Eccles, and Alexis Carrel. The Jesuits were and remain quite active in astronomy.[17]

So it is difficult to square the numerous devout Catholics in science with the charge that the Catholic Church opposed scientific knowledge and progress.[18]

There was a date certain before which "science" did *not* exist and a date certain after which there was "science." Many today believe Galileo was the first scientist, not only outside the church but a great fighter against the close-mindedness of the church. They would be wrong on both fronts: he was not the first (he was just famous for his battle with the Church). Further, he was a devout Catholic.[19]

Contrary to the notion of a division between science and faith, it was the *Church* that developed what we now consider "science" the way we think of it.[20] The church, specifically Catholic monasticism in the Middle Ages, created the university and founded the great European universities during this extraordinary time:

Bologna, Coimbra, Paris, Oxford, Salamanca, Cambridge, Montpelier, and Padua. The church produced scholars like Robert Grosseteste, Albert the Great, Roger Bacon, and Thomas Aquinas, who helped establish the scientific method.[21] Why did it do so? To be the center for growth and science.[22]

The present Papal astronomer Guy Consolmagno hails science as an "act of worship" and as "a way of getting intimate with the Creator."[23] As Pope John Paul II himself famously noted: "Truth cannot contradict truth."[24] Because of this time of scientific exploration and openness, the era saw the birth of extraordinary new inventions and concepts such as musical notation, windmills, eyeglasses, printing, and improved clocks.[25]

Likewise, the Roman Catholic Church gave more financial aid and social support to the study of astronomy for over six centuries, "...from the recovery of ancient learning during the late Middle Ages into the Enlightenment, than any other, and, probably, all other, institutions.'"[26]

Christianity advanced science from almost its very beginning, through today. Catholic scientists, both religious and lay, led scientific discovery in many fields. After Rome's fall, monasteries and convents remained key centers of scholarship, and clergymen were the leading scholars of the age—studying nature, mathematics and the motion of the stars.[27]

Some will still challenge the notion of the church as champion of the sciences. They will say that it has a checkered history here, pointing almost exclusively to the Galileo affair. They will say there has always been an inherent intellectual conflict between religion and science.

There isn't much meaningful evidence to support such a claim. Quite the contrary, the church saw itself quite the opposite: the Vatican Council (1869/70) declared that "Faith and reason are of mutual help to each other."[28] The Catholic Encyclopedia of 1912 stated its position that "[t]he conflicts between science and the Church are not real,", and such naysayers may be basing belief in such conflicts on false assumptions.[29]

Over the past fifty years, historians of science have started to concede this as well. They soon "drastically revised" the conventional wisdom that the church was somehow anti-science.[30] The mainstream view now is that the "Church [has] played a *positive role in the development of science* . . . even if this new consensus has not yet managed to trickle down to the general public"[31] (emphasis added). Science historian Ronald L. Numbers has confirmed this view, writing that "Historians of science have known for years that . . . [claims of a conflict] are more propaganda than history . . . Yet the message has rarely escaped the ivory tower."[32]

I have focused primarily on the contributions of the Catholic Church primarily because it has presided the longest over Western Christian civilization compared to its offshoots (such as Protestantism, Mormonism, Seventh Day Adventists and Jehovah's Witnesses), and because the Catholic Church has suffered the most obvious attacks from the godless (arguments focusing on the Crusades, the Inquisition, etc. See discussion above).

However, history shows that enormous contributions also came from the other branches of Christianity and from Jews, in math, the sciences, education, medicine, psychology, the arts, music, law and justice, entertainment and architecture. It seems many ignore that it was their collective sense of community and duty to seek out God's truths which *compelled* them toward such work.

The religious pursued their achievements precisely because of a sense of calling from their faith. A longer list would be too lengthy and is not the subject of this book. But suffice it to say, very few of the godless historically sought out scientific truths because of any non-belief in God. By definition, the godless have no inherent sense of duty, mission or community. They may seek it out on an *individual* level, but that quest still runs afoul of the essential emptiness and lack of purpose in their atheism.

Don't believe it? That's fine. But do this homework: compare the innovations of the historical religious communities to the innovations under communism and fascism, or under any other godless society. You will conclude what is inescapable: there is no real comparison.

Yeah, But Other Than *That*, What Has Religion Ever Done for *Us*?

In one of the iconic scenes from the Monty Python movie, *Life of Brian* (1979), we see a band of Israelite rebels during the time of Rome's occupation of Israel, sitting around a table in a small shack of one of their members. They're developing their secret plan to kidnap Pilate's wife for ransom. While they do so, they discuss their disdain for all things Roman.

Reg, their leader, tries to rally his gang by bemoaning all that the Romans have taken from them, and then rhetorically asking: "And what have they ever given us in return?"

There's a pause. But soon, contrary to Reg's expectations, his crew starts offering up examples, one by one: The Aqueduct... sanitation... the roads... irrigation... medicine... education... wine and public baths... law and order.

All the while, Reg is tapping his fingers on the table, rolling his eyes. These guys are just not getting the point. Finally, he blurts out: "All right... all right... but apart from better sanitation and medicine and education and irrigation and public health and roads and a freshwater system and baths and public order... what have the Romans done for *us*?"

At least the Israelites could appreciate what their hated occupiers, the Romans, had done for them. But when it comes to the atheist's target of scorn, Judaism and Christianity, he has no idea what they've done for him. In fact, while the atheist complains of renegade crusaders and some kings and queens who did bad in God's name, he knows very little of the *good* that religion has done in God's name. He fails to appreciate any of it.

Ask an atheist. *He won't know.* In fact, it has never dawned upon him even to ponder such a question.

So what *has* religion done for us? Let's be like Reg's crew and lay it out for the atheist:

It was the Jews who created the judicial system and notion of justice as we think of it today. It was Judaism that gave us the basic moral code of the Ten Commandments, the foundation of most everything that even the atheist speaks of when he talks of morality. It was the Jews who gave us the notion of time, and ultimately, progress (see more, below).

When the Catholic church was founded, no hospitals existed. Today, approximately one out of five people in the U.S. receive their medical care at a Catholic hospital: The Roman Catholic Church is the largest provider of health care services in the world, outside of any government. Today, it has around 18,000 clinics, 16,000 homes for the elderly and those with special needs, and 5,500 hospitals, most of which are in developing countries. According to the Church's Pontifical Council for the Pastoral Care of Health Care Workers, the Church as of 2010 manages 26% of the world's health care facilities.[33]

Early on, the Christian push for practical charity gave rise to the development of systematic nursing and hospitals, which makes the church the single greatest center for not only hospitals and medical care but for research facilities.[34] The Church's involvement in health care has ancient origins, all which it premises on God's teachings.[35] As Thomas E. Woods, noted Catholic historian, points out:

The early church also institutionalized the care of widows, orphans, the sick and the poor in ways unseen in classical Greece or Rome. Even her harshest critics, from the fourth-century emperor Julian the Apostate all the way to Martin Luther and Voltaire, conceded the church's enormous contributions to the relief of human misery.

The spirit of Catholic charity—that we help those in need not out of any expectation of reciprocity, but as a pure gift, and that we even help those who might not like us—finds no analogue in classical Greece and Rome, but it is this idea of charity that we continue to embrace today.[36]

Likewise, in addition to the creation of the university, the church has contributed enormously in the creation and advancement of schools and local social programs for all, throughout the world. Virtually the entirety of the way we look at education and social programs come to us thanks to what the church created.

And when it came to ending one of the world's oldest but most evil institutions—slavery—Christianity deserves most of the credit. Although some Enlightenment philosophers certainly opposed slavery in principal, it was Christian activists in both Europe and America who organized and effectuated the abolitionist movement.[37]

One of the key abolitionists was Parliamentarian William Wilberforce in England, who wrote that "God Almighty has set before me two great objects, the suppression of the Slave Trade and Reformation of Morals."[38] Despite determined opposition, he was instrumental to ending the slave trade in the British Empire.[39] Further,

The famous English preacher Charles Spurgeon had some of his sermons burned in America due to his censure of slavery, calling it "the foulest blot" and which "may have to be washed out in blood." Methodist founder John Wesley denounced human bondage as "the sum of all villainies," and detailed its abuses. In Georgia, primitive Methodists united with brethren elsewhere in condemning slavery. Many evangelical leaders in the United States such as Presbyterian Charles Finney and Theodore Weld, and women such as Harriet Beecher Stowe (daughter of abolitionist Lyman Beecher) and Sojourner Truth motivated hearers to support abolition. . . . Repentance from slavery was required of souls, once enlightened of the subject, while continued support of the system incurred "the greatest guilt" upon them.[40]

It didn't stop there. As early as 1688, Dutch Quakers in Germantown, Pennsylvania, sent an anti-slavery petition to the Monthly Meeting of Quakers. By 1727 British Quakers had expressed their official disapproval of the slave trade.[41] Three Quaker abolitionists, Benjamin Lay, John Woolman, and Anthony Benezet, devoted their lives to the abolitionist effort from the 1730s to the 1760s.[42] In 1783, 300 Quakers presented a petition to Parliament protesting the slave trade.

In 1787, the Society for Effecting the Abolition of the Slave Trade formed, with nine of the twelve founding members being Quakers. Eventually, Abolitionist pressure had changed popular opinion, and in the 1806 election enough abolitionists became members of parliament to pass the Slave Trade Act 1807. The Royal Navy subsequently declared that the slave trade was equal to piracy, seizing and liberating any slaves it found on board slave ships. Doing so effectively crippled the transatlantic trade of slaves. Eventually, through more abolition agitating, popular opinion continued to grow against slavery, and in 1833 Parliament outlawed slavery itself throughout the entire British Empire.[43]

While the United States took longer to end slavery, it went through much the same story. The Christian abolitionist movement alarmed ordinary citizens and politicians, who claimed abolition would end white society and American democracy itself. Speakers at rallies and editors of conservative papers would denounce abolitionists as "radical reformers" who were nothing but "the same old 'church-and-state' zealots," who tried to shut everything down on Sundays. Mob violence sometimes ensued.[44] Even facing such opposition, many Christians of all denominations freed their slaves. They even sponsored black congregations. In 1801, American Methodists made anti-slavery sentiments a condition of church membership. Abolitionist writings, such as "A Condensed Anti-Slavery Bible Argument" (1845) by George Bourne, and "God Against Slavery" (1857) by George B. Cheever, used the Bible, logic and reason to reject slavery.[45]

Roman Catholic statements also became more and more vocal against slavery. In 1741 Pope Benedict XIV condemned slavery. In 1815 Pope Pius VII demanded the Congress of Vienna to suppress the slave trade. In the Bull of Canonization of Peter Claver, one of the strongest voices against slavery, Pope Pius IX branded the "supreme villainy" (*summum nefas*) of the slave traders. In 1839 Pope Gregory XVI condemned the slave trade.

One does not have to accept God as real, but one must accept that Christianity—adopting much from its older brother, Judaism—sought out truth, promoted justice, science and the general welfare, and battled scourges such as slavery, more so than any other single institution in Western civilization.

In the meantime, those with little or no faith in God showed no such fight, whether in the name of secularism, godlessness, or otherwise. No atheist institution or other group pushing godlessness created any schools, hospitals, or social infrastructure of any kind. It can't even claim it once painted the walls of a school or YMCA.

What *does* the atheist offer? The mockery and tearing down of the social fabrics that Christianity and Judaism have built.

Godlessness is that thirty-five-year-old man who still lives in his mother's house, never paying rent nor seeking a job. You can see him now; playing video games all day, sometimes getting high with his friends, sometimes just alone. All the while, he complains about the world—the same world that gave him his shelter, health, food, entertainment, and freedom.

Just like the unappreciative Reg from *Life of Brian*.

The "God of the Gaps"

The atheist's ultimate argument is that, as we have progressed in our knowledge of science and have otherwise advanced in civilization and culture, we started chucking away the god of the sun, the god of the sea, the god of war, and so on. Why? Because we came to understand how the sun works, how the sea works, and so on.

So take it one step further, the atheist argues: God is merely a last vestige of all those nature gods of the Greeks and Romans (and every single culture before those empires). At best, it is the one "god" who remains to explain the "scientific gaps" we have *yet* to explain. Hence, this God is the "God of the gaps," meaning the *remaining* gaps. Just give science a chance to figure out everything else and this God will suffer the final blow soon enough, too.

But those who suggest that God is just the last among a series of nature gods base their argument on a faulty premise. *This* God is no "nature" god like the others. He is outside of and above nature. *This* God *created* nature. This point alone of course doesn't prove the existence of God, but it rebuts the notion that God—the Judeo-Christian God—is somehow the caboose in a long line of gods before Him.

This God is different. He has no similarity to the "nature" gods who preceded Him. When you compare the Greek and Roman gods to how the Bible portrays what *the* "one" God is all about, you see there is almost nothing similar. You might as well declare the space shuttle and a paper airplane are the same because they both have wings.

The Judeo-Christian God is wildly off-course from the so-called "rest of the gods," so much so that one can say it came out of the proverbial left-field. The differences are enormous, but here are just a few:

- The Judeo-Christian God demands justice and expects that we be good to each other. By contrast, the gods demanded only your loyalty.
- The Judeo-Christian God has a relationship with every individual. The gods had no such relationship.
- The Judeo-Christian God wasn't created to explain the world; He provides a guiding light toward goodness and justice—standards. The gods did not demand such standards; there was little to no sense of moral direction at all.
- The Judeo-Christian God isn't capricious or mean; on the contrary, humans can expect to reason with Him. There was no such predictability or reasoning with the gods.
- The Judeo-Christian God wants you to be *free*. There was no such concern from the gods.

The point is: there is just no comparison. It is like comparing an amoeba to a human being. Madonna to Dostoevsky. Rap to Mozart. They are just not in the same league.

Taking Things Literally

As to the written testaments of various faiths, atheists dismissively argue that adherents read these books as literal in every sense. First, it is interesting how the atheists think they know how each faith interprets or appreciates its own holy books. How did atheists come to this conclusion? Did they do some independent research and talk to the leaders of all the major faiths, all of whom have said, "the Bible is exactly literal as it is written"?

This is intellectual laziness. Most faiths understand, for example, that the creation story of the Bible that God created the universe in six days is expansive in meaning: "days" does *not* refer to our present notion of six twenty-four-hour periods. That is simplistic. The atheist likes to point to the Bible's language selectively, usually to highlight language that he finds to be ridiculous or offensive. The atheist doesn't like to look beyond. He should: the Torah has made clear that in the workings of God "a thousand years are like a day" (Psalm 90:4).

For many Jews and Christians, moreover, many of the stories of the Bible are allegorical (such as the Garden of Eden story). Strangely, atheists dismiss any value from Bible stories because they believe those stories are fiction. At the same time, most atheists still appreciate lessons from classic fictional stories such as *Hamlet, Moby Dick,* and *The Godfather.* They even quote them often, so we might derive wisdom from them.

After all, we can learn from *Hamlet* (the frailty of human nature and hesitation, "To be or not to be...") or even *Star Wars* (as Yoda says: "You must feel the Force around you. Here, between you, me, the tree, the rock, everywhere!"). We don't have to believe that an actual little green alien Muppet uttered these words.

One can believe in God without believing every story specifically as the Bible tells it. In fact, one can believe in a higher being without believing in the Bible at all. That is the importance of this section and, in many ways, the point of this book: it is difficult to deny that a *Creator* exists, that He motivates our lives, that He is necessary in our lives, and that this Creator is already in our lives—whether we accept Him or not.

Think of your own family: Imagine what would happen if your children no longer saw you as the center and source of rules. Imagine what would happen if your children figured there were no absolutes; that rules just changed from day to day. The family would quickly fall apart.

If we take God out of our lives, we take away the backbone of our society. It is why we can conclude that, without God, no true sense of justice nor wisdom exists—both require and assume an underpinning of universal truths of human nature and of what is "good." Without those, the very structure of our society starts collapsing.

But that alone does not show God exists. It only shows that, as Voltaire famously quipped: if God did not exist, it would be necessary to invent Him. By definition, a world without God is a world of chaos which destroys virtually everything it touches.

God—The Guarantor of Only Good Things?

Whenever I hear someone doubting God because there's evil in the world, I think of the story of a town rabbi. His faith in God was so resolute he didn't even prepare for a major storm that everyone knew was soon going to flood the town.

As the rabbi walks the city streets, the water rises to his ankles. A jeep with some soldiers comes by; they're helping evacuate the town. "Jump in, Rabbi. The water's coming up fast."

"No, thank you," he says, waving them off. "God will take care of me. God will provide."

Another hour passes. As predicted, the water is now above his waist. Some fishermen from the town pass by in their motorboat on what used to be town's Main Street. They tell him to hop in, too.

Again, he waves them away. "Thanks, but God will take care of me. God will provide." The fishermen shake their heads and motor away.

Another hour passes, and things have gotten really, really bad. The rain is coming down in sheets, and water is now up to the good rabbi's neck. Soon, from above, he hears the thudding noise of a helicopter's blades. It's the fire department's rescue team.

From the helicopter, men toss him a rope ladder. With a megaphone, a rescue worker's voice booms from above: "Rabbi, grab the ladder and climb up! The water's about to rise another foot in the next few minutes!"

But the rabbi remains steadfast. He doesn't change his tune: "No, thank you," he says, waving them off, too. "God will take care of me. God will provide."

And they fly away to safety, shaking their heads, too. Silly rabbi.

Then another half hour passes. The rabbi is now totally alone.

And then what happens? Well, the good Rabbi dies, of course.

So, his soul now rises and soon reaches heaven. But he is one furious rabbi. I mean, super, *duper* furious. He is talking to himself, muttering up an angry storm. Hadn't he been an outstanding exemplar of goodness for the community? Had he not spread the word of God to everyone? How could God have abandoned him?

Finally, he sees God at the entryway of the gate to heaven. His soul (still sopping wet) charges right up to God: he's going to give God a piece of his mind.

"I can't believe You'd do this to me," the rabbi says. "I've been a messenger for You my entire life. I ate, drank, slept, breathed, and sweated for you with every fiber of my being for every single moment in my life. All I wanted in return was that in this moment of crisis You would be there to provide and rescue me. But You were nowhere!"

God turns to him, hearing this rant. After the rabbi finishes, God puts up His hand in the air, starting to count one by one with His fingers. "What are you talking about? First I sent you a jeep, then a boat, ..."

I love this story for many reasons. But one is that it underscores how we don't appreciate what we have—including the little jeeps, boats, and rope ladders that come to us all.

But most significantly, I like it because it tests the question of what is good and how to deal with evil. While the atheist sees the evils of disease, earthquakes, and men who would butcher little children, the believer sees the gift of medicine, first responders, and soldiers who not only fight bad men but who seek to spread liberty.

In a sense, none of these people would even exist without the existence of their evil counterparts. After all, a fireman makes no sense without a fire, a brain surgeon makes no sense without someone suffering from brain cancer, a charity makes no sense without poorer people to give money to, or a war hero without a group of bad guys who outnumber him. We cannot meaningfully talk about "good" without implying there is a correlating "bad" that goodness (hopefully) overcomes.

That's not enough for the atheist. For him to even be open to the *possibility* of God, the atheist must *first have no evil in the world at all*. Then, and only then, will he deign to start the discussion about whether God created the universe, and all that stuff.

This is one of the great canards in the atheist's deism debate. He sidesteps any discussion of God's existence whatsoever because of his demand that God must deliver a *perfect* world—a world *entirely* without evil. "If God is so good and powerful, why hasn't he eradicated all evil and bad fortune, and particularly against innocent children?"

But who said God's role is only to provide goodness to the world? Nowhere in the Bible does it say God will bestow a perfect life for all who are kind or innocent. Nowhere.

This "God means no bad things" argument is entirely the construct of the atheist. *He* has decided that's what any god worth his salt must do—protect us from all bad things. So, if bad things happen to good people (your four-year-old daughter dies of cancer, or your wife is brutally raped and murdered), well then God isn't doing His job. He's supposed to step in—like the principal in a school who stops the bully just before he lands his next punch on the little kindergartner.

The fact that horrible things happen on this planet, even to the most innocent of people, is entirely irrelevant to whether God exists. But the atheist has decided the definition and standard of God is, and then proclaims Him not to exist because God has not met that standard.

So the argument is circular and conveniently sidesteps the *believer's* standard of God. It also makes no sense: We would never reason like this in virtually any other circumstances: a daughter may want her father to give her horses and a stable, but there is a good chance he can't do so. That doesn't mean he's not her father. I may want my son to be a professional basketball player, but he may have a different vision. That does not make him any less of my son.

Let's take the argument one step further. That not only applies the horrible things to the daughter and wife I described above, but also to horrible massacres such as the Holocaust and even natural disasters such as the 1985 Mexico City earthquake or the 2004 tsunami in Thailand.

You might as well make this argument: John's parents gave him life, raised him in the world, gave him an education, and fed, clothed and bathed him. They taught him boundaries and manners and to be good to his neighbors. They took care of his braces and gave him his shots. They helped John become a productive and respected member of society.

After a while, John got married and had a family of his own. But then he lost his job and all his money in a financial pyramid scheme. Things eventually got so bad that John had to go on welfare. Unable to support his family anymore, John's wife left him and took the kids. Soon he was on the streets, playing a banjo for passersby tips. If things went generally well, he'd get beaten up only two times a week. And those coughing fits? Hopefully it's not tuberculosis.

John's life has met total ruin; he has nothing. Even his own kids wouldn't recognize him—not that they would want to see him after their mother poisoned them against him. There's also a warrant out for his arrest for that third DUI he got just before he lost his job.

Here's the ultimate question: Does this mean that John can claim his parents were never real? Is it reasonable for him to blame them for not protecting him from the bad things of life? Perhaps they should have been there all along, even in his adult life, making sure nothing bad ever happened to him. When financial troubles came, they should have put more money in his bank account. If his wife had arguments with him, they should have tried to force her to like him. And they should have made sure that John's boss promoted him rather than fired him. If a hurricane threatened John's house, they should have provided appropriate materials to board up the house—or alternatively, relocate him and buy a new house for him.

This is how the atheist argues. This is what he thinks God is supposed to do. Defining what God is and then slamming God for not meeting that definition is the ultimate "straw man" argument. People use this technique in debate, but it is a form of cheating in debate, and intellectually dishonest.

To Dream the Impossible Dream

To dream the impossible dream . . . .

To right the unrightable wrong . . . .
To reach the unreachable star

This is my quest
To follow that star
No matter how hopeless
No matter how far

— "The Impossible Dream,"
from *Man of La Mancha*
(1972; music, Mitch Leigh; lyrics, Joe Darion)

Let's play out the atheist's interpretation anyway. Here's a thought experiment: we'll pretend the role of God is indeed to prevent all evil in the world.

The first question that comes to mind is, just *what* evil should God be stopping? I understand the classic argument of my late grandmother, who insisted there could be no God who could allow a Holocaust to happen. I get that.

If you are an atheist who wants proof of a "good" God who wouldn't let "bad" things happen, here's a question: What amount of "bad" *is* acceptable to you? Ice cream headaches? Stubbing your toe? People who let their dogs do their business on your lawn?

There's a world of difference between "evils." And that's my point: Is there some evil short of a Holocaust that would still make you say there is no God? Or conversely, is there *some* acceptable level of evil, suffering, or general unpleasantness that *would* make you receptive to the idea of God? Say, for example, only 100 murders per year throughout the world—and absolutely, positively, not one more.

Let's go through a thought experiment, and see how things turn out:

Pretend first that God does what the atheist would demand of Him and has erased our ability to commit mass murder (such as the Holocaust, Mao's cultural revolution, the Turkish genocide of Armenians, etc.). In such a case, my grandmother might have returned to believing in God.

But not for the typical atheist. Remember: we now live in a world where genocide or slaughter is simply unimaginable (God in our scenario doesn't even allow that possibility). The atheist might nevertheless look around the world and still see serial murders and horrific tortures. "How can there be a God where serial murders and torture happen?" he would ask.

So, God takes the next step: He completely wipes out our ability to engage in serial murders and horrific tortures.

Again, this is not enough for the atheist, so God takes the next step: He wipes out our ability to engage in *any* kind of killing at all. This, however, still might not appease the atheist. "How could God allow a world where there is rape and mugging and gang brutality?" he asks rhetorically, shaking his head. He can't have any part of such a God. No sir.

Now imagine a God who erases all possibility of even rape, muggings, or gang beatings. Still, this next alternative world again does not satisfy the atheist. "How could there be a world where people steal from each other and defraud each other?" shaking his head yet again—not being able to contemplate the much more violent world we already wiped out as a possibility.

So, we go to the next step. Imagine a God who doesn't allow us the ability to even steal or defraud. Again, this would not be good enough for our atheist friend: "How can there be God in a world where people yell at each other or even humiliate their fellow man with gossip?"

Then we erase *that* world, too. The atheist would then complain about disease, famine, and natural disasters. Then we would wipe out those matters as possibilities. And soon enough, the atheist would complain about how we can live in a world where some people are better-looking than others, taller than others, or skinnier than others. Or a world where people have financial problems, tension at work, or sexual incompatibility. Maybe our son didn't make the basketball team.

"How can your God allow *that*?" our atheist will ask, again not realizing God had already taken away the possibility of all the other disfavored behavior.

On it would go, to the point that the atheist would still complain even that some people get ice cream headaches.

The point is, there will never be a dividing line acceptable to the atheist. What becomes utterly unacceptable in one situation (the ice cream headache, a bee sting) wouldn't be any concern to, say, someone surviving a Nazi death camp during a cold winter. It wouldn't even enter his mind to think of headaches and stings as issues. Likewise, two hundred years ago a woman who suffered as a sex slave thought only to get out of her slavery. The fact that she might not enjoy air conditioning on a humid day was probably less important to her.

Pain and discomfort are all relative. In my early twenties, I rented an apartment in Los Angeles, and there was one problem: my bedroom was right under the building's Jacuzzi. And boy was it loud. Worse yet, people used that hot tub at all hours of the night.

I asked the property manager to restrict the hours of the Jacuzzi, so people couldn't use it after 11:00 p.m. He said he would consider it, but weeks went by and nothing changed.

When I followed up with him, he said he wouldn't limit the hours: "When I told people that they shouldn't use it after 11, they got angry and said, 'What is this? A concentration camp?'" He then threw up his hands, as if that made all the sense in the world.

You see? Not having use of the Jacuzzi after 11:00 p.m. is like suffering in the Holocaust.

The atheist doesn't see the relativity of what "suffering" is, either. He will never accept any world with God as its driving force because God can never make a world that is good enough for him. Ever. For the atheist, something always will be unacceptably unpleasant. So God must deliver perfection—whatever that means.

But civilization as we think of it *is the result* of imperfection. In fact, virtually every invention anyone ever created is in response to a *problem,* a *need,* or in quest of greater *convenience.* Otherwise, no one would need any invention. To have none of these things would be to expect perfection, or some kind of heaven. A Garden of Eden, if you will. And hell, we know *that's* a fiction, right?

Even our human impulse to have a roof over our heads stems from dealing with the unpleasantness of rain and a scorching sun. We would never improve without our wanting to alleviate such unpleasant things.

The atheist does not believe in God because of the existence of evil and—if he were intellectually honest—the existence of all unpleasant things. But in insisting on such a perspective, he expects us to live in that Garden of Eden.

What's that word again? Irony.

Now let's bring it back: the atheist can't appreciate the exceptional world that we actually *do* have—one where we can explore the stars, advance in science, create and innovate, and help make the world better for others. It is our free will, our quest to fight evil, to overcome the obstacles that nature, disease, and evil throw at us, that *make us the better men and women we can be*. By contrast, a "Garden of Eden" offers no growth to anyone.

It is the bitter cold and rain that made us develop houses with roofs and fireplaces; the scorching heat that created air conditioning; the need to conquer distance that made us domesticate the horse, and then create the boat, the train, the bike, the car, and the airplane. It was disease that pushed us to cleanliness, which in turn led to longer life for everyone.

Don't you see? If you want a world that improves, you couldn't have fashioned a world any better. This *is* the world you would create if you had to start from scratch. The world the atheist claims to want would be a world without challenges or obstacles and, therefore, without innovation and improvement.

It's like the line from the classic movie, *The Third Man*, where Harry Lime notes how Italy under the Borgias had warfare, terror, and murder, but they nevertheless produced the artistic wonders Michelangelo, Leonardo da Vinci, and the Renaissance. By contrast, he notes that Switzerland had 500 years of peace, "… and what did that produce? The cuckoo clock."[46]

A world without obstacles—and yes, even without horrific evil—is a world where we can't ultimately learn to become the men and women we strive to be.

My friend and producer Ari David once pondered that perhaps the reason people advance socialism, knowing the empty and dehumanizing aspects of it, is only to keep us on our toes, to serve as the proverbial whetstone that allows us to sharpen our debating knives. Such people make us vigilant; they make sure we never take anything for granted.

And likewise, perhaps evil is the whetstone that allows us to sharpen our "goodness" skills, and to appreciate and bring out the beauty in our lives and to understand what freedom truly means.

God knew what He was doing. God *wants* us to find Him. But we must climb the mountain to reach Him, one challenging step at a time. Take those challenges away, and we lose what makes us human and what we are intended to be.

God kicked us out of the Garden of Eden for a reason. He wanted us to grow, and to create. No adversity means neither of such things.

CHAPTER III

THE FIGHT AGAINST GOD WITHIN US

The God Impulse

I briefly talked about instinct and believing in God, particularly the "God Impulse." The atheist also should acknowledge this has always existed. In fact, it is part of his very argument: he, too, recognizes praying to higher beings is hardwired in our history, even instinctive. Even the cavemen prayed to gods, an atheist will say. So we are only as primitive as they were when we believe in God now. Let's discard this God nonsense and move to Science, with a capital "S."

But here's what the atheist doesn't factor: Maybe there is *meaning* to the fact that our species has always prayed to the skies and believed in higher powers. It's not as if God is a new concept in belief in the past one hundred years (such as, say, global warming/climate change). The Judeo-Christian God has been in our society for more than four thousand years. More significantly praying to higher powers of some form or another has been around ever since the dawn of humankind. It is likely that there were few atheist cavemen. Indeed, it is atheism that is the relatively recent arrival of the past 150 years or so.

Why is it that humans have always—repeat, *always*—prayed to forces they perceived to be in charge and more powerful than they were? Why is it that humans have always believed some outside supernatural forces affect human events?

It is worth not only noting the fact, but asking the question why the fact is so *consistent* in our species' history. And it cuts across all cultures, even where there was no interaction among them whatsoever. The Native Americans had their spirits, none of whom they borrowed from the Greek gods, for example. Every culture and every people has had their own gods or spirits.

It seems we humans have always had an instinct for a higher authority. For now, we don't even have to call it God. But we seem always to have gravitated to a supreme being.

But then this begs the question: Why do we humans have that impulse? And if it is evolutionary, why don't animals seem to have it? If believing in God is somehow "mere evolution" to give us a sense of structure and purpose, why doesn't that need for structure and purpose apply equally to animals? After all, we see no animals making sacrifices. The lions never seem to look up to the sky, praying to their god (let's call him Simba), who might bless them with an extra bounty of gazelles this spring.

Why are we humans the only animals this nature has conferred this "evolutionary" instinct? No matter what society you look at, from the cavemen to the present, it seems our impulse for God must get satisfaction. And as I show below, ignoring it leads to great peril.

Dr. Francis S. Collins, head of the Human Genome Project, explained the nature of this instinct in his superb book *The Language of God*. Our instincts are critical to our very survival. By this, he notes there is no instinct for which we do not have some way of satisfying it. For example, if we are hungry, we can eat food. If we are thirsty, we can drink water. If we are feeling aroused, we can pursue sex.

Here's the point: the atheist admits that we have an instinct for a higher being, from the beginning of humanity itself. But by denying God, he also is saying there is no ability to *satisfy* that instinct on the other end. There's no one else on the other end of that phone call, as it were.

Collins argues this would make no sense from an evolutionary point of view. Why would our biology imbue us with an instinct for God only to learn that there is no one to satisfy it?

It would be a cruel, cosmic joke, like the proverbial man in the desert reaching out to a mirage of an oasis, only to have it vanish as he reaches out for it. Or worse yet, it would be like saying there is a mineral that our bodies must have for our survival, but we can only get that mineral on the moon. We would stare longingly at the moon, like the proverbial wolf howling at it, forever unrequited.

The atheist instead points to our primitive beliefs in higher beings to mock the notion of a belief in God. He'll say our belief in God is only a slightly more sophisticated adaptation of the "nonsensical" prayers to the many gods of cavemen days. Once we recognize that, then we'll see how pursuing our present "God" is just as nonsensical. How embarrassing it'll be for the believer.

Rabbi Brandon Gaines had an intriguing point about this: We've always had a "sense" of healing, with potions and leeks and other remedies we now consider backward. Does that mean our sense of healing today (which is more sophisticated with its hospitals, drugs, and so on) is somehow not valid?

Likewise we've always had communication, which probably started with grunts and a lot of finger-pointing. Today's communications are far more sophisticated (emails, video chats, social media). Shall we mock the notion of communication?

You get the idea. The fact that we have always looked up to the heavens for answers only serves as evidence that there *is* a higher being, not evidence that undermines it.

The "Isms" Whack-a-Mole Game

Neither the atheist nor the believer can meaningfully deny the God impulse. The nuance is only that atheists will claim the impulse, as such, is an obsolete artifact of the past, like the buggy whip, quill pens or newspapers. It may have been necessary once, but we've outgrown it, like that butterfly leaving its cocoon.

But have you noticed a correlation? The avowed atheist usually seems to be passionate about some other "-ism." It's usually a cause that he will advocate with great passion, like environmentalism, climate change, same-sex marriage, income inequality, and so on.

It's as if they must find an outlet to express their instinct for God, one way or the other. If not for God, then he will seek it out in some other all-encompassing ideology, usually one that comes with a lot of rules. In fact, like all religions, it must have dogma, irrefutable truths, a charismatic leader, and a Satan. As a result, you often see many atheists who are quite supportive of greatly expanded government, which is to assume ever-growing involvement in all aspects of our lives. Those who disagree are greedy and evil.

The God impulse is so powerful that it is impossible to ignore. We must satisfy it. If one truly rejects God, one must find another god. It's a whack-a-mole game where the impulse keeps popping up somewhere. After all, if there is no God to govern the general rules of human behavior, we must have *something* in charge. Socialism, communism, and fascism offer that. Indeed, totalitarianism is the ultimate God-replacer—not only will it provide you for all you need, but the government will tell you what to think.

Years ago, my wife and I visited Vietnam. We went to Hanoi, where one of the attractions was the embalmed tomb of Ho Chi Minh. The tour required us to quickly move along around his glass sarcophagus where we could see his body. Guards stood at serious attention, a great sense of solemnity pervading the room. It was more serious than the Notre Dame church during Easter services. The booklet the official tourism ministry gave us advised that we were not to laugh, smile, or even whisper during our pass through this hallowed room.

It dawned upon me that we would never see such a thing in the United States, Israel, England, or any other democracy rooted in God. Only dictator nations seem to have this sort of idolatrous fixation on their former leaders.

And even those dictators who still rule their countries seem to enjoy almost deity status. Take a look at any dictatorship, and you will see posters of the dictator everywhere about the town and country. This applies almost equally to dictators of both past and present: Saddam Hussein, Adolf Hitler, Mao, Castro, Ho Chi Minh, Vladimir Lenin, Stalin, Kim Il Jung, and Che Guevara. In fact, it seems to be a hallmark of a dictatorship that you get to see their brave and glorified faces on posters everywhere in their countries.

It is not so much a question of ego—although all dictators do seem to have exceptional egos. It is more that the dictators expect people to treat them like gods, especially in those countries where God is not a factor. So, they assume the role of a god; after all, aren't they imposing their will on the people in almost every respect?

The rule is simple: Where a dictatorship has no God, a human will become God. Plenty of evil men will be happy to oblige. And many are willing to follow them.

What Matters Most

What matters most to humans? It's that we matter.

We manifest that in many ways. Some want buildings named after them, or to show awards that this or that organization has conferred upon them. Many showcase pictures of themselves throughout their offices, standing with famous people. Others buy expensive cars and other items to show how successful they are.

Sometimes people just want to be famous. In fact, most pre-teens and teenagers no longer seek to achieve or "be" anything (such as a policeman, fireman, astronaut, supreme court justice). At this point it appears they seek *only* fame: it doesn't even matter what they might be famous *for*.[1] The combination of reality television, social media, and a strange obsession to have as many "views" seem to have fostered the perfect storm for such a quest.[2]

Even many young women in pornography are in it just for the possibility of becoming famous.[3] Do an Internet search for "porn amateurs do it only for fame" and you'll not only get links to articles about precisely such motivations, but actual links to hundreds (if not thousands) of women's porn pages who themselves say that they want you to see their porn videos *precisely because they want to be famous.*

It is the quest for fame for fame's sake, with no appreciation for the hard work that often precedes fame, even in the case of celebrities and athletes. More strangely yet, they often seek fame regardless if it comes with money. Money seems to be secondary to them, an afterthought.

What explains this bizarre new singularity of focus for fame—and only fame—*sans* the hard work and even *sans* the money? It's like they want to become rich and they think the only way to do it is by going to Vegas (work is for fools). Or they want great sexual thrills, but without the effort and time one normally needs to put into a relationship to make that sexuality meaningful (relationships are for fools).

It is a culture that has lost God. But God has infused us humans with this sense that we matter and that we need to do things that matter—that everything we do is indeed for a greater purpose. It might be in the form of art, music, literature, movies, philosophy, psychology, medicine and science.

But without God, the "mattering" thing is pointless. It's like they don't know what to do with this instinctive sense. They're like dogs which are bred to herd, but who are now just pets in a home, without anything to herd.

But the need to matter itches within them. So they manifest it whichever way they can. They seek out fame, mistaking it for mattering. They want people to remember them, to know who they are as they walk around in public. They want desperately to *matter* in other people's lives. But they don't ask what makes them *want* that so badly in the first place. For the religious, by contrast, all such things are part of the search for God.

I rarely meet anyone who does not yearn for something better. Beyond money and comfort, he seeks a purpose. If he doesn't yearn for it, he becomes restless, even depressed. And if he has a family, he seeks a better world even more so—a sense of imperative that his children grow up to be good and caring. Barring true sociopaths, it is a rare person who truly does not think of some sort of future and what his purpose in the world might be, how he figures into some larger scheme.

Putting it another way, there are few people who do not desire a legacy after they die. Not only do they seem to want to matter, they feel they *must* matter.

That we want to matter can be a primary motivator for evil, too. The insane shooter who wants us to read his manifesto is doing so because he wants to make his "mark." He'll do it even if it means killing many people who are innocent. It's misguided and horrible, but it's often the *same* driving force that drives him—the compulsion to matter.

Why should it matter, though, that we matter? After all, the lion doesn't care if he matters. He doesn't yearn to be famous. He just wants to survive and get food—and make little lions.

He doesn't suffer depression or go on killing sprees, nor try to be the best example for lions everywhere. He doesn't care if his grandchildren remember anything about him. The same applies to the cat, the dog, the giraffe, and every other non-human life form.

But for some reason, we humans seem to give a damn. If we don't, we somehow feel out of place or even lost, like we've failed some sort of legacy or responsibility.

It's as if we know we must live up to some *expectation*. It's as if we have an innate, visceral sense that we must do something with our lives beyond mere existence. It runs through every human being. If we don't do it through God, we manifest it in other ways. We're all going to make sure that we matter, one way or the other.

Any legitimate atheist must concede that atheism implies randomness and meaninglessness. But this runs counter to humans' instinctive need to matter. And "mattering" still courses even through the veins of an atheist. For that reason, it is ironic that atheists such as Christopher Hitchens, Sam Harris and Richard Dawkins ever seek to advance atheism through books and lectures.

They want to matter, to make names for themselves, all in some quest to matter, to have everyone know who they are. But as atheists, why should they care?

The notions of purpose and mattering should burden and trouble the atheist. It should confound him. Everyone must feed his sense of purpose, yet it is a sense which the atheist can't meaningfully ever explain without a "giver" of that sense. He in fact is answering to the God impulse within him—whether he realizes it or not.

Answering the Call of Anything

Those who stand for nothing fall for anything
— Alexander Hamilton

Although atheists will dismiss the God impulse as a pointless vestige of a by-gone era, useful in its day but no longer relevant in the modern era, we *all* tend to answer "the call of duty." Most of us feel a need, an imperative, to answer that call. For the believer, it may mean attending church and synagogue and following the tenets of his faith. They can have many other "callings" that are meaningful to them, but they keep it in perspective.

For the secular, they may answer it in other ways: through their art, writing, filmmaking, or political or activist involvement (such as an "ism"). The point is, they'll want to step outside of who they are to make an impact. They are, in effect, answering their own call of duty.

But they rarely ask themselves *what* is compelling them, or even acknowledge that they are answering some call of duty. All they know is that what they are doing is quite important.

In the end, it is all a mission without purpose. The "isms" (environmentalism, socialism, and so on) underscore humanity's search for structure, if not meaning. This shows we never truly "evolve" from the formidable God impulse. And we gravitate toward the "isms" because we crave purpose, a purpose that God has given us to seek Him. When we reject Him, we move toward anything else. Like the wayward girl who runs away from home, she'll run to the pimp because she still needs a male figure in her life. And that's all these "isms" are: pimps who play off our need for purpose.

Take a soldier: you can give him a gun, but you should explain why you are giving him the gun. Evil forces are out there wishing to destroy America. So, stop the bad guys. And while you're at it, here's how to make sure that you use the gun safely. Also, let's train you to figure out who the bad guys are and how things can go wrong. Watch out for the landmines. Develop a code by which you make sure to leave no man behind. Learn and control your emotions so that you can be the most alert and protect yourself and your buddies.

If you give just any man that same gun and tell him to use it but without any training, he becomes a dangerous man indeed. He won't understand what to use it for, or how. How can he discern the good guys from the bad guys (if there is even such a thing as a "bad" guy)? Is there any code at all by which he should live? What is the mission anyway?

And so it is with the God impulse: without an appreciation for the impulse, knowing what it means and what it is actually for, we are doomed to create only chaos. We will be as aimless—and dangerous—as the lone man receiving a gun from nowhere and for no apparent reason.

Once I went to a movie with some friends. The plot made absolutely no sense to me. Characters were coming in and out, and they seemed to be old in one scene then young the next, only to be aged again twenty minutes later in the movie. Nothing seemed to be in sequence.

When we left the movie, my friends and I were divided into two groups: those who believed the movie was wonderfully artistic and those who thought the movie made no sense at all. Those in the "artistic" group found all sorts of meaning and intention by the movie's director. They felt he had really "broken out" from his earlier, simpler, films.

Well, we found out the issue pretty soon: the film projector guy had put in the reels at the wrong time; he had shown the movie out of sequence. He had also missed a reel. The movie was in fact supposed to be a simple story, with a beginning, middle, and end. The good guys won.

And we all felt like idiots.

Still, the experience had a lasting impact on me. It dawned upon me that there were those who were trying to find structure where there was no structure, like the proverbial monkey who throws paint on a canvass, and people then mistake it as masterpiece work of human genius.

People crave structure; something seems to imbue us with a deep yearning and sense for order and purpose. But some do not wonder where it comes from, so they seek it out in the oddest of ways. Someone is always ready to give them a structure, a paradigm, that might pass as an explanation for all the confusion life seemed to have thrown at them. Hence the success of cults (Scientology, the Moonies, EST). Each of them offer quick answers and a framework by which to look at life's complexities. And all followers must do is give up their wealth.

It doesn't stop with cults. Ideologies such as socialism tell secular individuals that all life's problems can disappear if they consider themselves part of a collective whole. Just share everything, and no one will be rich or poor. Medicine, education, and the basics of a society's infrastructure will all just appear. The appeal is great: someone is offering structure, with virtually no input or effort on your part. The only obligation? Submit.

And naturally, there will be a charismatic leader to such ideologies. Vladimir Lenin was the first true communist leader to advocate for communism during the Bolshevik revolution. Many American intellectuals fell for it, almost all of them secular. They went to Russia, where they hoped to sacrifice their time and efforts for the greater good of Russia. Those who didn't stay came back and reported how great Russia was.

Lenin was a smart man, however. He knew communism was an absurd ideology that could never work with human nature. Lenin wanted only power, and he understood the best way of getting that was to answer people's basic craving for structure. And how did history refer to these American friends who helped advance communism for him? "Useful idiots." The epithet has become synonymous with suckers who unwittingly do the bidding of evildoers.

It did not stop with socialism or communism. It also applied to fascism, environmentalism, even vegetarianism and animal rights. People can strive so hard to find meaning in their lives they will stop all they are doing and sacrifice much of their lives to the cause *du jour*. Just tell them what it is.

Usually it involves a messiah or two, some great "leader of the movement." When we think about global warming and environmentalism, we think about Al Gore. When we think about socialism, we think of Karl Marx. Fascism makes us think of Hitler or Mussolini.

Scholars advise that it was these men's charismas which gave rise to these ideologies, even though the ideologies were based on massively absurd lies. But this is only half the answer. These men also understood something far greater at play: man's inherent desire—his need—for structure, and to matter. If you can give him an outlet for that, he'll believe and do almost anything you tell him.

As Homer Simpson once said, trying to make excuses when his wife catches him in a big lie: "Now Marge, you know it takes two to lie: one to lie and one to listen."

And without God and the structure He provides, we are all too willing to listen.

Man Makes Himself God

When you believe in God, you believe He created each of us equally in His image. As a logical follow-up to that, you believe no one is superior to anyone else, at least in God's eyes.

When you do not see God as a force in your lives, a pecking order soon surfaces; you necessarily believe that some people are inferior to you, based upon what they do, what values they hold, how much money they make, how pretty or handsome they are, how much influence they exercise, and so forth.

Of course this all becomes an exercise of relative judgment. Lady Gaga, Snoop Doggy, MC Hammer, Pee Wee Herman, and many other entertainers have come and gone in influence. But they are influential only to the extent that we *let* them be influential.

I'm not an avid follower of sports. I love watching professional games, but I generally don't buy tickets to games. (I'll almost always say yes if you have a ticket available, however. Ahem.) When I was general counsel to an NBA team owner in Los Angeles, I often bumped into basketball stars. But with few exceptions (say Magic Johnson, Kareem Abdul-Jabbar, and Kobe Bryant), I really had little idea of who was who.

I noticed, however, that many of my friends who know them became utterly star-struck as soon as any of these stars came near. On me, however, their presence had zero effect. Not knowing them, I could talk to them easily. For me, had I been somehow able to meet Churchill, Dostoevsky, or Ronald Reagan, I would have been equally star-struck and speechless.

It dawned on me that "celebrity" was relative. Even celebrities and well-knowns understand this. They are "influential" only to some. But *we* ultimately decide who will be influential. *We* decide what moves us, and we throw ourselves into life accordingly.

The same is true for ideas and positions. With God, we know that everyone's life is infinitely and equally valuable. But without God, anyone can determine for us what is important and, for that matter, who matters. And they can decide to whom we should listen, and whom we can subjugate, marginalize, scapegoat, demonize, or treat in any other inferior way.

A world without God opens all such doors of horror. Hitler understood this well, managing through his godless regime to manipulate millions into his murder spree of millions of innocents. After the war, Germans looked at each other like a spell of madness had overtaken them, and now the spell had been broken. How could all this have happened?

Because it was exactly that: a spell of madness. It was a spell that they were all too willing to fall under.

No Higher Power

By definition, atheism can only result in one of two paradigms: chaos, or heavily structured dictatorship. Atheism understands no order, no hierarchy. In fact, the only thing consistent in atheism's theory is randomness and disorder—and the Law of the Jungle that must flow from it.

Ironically, if an atheist advocates for goodness in *any* form, he unwittingly advocates for an exception to his own ideology, even the opposite of it. To be consistent, the atheist should advocate *for* the killing of all weak and socially "undesirable" people (whatever that might mean), because they are a drain on society. He should be a eugenicist, as it were.

This is the reasoning of the main character in Fyodor Dostoevsky's classic *Crime and Punishment*. The character Raskolnikov sets about to kill an old woman neighbor in his apartment building. Why? Because he's an intellectual atheist who's determined that he should act consistently with his atheism. She is old, decrepit, and therefore useless. She's also mean. For the good of society, he reasons, she must go. So, Raskolnikov sets about to kill her in her apartment. He soon does exactly that—along with her sister whom he didn't expect to be there.

Raskolnikov gives no consideration to the possibility that the women might have infinite worth just for being human. How could he? Without God, there is only mere existence from cradle to grave. You are but a carbon unit with no extrinsic value beyond what you can contribute for the "good" of society (however you might define that). From his point of view, it was *logical* and even the "right" thing to kill the old women.

In a world without God, there must be no higher power above mankind. Mankind must be supreme. He is in charge, by default.

But a problem bubbles up: many have differing opinions about how to govern, what is right and what is wrong and what other values we should enforce. All sorts of complications start flowing from this, which perhaps is the impetus for the universal governance movement—the notion that there should be one defining set of rules for everyone.[4] But those who believe in universal governance generally do not embrace conservative values nor the spread of freedom. Why? Because conservatism seeks to *lessen* government involvement and *increase* individual freedom. Universal governance contemplates a more uniform "one size fits all" approach to governance. Or better yet: Once size *will* fit all. Or else.

But no one can deny this simple point: we will never all believe in the same set of values. Billions of people are on the planet with multitudes of contrasting and competing cultures and histories that inform each of them. Many versions of what constitutes "right" and "good" compete. As many will point out to you: One man's terrorist is another man's freedom fighter.

Here are some examples: In America, many believe the death penalty is not only appropriate but a core, good value, that it reflects our deep contempt for the wrongful taking of an innocent life. That is logical to many in the United States. By contrast, most in Europe see the death penalty as horrid under any circumstances. To them, it is illogical and inherently wrong.

The story of convicted serial killer Anders Breivik in Norway illustrates this dichotomy. The *New York Times* reported:

> Convicted of killing 77 people in a horrific bombing and shooting attack in July last year [2011], the Norwegian extremist Anders Behring

Breivik was sentenced on Friday to 21 years in prison—fewer than four months per victim—ending a case that thoroughly tested this gentle country's collective commitment to values like tolerance, nonviolence and merciful justice.

Mr. Breivik, lawyers say, will live in a prison outside Oslo in a three-cell suite of rooms equipped with exercise equipment, a television and a laptop, albeit one without internet access. If he is not considered a threat after serving his sentence, the maximum available under Norwegian law, he will be eligible for release in 2033, at the age of 53.[5]

As noted, this was the "maximum" sentence Norway could legally impose upon him, despite the fact that he killed more than seventy-five people.

This is what Norway considers proper, tolerant, and merciful. These are Norwegian values. For many other countries in the West, not imposing a far greater sentence, and perhaps the death penalty itself, was an abdication of a collective duty to pursue justice and to publicly express our shared contempt for such horrid acts.

Likewise on the abortion issue, the pro-choice movement considers it good and even kind to allow a mother to choose whether her fetus should live. The pro-life movement considers the exact opposite to be good, that a pregnancy immediately signifies a life whom no one has any right to terminate merely because it is in a womb. In China, it appears not even to be a moral issue: the government even encourages abortion and has even forced sterilization and abortions upon mothers, for population control purposes.

Another example is the Muslim world, which not only allows men to marry multiple women but encourages them to do so.[6] In the West, we see this as an affront to women and bad for society. Also in the Islamic world, some see so-called "honor killings" as good and proper (where a family kills a female relative if she is raped or if she converts to another). In the West, we call this murder.

Without God there can never be any universal interpretation of what is right and what is wrong, what is good and what is evil. The atheist's notion that goodness and fairness will flow from some universal understanding of logic (or from the "heart") naively ignores that logic and good are at best floating-point standards. We all bring with us our own culture, our own history, our own perspective. The American South versus the American North. The British versus the Americans, the Arabs versus the Israelis, the Jews versus the Romans (and versus the Greeks, the Babylonians, the Spanish, the Germans, etc.), the Native Americans versus the European Settlers, and the Federation versus the Klingons.

Floating-point standards only invite disorder and chaos. Why? Because it invites everyone to clamor to advance their own particular values—many of which will be at direct odds with the values of others. At some point, a strongman dictator must step in to bring order to it all. History has shown it has always been this way—until the arrival of God-centered liberty.

In a world where the Human reigns supreme, you can expect only two outcomes: a world descending evermore into chaos, or a world without liberty. Usually it has been the latter because history abhors a vacuum, and a strongman dictator will always eventually come to fill it. Hitler came after the chaos of the Weimar Republic. Napoleon arose following the chaos of the Reign of Terror. The North Viet Cong descended into South Vietnam when America retreated in its financial support. Islamic State (ISIS) filled the void after America's pullout from Iraq.

A world without God in charge means a world only of men in charge. It has never turned out well.

CHAPTER IV

SEE? I *TOLD* YOU NOT TO TURN SKYNET ON

Remember the *Terminator* movies? They imagined a post-computer-age apocalyptic world where robots have mistakenly re-interpreted their programming to treat humans themselves as the enemy. For a while, the robots massacre or enslave humans. But good news: a resistance has begun, and the humans' fearless leader, John Connor, has begun to turn the tide of the war around against the machines.

So naturally, the robots send a cyborg back to the past to kill John Connor's mother before she can ever give birth to him. The humans in turn send back a man, Kyle, to stop this cyborg from doing so. Think *Back to the Future,* but with a lot less Biff and a lot more guns.

Well, Kyle manages to protect the mother, but not after knocking her up with the very baby that ends up being John Connor. The story continues in *Terminator II,* during which we learn of the "inevitability" of Judgment Day, as the re-programmed "good guy" cyborg tells it: Skynet, the program that the humans have created to protect humanity, will become self-aware, take over the military computer network, and ultimately turn on humans and start taking over the entire planet (and you were worried that *Jurassic Park* could happen).

There is no way to stop it, we learn. Well, except in one way: Don't let Skynet take over all the military infrastructure in the first place. Just keep humans in control, no matter what.

It is the same with atheism. Give atheism control of the "network," and all hell breaks loose. Not the futuristic, cool kind of apocalypse you see in the *Terminator* future, though. At least *that* might involve some cool new gadgets and the possibility of time-travel. No, this one will be more like an apocalypse of the past—one we've seen many times before: Sodom and Gomorrah, pre-Israelite Canaan, or the Germanic tribes of the first millennium, and just about anywhere outside of ancient Rome and Greece. If you prefer, it'll be like the struggling survivors in the post-nuclear age in *Max Max: The Road Warrior*. But without the weird fashion choices.

Godlessness and Big Government

Without a paradigm of absolute standards, we have to invent rule after rule to enforce good behavior for the sake of the whole. But to borrow from climate change language, this creates a runaway "greenhouse effect," in which rules beget more rules. Besides, no one can accurately predict how people will respond to basic rules, so we must cover every possible scenario that may come into play (as opposed to applying "natural law" considerations of punishing general fraud, negligence, and breach of contract on a case-by-case analysis).

Regulations soon creep into every aspect of life because we can never assume people will do the right thing. So your children's car seats have to be virtually identical. Ice cream must have an exact percentage of "cream." After a certain number of employees, you are required to provide health insurance to all your employees. When it comes to sex, both partners must sign some written agreement. And to start a business? Here's a telephone-book-size manual.

Investors in stocks must pour over a labyrinth of indecipherable rules before and after they invest in anything (and no one reads them). Stores must have the same toilet sizes, with the paper roll being just so many inches away from the toilet seat, for disabled people. Buildings in must include notices that they "may contain" substances the state considers hazardous.

Rules abound at the workplace regarding what you can and can't say to interviewees or employees. Employers can't even comment that their employees look nice. Businesses of certain sizes must hire in the same proportion of the general diverse culture of the neighborhood. Drug companies must disclose every conceivable side effect. Carrying a gun requires ever more extraordinary background checks. How you speak to, act with, or educate your child becomes more and more the domain of the State. An environmental agency threatens to foreclose on your house with penalties you've accumulated of $35,000 a day for having drained a swamp in your backyard. You can't contribute more than $2,500 to any political candidate.

Soon, the government expects people to cough up more and more of their income to feed the enforcement of its mountain of rules, many of which are for too complex and lengthy for anyone to understand or read, which change all the time, or which contradict one another. And then there are the rules for your taxes and what you can claim as an expense, can defer, can shelter, can partially reduce as an offset, can claim as a dependent, can consider passive income, a capital gain, or an unrealized gain or loss.

Then you don't know where the money you just paid actually goes to, despite purported rules regarding how government can spend your money. The government assures you that it's going to create an important new committee or regulatory body to oversee a problem you didn't even realize existed, to pay for a major public transit system you probably won't use, or to fund a study of an area you wouldn't think needed studying.

Without God, the rules keep pumping out of the state and federal bodies, piling up like landfill waste. Why? Because government believes it needs to be ever vigilant to plug up this or that "hole" in business or personal matters where a business or individual might be in danger of having too much discretion. Discretion to the godless is worrisome, even frightening.

The human condition needs a sense of what is right and what is wrong. We need absolutes. And where there is no God to give us the sense of what is absolute, Big Government, like the dictator, races to fill the void. The problem is, without a guiding sense of what constitutes true absolutes, you'll always be making more and more "small" rules, piling one upon the other without end.

Imagine telling a driver he can drive his car, but he's not allowed to look at the road itself. You'd have to set up a myriad number of rules based on everyone's car's proximity indicators, gas and water gauges, echo-location and GPS enabling. As if that weren't difficult enough, you'd have to synch that car up with all other cars in the road, ensuring only so many cars are on the road at certain precise times. The complexity would be never-ending, as each new car on the road would geometrically amplify the number of possible problems to resolve.

But we don't do this. In the end, we expect drivers to use their judgment, and most moving violations are about errors in judgment, such as running a red light, or speeding. We seem to know and sense that collective driving can only work that way. You must count on the judgment of individuals acting in concert with one another on the freeway and otherwise, each one giving way and understanding from time to time he must wait his turn, and that each of us has a communal duty to act with some degree of care.

And the funny thing is, that gut "sense" of duty has little to do with whether we are following all the myriad traffic regulations. We do it because we have a natural sense of obligation to drive carefully.[1] In short, it is the individual's common sense and awareness of his surroundings which makes traffic "work."

By contrast, big government lacks any vision of the individual, let alone respect for the judgment of the individual. At best, big government *tolerates* the individual, and even then only to a degree.

Godlessness must lead to big government. And big government enables big evil things.

Big Government and Big Evil Things

It is difficult to imagine more brutality than what the twentieth century threw at us. Up to 200 million people were killed. Most were not even soldiers. Most died because some ruling dictator or regime perceived them to be in the way of some beautiful utopian vision. To add to this nightmare, totalitarian regimes enslaved over a billion people.[2]

In every case, it was a big government that did all this massive killing and enslaving. How so? The bigger the government, the greater the opportunities there were for doing great, organized, mechanized evil. By contrast, evil individuals without power can do only so much harm.[3] They may take a machine gun and shoot many people in a crowded movie theater, such as the monster who did exactly that in Aurora, Colorado, in 2012. As devastating as this was, such a crime was nothing on the order of what Hitler, Stalin, Che Guevara, or Pol Pot managed to achieve. Those leaders employed the machinery of government to do their bidding. And the bigger that machinery was, the more horrific and widespread they could project their evil.

Of course, this does not mean all large-sized government is evil, but it does mean such massive and orchestrated killing can only happen with large-sized government. The point should be obvious, but the same people who believe in massive government programs because of what good they supposedly can do usually fail to see the dark side of such great power. The citizens of these countries can do little but watch as their boundaries become jail bars and their countries turn into little branches of hell.

I have yet to meet an atheist who is *not* enthusiastic about big government, big rules and big regulations. In this sense, the atheist is consistent: he knows that order must come from somewhere. He recognizes that society must in some way bridle humanity's greed and opportunism, like ranchers must "break" wild horses and ultimately fence them in. Without God, that is the only way to perceive your fellowman. Rules must exist to accomplish this—lots of them. But by embracing big government, the atheist can become an accomplice to the one thing that can foster such expansive evil.

You can judge a man by the company he keeps. And the atheist has a lousy friend in big government.

Who Really Imposes Values

On September 17, 2011, a group calling itself Occupy Wall Street (OWS) took over Zuccotti Park, located in New York City's Wall Street financial district. It quickly received global attention, soon spawning Occupy "movements" in numerous other cities. The common refrain was passionate anger against perceived social and economic inequality worldwide. It stemmed from anti-austerity protests in Spain. The Canadian magazine *Adbusters*, known for its anti-consumerist, pro-environment beliefs, had initiated the call for a protest.

Occupy Wall Street perceived great social and economic inequality, greed, corruption and undue influence of corporations upon government—particularly from the financial services sector. The OWS slogan, "We are the 99%," referred to income inequality and wealth distribution in the U.S. between the wealthiest one percent and the rest of the population. To achieve their goals, protesters acted on consensus-based decisions made in general assemblies which emphasized direct action instead of petitioning authorities for redress.

According to its own website, its adherents "… are daring to imagine a new socio-political and economic alternative that offers greater possibility of equality. We are consolidating the other proposed principles of solidarity, after which demands will follow."[4] Those demands included a long list for change, including stopping the profiting from torture, allowing employees to bargain for better wages, ending racial and sexual orientation discrimination, ending the "selling of our privacy as a commodity," ending the use of the military and police force to prevent freedom of the press," and misuse of animals—and the covering up of that misuse.[5] Sure it may have been short on specifics, but that wasn't important. The task was to resolve the worlds' problems then and there, because you know what? It was high time.

Notably, neither the list for demands, nor the mission statement of OWS, included a call for more religion nor adherence to the Ten Commandments. Also, there appeared to be no serious mechanism for enforcement of a code of conduct. But that was okay, since no one had developed a code of conduct *to* enforce.

Equally vague to their mission and demands was any sense of internal structure, particularly for consideration for any difference in opinion, or for more base things like sanitation or safety. Almost immediately (and not surprisingly), the unstructured movement descended into multiple incidences of theft, rape and attempted rape, groping, and incidents of other violence.[6] Also notable was the extensive use of tents, food stuffs and deliveries, clothing, medical supplies, music paraphernalia, computers and smartphones, all made possible through the outside structured society and corporations they condemned.

The city police forced the protesters out of Zuccotti Park on November 15, 2011. Protesters eventually turned their focus to occupying banks, corporate headquarters, board meetings, fore-closed homes, and college and university campuses.

In the end, no corporation nor government changed a single policy in response to OWS' numerous demands. The protestors ended up being more like the termites that suddenly invade your home: You don't change much in your personal lives; you just wonder how you can avoid the termites from ever coming back again.

Famed "shock" documentarian and multimillionaire Mi-chael Moore joined in the protest *in sympatico* bonding with his people. Well, he considered them his people. Or at least he visited with them.

During the visit, a reporter asked him about his feelings about the movement, to which he replied excitedly that they would change everything in capitalism. The reporter then asked what system he would replace it with. "I don't know," he said. "We'll just have to see what happens."[7]

This is the classic response of many who seek revolution of the status quo, particularly among many of the godless. They imagine a utopian world, but don't know quite how to get there. It's gonna be great: Just you wait. Never mind the specifics, and don't be a negative Nelly.

But in the end, to reach utopia means imposing some sort of structure by decree, by dictatorial rule. Like we discussed above, it *must* mean this. It necessarily means a vision that they think is superior to yours.

After all, they know better than you.

Not a dictator in the world has ever imaged himself as evil. On the contrary, every dictator imagines himself to be doing the best for society, and that his vision is the best way to get there.

But that means the mandating of that vision upon everyone else. But surprise: nobody else will necessarily agree to it.

If there was one overarching reality of the atheist ideology of communism it was that *everyone had to get with the program.* Or you died. Many argued the reason why communism was so destructive was because of the general communist ideology.

I think this misses the mark: what was deadly was not the ideology of sharing resources equally. That alone would not be sufficient: What made it deadly was the *godless* nature of it.

It's not the snake's body which makes him so threatening, it's his *venom.* The body just acts to deliver the venom. Likewise, it is the *godlessness* in these ideologies that makes them murderous. Everything else is just a delivery system.

Atheist regimes always ultimately sought to impose their atheism on the believers of their countries. This was true in French Revolutionary France in 1789, Revolutionary Mexico in 1917, Post-War Albania, the Soviet Union, China, North Korea and virtually every other atheist society.[8] For many of these governments, they considered religion not only backward but a foreign "import," an attitude which would justify expelling or exterminating all clergy.[9]

By contrast, governments of faith (certainly those of the Judeo-Christian variety, but others as well) tended not to criminalize atheists for their beliefs in atheism. Yes, drunken locals may have picked on atheists (and others of differing religious backgrounds for that matter) but that is not the same as *criminalizing* a belief itself.

What was unique about the advent of democracy—with its novel notions of free-market capitalism and freedom of religion—was that by definition, it did *not* impose what you must believe. Every other system, in varying degrees, imposed its will upon its people. If it appeared not to, it's only because the dictator *du jour* was feeling charitable for the time being. It was never because there was something inherent in governance that made it tolerant of faith.

A final, but important, note before we leave this topic: Remember that it is the atheist (as opposed to an agnostic) who is far more dogmatic than the believer. He is far more certain of his belief in the Non-God than most believers are in God. The believer often finds himself questioning God's commandments or even his existence. Indeed, the believer will tell you that it is this doubting that ironically makes his faith all the stronger.

But the atheist does not question the absence of God. The atheist tends to be far more "certain" that he is right. And so he'll be far less squeamish about imposing his will on the rest of us. Yet he'll claim every step of the way that it is the believer who seeks to impose his values upon the rest of us.

A fantasy, indeed.

Take a Couple of Cynical Pills and Call Me in the Morning

We have discussed how only big government can inflict the kind of massive evils we have seen through the French Revolution, communism, fascism, and other horrific programs. Big government in general needs to get everyone on board with the proverbial program—whatever that program might be. And big government usually needs to "sell" that program to you. They don't want you to question it.

Cynicism often gets a bad rap. But there may be a reason why God gave us an eyebrow to raise. Cynicism is at least one part skepticism, and another part experience. It allows us to separate the scams from the opportunities, the dangerous from the idealistic. It's that thing that tells a woman that something may be off with that hairy-chested man with the many necklaces wearing heavy cologne and who tells her that *he* knows how to satisfy a "hot mama" like her, as he looks her up and down.

Had the West been more cynical and questioned the true nature of fascism, we might have resisted it sooner, and reduced the numbers who died in World War II by tens of millions. But instead we believed the Nazi propaganda that Germany would not seek more territory, that they only wanted to climb out of economic ruin, and that they just needed more living space.

Had we opened our eyes to the evils of communism, we might have defeated it sooner, and spared tens of millions of lives more. But we believed the communist propaganda that communism fought for the working man and for a world where everyone is "equal." Had we recognized the true nature of Eugenics and China's One-Child Policy perpetrated, we might have ended those horrific programs earlier, too. But we also believed their propaganda that getting rid of "misfits" and other undesirables was good for the world.

Had the world questioned the Revolutionary Guards' intent to overthrow the Shah of Iran, which led to the Iranian Revolution of 1979 and the subsequent creation of the most dangerous Islamic state the world has known and the metastasizing of terrorist groups such as Hezbollah and Hamas and other terrorist groups throughout the world, we might have worked to keep the Shah in power. Instead, we believed the Mullahs' claims that they were just seeking to overthrow a despotic regime and replace it with a Republican form of government respecting the rights of all Iranian citizens.

In 2015, had Europe considered the consequences of letting in a million immigrants from dangerous countries such as Syria, it might have avoided the pervasive violence, "no-go zones," rapes, and other cultural tensions that quickly proliferated throughout the continent. But it did not, instead believing the media and European leaders that all the immigrants wanted was a better life in

Europe, to adapt peacefully and gratefully to the culture of their new host countries.

We didn't question, when we should have. We weren't cynical, when cynicism was necessary. We didn't think things through, when we needed to think of consequences.

But there were some people who knew of the impending disaster of each of these offerings. They wrote about it, spoke about it, and even campaigned against it. They predicted the parade of horribles each time. They did so with remarkable accuracy.

Who were these visionaries of truth and consequences? The ones who held a deep belief in God. Very few others had the clarity to see the developing storm of evil in all such moments.

We learned before that it was predominantly the Christians who led the charge to abolish slavery in the United States and in most of the West.[10] It was the Christian West which used force to stop slavery in other cultures, such as the Muslim slave trade off the coast of Africa.[11] As we noted, others did very little, if anything.[12] Before the Christian opposition, there were no opposition groups to slavery—least of all those with little or no faith.[13]

Likewise, we saw it was the Catholics, Protestants, and Jehovah's Witnesses who resisted the Nazis and who hid Jews and other victims. It was they, along with many devout Jews, who warned about communism. It was they who supported Israel against her enemies, and continue to do so. It was they who fought eugenics and China's One-Child policy.

How can this be? The blind and foolishly religious can foresee bad things happening before their godless betters do?

That's right. They can, they have, and they do. The religious are in fact *deep skeptics and sometimes great cynics when they need to be.* They question when someone offers a program that they know will diminish your freedom. They are the first ones to leave that crowd that's formed around the salesman hawking his snake oil.

To many of the godless, this premise will cause them to scoff. Religious people more skeptical? Aren't the atheists the ones who revere science, and follow it wherever the facts may lead? That's what they keep telling us, anyway.

Not so much. Many religious believers have in fact come to God through deep scientific and statistical analysis, as well as logical deduction (like myself). But even those who believe just because their parents have raised them to believe have steeped themselves deeply in the Bible. They've often done so decades, every Saturday or Sunday. And in those sermons, readings and prayers, they learn about the true nature of man, from fear of freedom (example: the Book of Exodus) to the destructive natures of jealousy and envy (examples: the story of Jacob and Esau, Joseph and his brothers), to how to deal with enemies, fear, and temptation.

Perhaps you dismiss these arguments because you claim they stem from fictional stories. But the important part is that the believer has been studying human nature for much of his life. And his study has in turn derived from centuries and millennia of study from others.

Like the professional tennis player who has trained his arm and mind for so many years so that he knows where to hit and receive the ball with such precision that it becomes second nature to him, the religious individual has trained his mind to see the consequences of temptations, the destructive nature of self-deceit, the need for justice, the misdirection in the glorification of nature, and the essential centrality of family, the individual and freedom.

The *religious* are the first ones to raise their hands in skepticism, to challenge the Big New Idea, to point out the "What Ifs," and the "Have You Thought Abouts." They are the ones who know that history repeats itself; that man needs to channel his inherent self-interest, not deny it; that family and marriage forms the cornerstone of civilization; that men and women are different; that absolute power corrupts absolutely; and that evil is real.

Contrary to their perception of themselves, those without God do not delve very often into skepticism. Why would they? Every day is the same as the next for them. They haven't set any time, let alone one day of the week, year after year and decade after decade, for self-awareness or the study of the pursuit of goodness. They haven't looked past their proverbial noses to routinely inquire about the great issues. Yet the godless claim to somehow know more about such matters than the religious.

Actually, wait: it's worse than that: As G. K. Chesterton famously noted, when you don't believe in God, you don't believe in nothing; you believe in anything. They will absorb whatever anyone tells them, so long as he's appealing or charismatic enough. All that matters is that the proposal or ideology makes them feel good.

Why wouldn't they? It is much easier for them to fall for evil ideologies, like eugenics, some of which are even based on "rational" arguments. That's because the godless rarely have moral underpinnings or even the notion of a universal "standard" which might help inform their decisions, to let them know clearly that something is "Wrong." It's as if they float in space without any bearings, not knowing which way is up or down. So they'll cling to whatever gives them a sense of stability and orientation.

In the end, then, it should not be surprising that it is the godless who are and have been much more likely to believe in nonsensical and/or horrific ideologies (fascism, communism, eugenics, global warming, world overpopulation, and other "Sky is Falling" scenarios). They have always been and remain far more willing to embrace dictatorship as an answer.

Don't believe it? Just ask them. Particularly "elite" men like New York Times columnist Thomas ("let's be China For a Day") Friedman and Woody Allen (see discussion, below). Ask the

American progressives who raced to Russia to support its new promising ideology of communism, and the same progressives who fell in love with Mussolini and his fascist order only a little while later. Ask the celebrities who embraced Castro of Cuba and then Hugo Chavez of Venezuela. Ask Jimmy Carter and other American and European supporters of Ayatollah Khomeini of Iran, who believed his fundamentalist, Sharia-oriented dictatorship would be better for the Iranians and the world than the Shah. Even now, very few among the godless fully appreciate the coming onslaught of Radical Islam, even as it penetrates deeper into Europe, year after year.

It is the believers, through their skepticism and resistance—based on standards which have developed over thousands of years—who have saved our civilization, time and time again. It was the believers who created the unique and enduring American system of checks and balances, precisely because they understood the frail and corruptible nature of Man. It was *their* skepticism of human nature that turned out to be right. It was *their* skepticism which caused America to become the beacon of hope, opportunity, compassion, liberty, innovation, and security, and to spread many such values to other countries.

Skepticism is not part of the world of the godless. They don't have time for that, what with them spinning wildly in space, desperately looking to cling to whatever shiny object might come their way.

To Hell with Your Freedom

Once on the news a few years ago, I saw a group of people in London protesting some perceived injustice (the British government had not condemned Israel enough about something). Many Arabs and Muslims protested, holding placards, and a news reporter was reporting their grievances. I remember he was hunching his shoulders; it was a cold day.

But there in the background, one protester caught my eye. She was holding a sign. Unlike the other signs which were bobbing up and down, she held hers steady. That, and the fact that the cold seemed not to affect her whatsoever, compelled me to her. And on her sign were some of the most frightening words I'd ever read. It was handwritten in paint.

Did it say "Death to America" or "Death to Christians" or "Death to Jews and Israel"? Or perhaps, "Prepare for Allah's will in Europe"? Maybe it read, "You will all die like dogs"?

No, nothing like that at all. It was simpler. Far simpler.

It read: "To Hell with Your FREEDOM."

This chilled me, because it was a revelation of something so basic that cut to the core of all things. And it a complete inversion of everything I once understood:

Not everyone seeks or cherishes freedom.

Let me repeat that: *Not everyone seeks or cherishes freedom.*

In fact, a surprisingly large number of people don't. That's right: what you always thought was so fundamental and universal to human nature is just not true. It turns out many people actually *despise* the notion of freedom—even many born-and-bred Americans.

Here is why: freedom ultimately requires responsibility. Freedom requires work, and *hard* work at that. Many people would rather have a "command and control" economy where, yes, one party may control everything, but just think of the benefits. The central authority promises *everything* to you—generously, consistently, predictably. As long as you get what you need, well then who really needs freedom?

And when you realize most people don't passionately love freedom, you begin to understand how freedom is *not* normal. People fail to understand the very meaning of freedom.

You see, freedom is *not* the absence of dictatorship. Freedom is *not* what occurs when no one tells you what to do anymore. No: Freedom is active and requires constant nourishment and attention. Freedom is a beautiful but needy garden, which only retains its beauty as long as many people continue to water it, weed it, and keep the overgrowth, rats, and other vermin at bay. Freedom is the right to think, the right to learn, the right to *self-actualize*. These are all *active* in nature.

Freedom seems wonderful in principle. But it is the difficult work of countless others before us that gave us the freedoms we now enjoy. It came after the smell of smoke from hundreds of thousands of rifles, frostbitten toes and fingers, desperate letters to superiors demanding more supplies, and letters of love to distant girlfriends and wives, many of whom would never receive them.

For many of us, however, freedom is something that just *is*, not something we must nourish. It's like a child who goes to the grocery store and doesn't know of all the hard work it took to make the food, transport it, pass all the safety inspections, and then stock it on the shelves in its proper place. For the child, the grocery store and its food have always been there.

The freedom we have today *wasn't* always there. It took centuries to develop into the institution of freedom we take for granted today. At times, we can be no different than the child at the grocery store. We gyrate and sweat to the music at the clubs, binge drink with our buddies, work just to pay the rent, and sex it up with anyone who's willing. Then we repeat the cycle the next week. But church and God? Who has the time? By the way, what's "God?"

And as God leaves the picture, a funny thing occurs: freedom, and fighting for it, seems so antiquated, as if it's relevant only to a time long passed—as relevant to us today as the horse and buggy, the ice man, or pagers. So we don't fuss much when college campuses impose "Speech Codes," when the government suggests forcing news channels to air opposite opinions (the so-called "Fairness Doctrine"), or when legislators consider criminalizing those who question whether humanity is primarily responsible for climate change.[14]

Not surprisingly, freedom is not a meaningful part of the atheist's utopian vision. He may pay lip service to the notion of freedom, but when he actually thinks about it, he'll be among a whole lot of others who advocate for a "dictatorship."

But don't you worry—they don't mean the "brutal" kind of dictatorship. Just one of those soft and sweet dictatorships, like the Stay Puft Marshmallow Man from the movie *Ghostbusters*: a huge monster, to be sure, but fluffy on the outside so he must be good. Or maybe the kind of dictator who really "gets" you and wants what's best for both you and everyone else. Heavy on the regulations and great efficient planning, but hold the guns and torture, please.

You know the kind of dictators I'm talking about. You see them all the time.

It is not surprising that atheists are more likely to prefer dictator rule. They *fear* a world with freedom—as I once did. If man has no free will and is little more than a self-centered sophisticated animal, then we must control him for all that he might do (yet, strangely, they somehow claim that man is inherently good, but that's another conundrum I'll leave them to deal with). We should view man no differently than a vicious dog. The last thing you would do is let him loose in the neighborhood. You must leash him. Watch him every moment. Control him.

To the nonbeliever and to the socialist nonbeliever in particular, democracy is a nuisance, an obstacle to all their big plans. They resent it. After all, in a democracy, the people might vote to undo the socialist's grand plans, whether that might be universal health care, requiring all to run their homes and businesses on solar/wind power, or mandating a new way of educating children. Hence Thomas Friedman's wistful appreciation for China's ability to control its people and the desire of some atheists who view dictatorship as a positive thing (see more, below).

And so, consistent with that, the godless will tend to push for as many laws to control as many aspects of life as possible. Little should be left to the discretion of the individual.

All of us—atheist and believer alike—intuitively know that *someone* must be in charge. No one quibbles that a city, state, or country must have a leader; that a ship must have a captain; that a team must have its captain or quarterback; that a child should have someone raising him; and that a company must have a CEO. But the believer's focus on God as the One in charge is what actually bestows the gifts of freedom and free will. The atheist's Man in Charge cannot.

The end of freedom is not a factor for the godless, nor the evil that always accompanies that end. We think our freedom has always been there for us and always will be. But it hasn't been, and it won't always be. It was God who gave the notion of freedom any meaning, and God who gives us the strength to fight for it.

And if we don't fight for it, we don't deserve it.

Freedom to Do WHAT?

If a man hasn't discovered something he is willing to die for,
he is not fit to live
— Martin Luther King, Jr.

Here's the next question to beg: freedom to do *what*? To make money? The freedom to complain about pension benefits? The freedom to look at Internet gossip? to download music free of charge? To use the opposite sex's restrooms?

Maybe it's something more noble, such as the freedom to vote. Maybe it's the freedom to speak your mind and disagree with your friends, to even write an editorial complaining about the latest missteps of your government leaders?

I don't think so. Let's be frank: is this *really* what you might be willing to *die* for? The right to complain or even the right to govern yourselves?

Let's do a thought experiment: What if your government gave you just enough goodies to not have to work hard, to feed your family, and to let you enjoy all the parks and museums you could want and go on vacation quite often? The work week would be pleasant—laws would prohibit any employer from making you work more than, say, thirty hours a week. You could look forward to a guaranteed pension when you retire as early as fifty-five years old. Your family would enjoy similar perks, too.

You'd get free university education and health care. Public transport and other services would come at minimal expense to you. You'd never have to worry about hunger or shelter.

You could have as much sex as you wanted, of course—no issue there (other than pedophilia and perhaps bestiality and incest, but that may change, too). Drug enforcement would still exist, but let's face it, not very strictly.

What's not to like? Others would have similar lives—not much better and not much worse than you. Think of it as one of those "sine and cosine" graphs during your advanced math days, where the amplitude in either direction is not so significant. Everyone is more or less in the same boat, so it's hard to complain that anyone is getting more than you.

The only expectation in return is that you don't fight the system, or expect anything beyond what the system gives you. Just do as the government tells you, and don't stand out. Remember, this whole thing only works if we all get with the program.

Now that you understand, here's the offer: You can keep all those goodies. Or you can give them up and fight for something different that could be much greater. Keep in mind, however, you might die in the process. I'll explain in a moment what you might be dying for.

But first, let me make it clear: you can go for Door Number One—with its promises of a seemingly satisfactory life, at least as you know it. Or you can choose Door Number Two—behind which is something that allows you the possibility of a more meaningful life. You just don't know exactly what that something else might look like, other than that it also involves work and risk. But trust me, it's so good you'd be willing to die for it.

So, what is it that could be greater? What is the thing you might die for?

It is the freedom to create, to innovate, and to discover—the freedom even to fail. And with those things is the ultimate purpose: the freedom to connect with God.

In the end, *that* is why so many have died for the United States and elsewhere. It is the only freedom truly worth fighting for, and the only freedom they actually *were* fighting for.

Still skeptical? Think of this, then: Without God, no real need for freedom exists. After all, if the government provides everything you need, then what is there really to complain about? And even if there is something to complain about—say, the government has not yet delivered enough milk to the supermarket, or the government should subsidize wine or provide contraception and abortion free of charge—are such things really enough for you to die for?

I didn't think so. What other than the quest and right to seek or worship God would you be willing to actually die for?

I assume everyone is willing to die for their family, but I am talking beyond this. Imagine taking a piece of paper and writing: "I am willing to die for the following: . . ." If you don't believe in God, your list will be short. In fact, it is likely not to include a single item.

This lack of will to die for virtually anything explains why so many had no problem saying "better red than dead" during the Cold War. It explains why the media so often attack Christianity and Judaism (neither of which seek to conquer the world nor impose a religious scheme over everyone) and condemn anyone who attacks Islam (a significant minority of which *does* seek to impose a religious scheme over everyone—and based on which almost all modern-day terrorism arises). It explains why men like former Secretary of State and Senator John Kerry can mock men and women who join the military.[15] It explains why the media and much of our own population grimaced and mocked Ronald Reagan for calling the Soviet Union the "Evil Empire" that it was. And it explains even now why public schools and governments are so willing to highlight and even teach Islam in public schools, while simultaneously banning the teaching of, and even reviling, Judaism and Christianity.

In a sense, every innovation, every great philosophy, every new scientific discovery, every effort to create and move the proverbial needle just a little bit further to make humankind more comfortable, enjoyable, or efficient, is but part of a greater quest to get closer to self-actualizing. And only with self-actualizing can we have the *ability* to get closer to God.

Still not convinced? Imagine yourself in a tribe of cavemen, and a recent storm and flood has forced you and your buddies out of your cave. You have no time to wonder about the wonderful machinations of the celestial bodies. No time to appreciate the beauty of art, let alone create it. No time to contemplate how you got here, let alone why you are here. Your mission for every moment of every day is simple: get shelter, get food, get water, and fight off enemies. Repeat, day after day.

There is no issue of "freedom" under such circumstances. The very idea of freedom is itself a philosophical luxury that can only come after centuries of innovations, and only after enough innovations eventually allow us to extract greater and greater amounts of free time away from the menial existence of survival. As a caveman, you cannot even contemplate freedom until you can rest, and are able to engage in contemplation itself. There is otherwise only survival. God and the notion of freedom are unnecessary in a world where you seek only to make it to the next day.

It's what any animal in the wild goes through every day.

No species other than humans has ever sought to improve its collective lot for future generations; the lifestyle of the elephant of today is no different than it was tens of thousands of years ago. No penguin will ever hope that her grandchildren will lead a better life than she did. There is no famous salmon that changed the way all other salmon think. No animal species has its own Plato, Abraham Lincoln, Martin Luther King Jr., or the Beatles (but to the animals' credit, they also don't have a Justin Bieber).

We humans are quite different. We crave to improve our lot. And it's only after innovation, artistic expression, and scientific discovery that we can even approach the discussion of God.

Dictatorships have always known that their greatest threat was religion—particularly a religion that seeks to connect to God through discovery, art, and science. It is the very reason communist, fascist, and other dictator regimes have always sought first to squash religion in their countries. The agenda of finding God pulls you away from the playbook of the dictatorship countries, or even the agenda of the socialist countries.

They've provided everything you could possibly want, at least the security and the part about the basic comforts of life. Yet you somehow want *more*? What more could you want?

Yes, the "more" is our quest for God, which is ultimately what makes us human, what distinguishes us—by leaps and bounds—from all the animals. And it is the end-game of all dictatorships and socialist structures—intentionally by dictatorships and negligently by socialism—to deprive you of your humanity. Take away the *quest* for God, and no one needs freedom. Once freedom is unnecessary, or at least so unimportant that people never think of actually dying for it, well, the populace is yours for the controlling.

Still skeptical? Ask any European today whether he'd die for freedom. I did. They'll give you an absurd look; of course they're not. They will tell you that fighting is a barbaric relic of the past. Fighting is unnecessary and even evil itself. They'll even look contemptuously at you and ask, "What do you mean by freedom?"

And that's what you'll hear from the thoughtful ones. More often, they just shrug their shoulders, as if you asked them to speak passionately of the difference between stalagmites and stalactites. The very question means nothing to them.

And then, just to wrap it up in a bow, ask them if they believe in God. Nine of ten will say no, or wave you off, like it, too, is a thing of the silly and destructive past. The tenth will say yes but in a whisper, as he leans in.

While Americans tend to be far more religious than their European friends, the trend even in the United States also leans to negativism, if not outright atheism. Church attendance is beginning to wane, as it did decades ago in Europe.

And we will soon be like Europe, wondering why we were ever so bent out of shape about freedom in the first place. Security, guaranteed pensions, going easy on the drug enforcement, and as much sex as you like. What's not to like?

By now you can see it: real freedom is the freedom to seek God. It is the only freedom truly worth dying for.

What so many socialist governments have done—quite effectively—is to change the risk calculation for its populations. In effect, they've convinced their people to choose Door Number One. They lose out on freedom, yes, but they'll get a lot of freebies. And in any contest between freebies and freedom, freebies always win. They don't quite know what freedom means anyway.

And that's what makes it so easy for someone to tell you to take your freedom to hell.

"China for a Day"

The dictatorial impulse is within all of us. Freedom is a threat to that dictatorial impulse. And make no mistake: the dictatorial impulse is strong, even within many Americans.

Writer and director Woody Allen famously declared in 2010 that not only did he think President Obama was "brilliant" and Republicans "should get out of his way" to allow Obama to achieve what he wanted to achieve, but that we should let Obama be dictator. As he proclaimed in an interview with *La Vanguardia*, a Spanish-language magazine, "It would be good . . . if [Obama] could be dictator for a few years because he could do a lot of good things quickly."[16]

Likewise, Harry Belafonte stated in an interview, with host Al Sharpton on MSNBC cable news channel, that the president's only recourse might be to act as a "third-world dictator" and put all dissenters in jail.[17] Oddly, Belafonte justified imposing dictatorship on the grounds that the Republicans were frustrating the "will of the people," and what choice does the president have except to jail people who dissent from him?

The temptation for authoritarian control goes beyond quirky entertainers. Writer and well-respected commentator Thomas Friedman of the *New York Times* suggested in his book *Hot, Flat, and Crowded* that America adopt his idea of becoming "China for a Day": Among other things, Friedman expresses his envy that China could order the banning of the plastic bag, and it is banned. He wonders: "Why can't we be like that?"[18]

And it would be great, he proclaims, because it would take only a day of enactment, and our federal government would then enforce it thereafter. He complains that in America right now, if there are various hodgepodge environmental regulations, we must wait for "a dozen public interest groups, led by the Sierra Club and the Natural Resources Defense Council [to] sue the violators (including the federal government) all the way to the Supreme Court."[19]

To Friedman, that is just so wasteful and frustrating!:

> That is why being China for a day—imposing *all the right taxes, regulations, and standards* needed to launch a clean power system in one day—would be so much more valuable to Washington than Beijing. Because *once the directions are given from above*, we would be overcoming the worst part of our democracy (the inability to make big decisions in peacetime), and the next day we would be able to enjoy the best part of our democracy (the power of our civic society to make government rules stick and the power of our markets to take advantage of them).[20] (emphasis added)

Did you get that? Read again carefully: "imposing all the *right* taxes, regulations, and standards." Yes, that's right, he wrote that. And they would all come "from above." This of course presumes that a "right" standard exists at all, and it's just various unseen forces who are warring with each other, blocking the path to that golden standard.

He of course doesn't define what that "right" standard might be. But what troubles me more is his implication that a dictatorship could ever get *anything* right, let alone the "right" blend of taxes, regulations, and standards. Indeed, if a dictatorship could get everything right in *one* day, then why not have a dictatorship, well, *every* day? Why settle for only one glorious day of greatness? If democracies are slippery and sloppy and inefficient, then why *ever* tolerate it?

His implication goes further: Democracy is quaint and might have made sense once upon a time, but let's face it: dictatorships are superior to democracies. In that sense, Friedman is no different than our progressive friends from the twenties and thirties, including Theodore Roosevelt, Margaret Sanger, and Franklin Roosevelt: Let's not let individual freedoms interfere with getting the job done, dammit.

The tautology in all this is dizzying. Friedman seems to forget that the very premise of democracy is not only to ensure and *encourage* competing views but also to *prevent authoritarianism*. Our Founding Fathers didn't *want* laws and regulations to flow liberally from Washington. Rather they wanted to *choke* that spigot. They did so by creating a complex set of checks and balances in a Constitution that sought to create gridlock, *not* efficiency, of government. Gridlock was a *feature* of the new Constitution, not a "bug." As Thomas Jefferson stated: "The best government is the one that governs least." It's as if Friedman—and so many others like him—forgot why America ever bothered to fight the Revolution in the first place.

Friedman's point also presumes that certain things just must get done, and we need to dismiss anyone who says otherwise—such as stopping global warming, adding bike lanes and imposing an infrastructure of high-speed trains, things that we can't afford to leave to local, state, or even federal "debate." It presumes that *his* vision of "right" is *the* ultimate right vision—and all of the rest of us are trying to impose something "wrong."

In his world, democracy is not only suboptimal but quite the frustrating nuisance and impediment to all good things, whatever those may be. Democracy is merely a technical right, mostly for the gun-wielding religious crazies. He's like the impatient judge who must hear out the *pro se* nut in the courtroom ranting about the aliens have taken over all our brains, and that's why he took the school's money. In the end, for thinkers like Friedman, Democracy is an annoying cultural vestige of the past we just have to suffer with, like neckties and pantyhose.

But this is exactly the problem that he fails to appreciate, and what makes his thesis so childish: *everyone* thinks *his* vision of what is right is the true "right." *It is why we have democracy in the first place.* I say it is childish, literally, because only really young children don't understand that people think differently (try telling your four-year-old that people speak different languages and have different values, religions, and cultural norms).

Another flaw in Friedman's argument is that it implies that only what *he* wishes to impose by dictatorial fiat is important but not other items (such as preventing abortion or stepping up enforcement against illegal immigration). In other words, *which* issues shall our "China for a Day" government decide on that glorious day?

Also, he fails to appreciate that being China for a day may entail some ugly things, too. Some examples include forced abortions, sterilizations, and forced organ "harvesting." There is little, if any, due process (it is still a communist country, after all).

Or perhaps Friedman means a "buffet" style approach to what he likes about China. I'll take the quick decision making, but I'll pass on the torture and middle of the night disappearings. But you have to take the bad with the good that you claim to like. Otherwise, why not argue to be Nazi Germany for a day? They were efficient, after all: The economy improved, crime went down, and those trains ran on time.

Friedman writes as if he's a young teenager who has entered the palace of a drug lord: he envies all the pleasures of the drug lord's palace, women, and wealth. He just hasn't considered the drug part.

Next, he fails to appreciate that it is American democracy—unseemly and unacceptably messy to him as it is—that created the lion's share of the world's innovations, inventions, and medical breakthroughs since the late 1800s. It also created wildly disproportionate contributions to art, music, fashion, and other cultural phenomena. What a mystery it must be to Friedman that all this could have occurred without a benevolent dictator to orchestrate it all.

How someone can think like this—thinking without consequences or a sense of the past that might inform him—is confounding, in some ways. It's even more bizarre that the literati would celebrate him as a visionary.

Friedman proves how those who do not incorporate God into their lives cannot truly understand what freedom is. This is why seemingly intelligent people like him, Allen, and Belafonte can so easily bulldoze over the most fundamental tenet of the American Revolution, without even wincing. They are like land developers who might look at the Louvre as only a building to tear down for a sparkly new shopping mall. They'll raze it, with no regard to the museum's extraordinary history and precious artwork.

Only someone who does not embrace God can let himself believe this nonsense. Not surprisingly, each of these men (Allen, Belafonte, and Friedman) are either avowed atheists or have expressed only a passing head nod to God.[21]

To Friedman, those who fight statism and who promote democratic debate are our enemies. Absolute power works. But as Lord Acton famously noted, history has shown that absolute power corrupts absolutely. To not learn from humankind's history and to willingly ignore the unique history of America, reveals a deeper truth: freedom is not only essential to advance society, but it involves great vigilance.

It also reveals a disquieting truth about human nature: we are flawed; we are not naturally "good." Perhaps most unsettling is that there are no easy answers. All the more reason we are to *resist* bigger and bigger government, not to embrace its supposed wonders.

It is rare to find the atheist who champions and seeks out *real* liberty. Without God, the door to authoritarianism is ever so easy to push open. It seems ever so logical, even seductive. But it is nothing more than the Sirens, calling you to crash upon the rocks of their island.

Truth, Justice ... And the Atheist Way

Who are you going to believe? Me or your lying eyes?
— Groucho Marx, from "Duck Soup" (1933)

In George Orwell's classic *1984*, Orwell presents a haunting futuristic world where an authoritarianism regime imposes socialism to strip the individual of his humanity, drilling into the mind of every citizen that his sole purpose is to serve the glory of the state. God is irrelevant. Big Brother, the state's ever-watching ruler, monitoring everyone's moves and actions, is all the God you need.

In one of its most chilling moments, the narrator writes:

> The party told you to reject the evidence of your eyes and ears. It was their final, most essential command. His heart sank as he thought of the enormous power arrayed against him, the ease with which any Party intellectual would overthrow him in debate, the subtle arguments which he would

not be able to understand, much less answer. And yet he was in the right! They were wrong and he was right.[22]

What is so striking in *1984* is not just the naked quest for power for power's sake, and not just the squashing of all things individual. Most striking is the pervasive effort to destroy truth. Following its publication in 1949, "doublethink" and "newspeak," became household phrases. In Orwell's dark world, a "Ministry of Truth" would generate official lies, a "Ministry of Peace" would pursue war, and a "Ministry of Love" would handle the government's systematic torture needs. Britain (referred to in the novel as Airstrip One) employs a fearsomely efficient government propaganda machine which controls all media, forcing all loyal and ambitious party members to follow the party's "official version" of the news and history, even though they know the opposite to be true.

All reality is constantly in flux. The government official news agencies will not even announce the switch of allegiances from its former ally, Eastasia, to its former enemy Eurasia. It just rewrites history accordingly: "Oceania was at war with Eastasia: Oceania had always been at war with Eastasia." All previous reports become irrelevant.

Citizens can write and say only certain adjectives, such as various variations of "good" (plusgood, doubleplusgood, etc., and so on), thus robbing its citizens of any creative or qualitative thinking. Loyal Party members learn to hold two contradictory versions of reality — party truth on the one hand, truth as they actually experience it on the other.[23]

More meaningfully, the notion of truth means absolutely nothing. All that matters is what information Big Brother mandates upon you.

Why does truth mean nothing in such a world? For that matter, was there something inherent in the nature of socialism, fascism or communism, or among any other "Big Brother" type dictatorship that made them uniquely hostile to the notion of truth, as we think of it?

It was the utter lack of God in these ideologies. Once you take God out of your civilization, you have no need for truth. It is almost axiomatic: One of the terrifying aspects of atheism is that it has no notion of, nor concern for, truth. Truth is as meaningful to atheism as the notion of etiquette was meaningful to Genghis Khan.

In Christianity, Judaism, and many other civilized faiths, telling the truth, and the quest for justice is front-and-center to their respective faiths' tenets. According to such faiths, without this quest for truth, civilization will ultimately descend and collapse. There is no point to any faith if truth is not at its core.

But atheism is different. Remember: atheism is about nothing. An individual atheist himself might very well appreciate principles of truth and justice, but that appreciation does not come *from* his atheism. Nothing *in* atheism informs or compels him to such principles.

Think of it this way: when a woman goes on a date for the first time with a man she just met, she tries to get a sense of what kind of man he is. She might ask him what motivates him or how he identifies himself. What are his passions, his sense of what marriage and children mean, his ambitions? If he brushes such questions off and only speaks instead of sports, the woman may conclude that this man is not right for her. He might be a good-looking "bad boy" who lives by his own rules, but he's revealed a great deal about himself by what he has *not* spoken about.

And so it is with atheism: here's an ideology that speaks nothing about truth nor justice. For that matter, it speaks nothing about compassion, innovation, freedom, the primacy of family, or the need for preserving or advancing civilization.

So, like the woman on her date, we may judge atheism based on what it does not advance. She can decide to marry him, but she shouldn't be surprised when the man, shortly after their honeymoon, acts like a selfish jerk, demonstrates no ambition, and shows no interest in making a family. As her girlfriends will no doubt reproach her later: Just what did you *think* would happen?

You may love the notions of truth and justice, but hitching your wagon to atheism isn't going to advance those noble principles. And forgetting God—the very source of our notions of truth and justice—means we can eventually forget about those principles too.

In atheism, truth is just something that you do when it's convenient. And if there are no consequences, then truth is not necessary. Truth is not a value, just like good and evil are not values. You do what you need to do. An intellectually honest atheist must recognize this.

If we all are to live without God, we'd be like the woman who marries that inadequate gentlemen friend, who now feels so unfulfilled, unloved and ignored, angry at the world and perhaps even more angry with herself, wondering as she looks out the window how things might have been so much better, if only she had chosen the other guy.

A Word about Your Word

You've heard it from countless stories of old. Here comes Hondo Lane, the hero from Louis L'Amour's *Hondo*, talking about how a man's word is his bond, and how he will not fight the Apaches in battle. Why? because he had given the Apache chief Vittoro his word that he would not. Here comes Atticus Finch, the protagonist and hero from *To Kill a Mockingbird,* who stands up for principle and honor to fight for the innocence of a black man accused of rape and murder, despite all the resistance from his town.

There are countless other such stories of a world where appearances, reputation, honor, your word, and even a handshake mean *everything.* Calling a man a liar could easily lead to deadly consequences, perhaps to a duel. Questioning a woman's chastity might devastate her, personally and socially. Right or wrong, your reputation and your integrity were cornerstones of your life.

Not so much today. All of that now seems at best yet another quaint relic of a time long gone. If someone tells you that he'll have your shipments delivered to you tomorrow, and that he gives you his word as a gentleman (or as a McCormick, or as a Lord of Commons, or whatever) and offers you a hand to shake, you'll look at him like he's just arrived from H. G. Wells's time machine. His "word" means quite little to you. You tell him you appreciate the gesture, but would he mind please just confirming it in an email? Thank you so much.

And you'd be right: lawsuits abound where one side weasels out of contracts and obligations. Your "word" sounds nice, but as they say: an oral agreement isn't worth the paper it's written on.

Honor is missing. In its place is a world where you take advantage of every situation as it may be convenient for you for the moment, wondering how and what you can get away with. Example: although you had a deal, another supplier has offered you a more lucrative deal in the meantime. So you take the second supplier's deal, and you tell the first supplier you never really had a deal with him. Instead of wondering whether what you are doing is right, you wonder whether the first supplier might have enough "evidence" to prove his case against you. If not, then onward to the better deal you go.

Why has our sense of our "word" gone? It is something we have lost over the decades. One might argue that it was because people usually confined themselves to their town and had to deal with each other much more than we deal with each other today. Today, if someone accuses you of fraud in your town? No big deal: everyone gets sued for fraud. And if it gets too hot to handle reputation-wise, just move to another business—or town or state.

But that argument doesn't explain real life rangers and ranchers, along with their whole families, who lived like Hondo Lane from the days of the Wild West, who *did* move about from town to town as a way of life. So why would such people care about their word so much?

And likewise, today, there are people who live in the same small towns for decades, and they don't seem to care much about their reputation at all. In and out of parole for one, a woman knocked-up by yet a different stranger, for another.

It's not that your integrity and reputations mean nothing. But you get a sense that such things are not as big a deal as they have been, decades before. To twist Winston Churchill's famous words: Never in the history of human civilization have so many felt they owed so little to anyone else.

Here's why: Because "honor" was never just about restraining yourself to avoid the watchful eyes of the community. The one thing that was common and central in the lives of such "quaint" people was their belief that *God* was always watching, even if no one else was. You still had to answer to *Him*. God always knew the Truth. You could fool your business partners, and you could even fool the judge. But you couldn't fool God. To the extent the community was "watching" you, and you reneged on a deal, the community was watching you violate your bond with God.

There was a reason why, back starting in 1938, the Superman TV series introduced and described not just how our amazing superhero was faster than a speeding bullet or more powerful than a locomotive. His main offering was that he sought "Truth, Justice and the American way."

Today's consumers of superheroes comics and movies are less concerned with such anchoring values. Even today's superhero characters themselves don't seem to understand why they're fighting, or if they stand for anything at all.

And that should come as no surprise: timeless values such as integrity, truth and justice can only come from something outside of us, something beyond: God. They arrived on the same train. And it was with God that we received them as gifts. He did so to better enable us to reach Him. When we abandon God, we lose these values as well. Or at least such values become pointless, like train tracks without their train.

To the atheist, maybe such values are only quaint, and belong in the past. But who are we, and what can we hope to accomplish individually, or as a society, when we think we can progress without them? Where do we *think* we can go? Where do we *want* to go?

How much longer does the atheist think a society can last when all these values disappear one day?

Hint: ask the next Roman you meet.

CHAPTER V

ATHEISM ON THE ONE HAND; HUMANS ON THE OTHER

The Battle for Free Will

We discussed before that any philosophy class will ultimately come to the same conclusion: true freedom or free will, or your ability to exercise any choice itself, can only come from an external force that gave it to you.[1] It cannot come about organically or randomly, whether through natural selection or otherwise. No amount of logic or feelings of the heart can create it. Someone or some "thing" must give or deliver it to you, no less than the newspaper boy delivers your paper (or some geek makes it available for you to download from the internet; work with me here).

The atheist will try to fashion an argument that free will can come about through the standard evolutionary process. How so? Who was the first one to receive free will? How did that adaptive mutation come about at all? We know what an arm or hand looks like, but what does free will "look" like? Where is it in the brain? How does free will offer a better chance of survival over the fittest than instinct, especially since all other animals operate predominantly out of instinct, and seem to be surviving as a species just fine? Why wouldn't there be a separate human species in evolutionary history, without the same degree of free will?

As with love, beauty, purpose, music, and so many other things we discussed earlier, you have to strain quite far to explain free will as the product of evolution. But that is the simplistic "one size fits all" explanation the godless will give (and must give) for *everything*. And this explanation is no more logical than the astrologer who thinks that all decisions can come from the movement of the stars, or the alchemist of old who thought all things were comprised of some combination of earth, air, fire, and water.

They are like the house goldfish who knows nothing but the world inside his fishbowl, and perhaps the living room his bowl sits in. He has no idea that the house was once built by carpenters and developers. He has no idea of where his owner goes to work, or what work is. He has no idea that the kids of the house go to school, or what they learn—or what even "learning" is. He has no idea of government, the roundness of the earth, the planets, let alone a "universe." For that matter, he doesn't know what lies beyond the reaches of the living room.

All he knows beyond his fishbowl is that, every once in a while, a big hand brings food from above. That is all he can see, and so that is all he knows of his world. And that is the way it has been for him and always will be.

That is the way of the godless. Without God, they are left to explain the world solely with what is within their immediate sensory, or extended sensory, abilities. They cannot fathom anything like free will because free will lies beyond their range of sensory abilities. It is well beyond their own fishbowl.

This is not something we should toy with. Free will is a reality within each of us. It is what ultimately makes us human. It is what make us free. When we toy with a world without God, we have no real freedom nor do we have real free will. Freedom and free will are irrelevant in the world of the dictator. They only matter in a world *with* God.

The Unbearable Impossibility of Being—Part Two

One of science's greatest questions, and some say the ultimate question, is the mystery of consciousness and self-awareness.[2] How do we explain the differences between our brain and our mind? Why are we aware of ourselves, and, further still, how can we even contemplate that awareness?

It is one thing to argue that life began spontaneously, and then adapted to greater and greater sophistication, but no amount of evolutionary theory can explain our own sense of self. We can build a car, a computer, a skyscraper, and even the most sophisticated spaceship. We can make them do the most impressive and complex things, but we'll never be able to give it a sense of self which even a lizard has. A computer will never feel startled, happy, or angry nor be curious or play with the mirror when it sees itself for the first time.

And for this same reason, we don't ever think of "loving" a computer, car, or building in the same way we might love a person, or even a dog. We don't criminalize someone for verbally abusing a frying pan. We don't talk about being cruel to a garden hose. Nor do we feel a sense of emotional loss and inner turmoil upon losing such things (well, maybe when I lose my iPhone, I'll give you that).

Consciousness and self-awareness are unknown qualities. We can't meaningfully explain it, nor will we ever truly understand it.[3] All of us have a sense that the "who" of "who we are"—the "me" of our existences—cannot be only a function of biological and chemical dispatches within ourselves, all of which evolved randomly.

Even if we believe that evolution brought us to our present sophisticated biological state, it feels as if the "me" part entered our bodies in a separate transaction. It's as if someone's built the train, and now some conductor has invited the "me" onboard.

In short, evolution cannot explain our "me." It can only come from something which bestowed that "me" sense within each of us.

There is no scientific proof of our "me." No amount of probing with microscopes, mathematical formulas, or surgeries will find it. Like free will and time (which I will discuss later), it is a fiction, at least from a scientific point of view.

Taking away God or some other creator from our understanding of the "me" in each of us means that we must ignore our consciousness and self-awareness. And in doing that, we dehumanize each individual. It means we have to view ourselves at best as sophisticated automatons. There is no basis for accountability or responsibility. Worse yet, humans are expendable and any opportunistic leader can use and manipulate them.

Does that sound far-fetched? You need only look at the past century for ample examples of just that. Remember Lenin, Stalin, Mao, Pol Pot, Castro, Hitler, and Ceauşescu? Each advanced the godless principles which fascism, communism, and even eugenics embodied. Each saw humans as little more than worker bees who were supposed to do the queen bee's bidding. If anyone even appeared to express a whiff of individualism, they disappeared into concentration camps, gulags, or the killing fields. They never considered anyone's "me."

"Me" is the ultimate conundrum to the atheist because he cannot deny it is the essential part of our existence. It may *seem* to be fiction, yet there is nothing more real within each of us, nothing that better defines each one of us.

"Me" can only come from a Creator. Unless we appreciate that, we will see ourselves only as locusts devouring a field. And if we are merely locusts, we will soon have as little regard for our lives as we would the lives of such insects.

It's a dangerous outlook, and so surprisingly easy to get there.

Purpose

If you were a convict in the early 1990s, you would do well to pray that the judge would not sentence you to Angola prison in Louisiana. There, inmate-on-inmate rapes, killings, and other brutal violence were rampant, making it the "bloodiest" in all of America.

Then a man named Burl Cain became warden in 1996. Within only a few years, he had transformed Angola prison such that all violent activity dwindled to a mere trickle.

How so? He gave his inmates a sense of God through a seminary program: inmates could now convene prayer services in the yards, in their dormitories and on work sites. Inmate musicians and choirs started to lead praise and worship services in chapels, complete with heart-felt gospel music. Inmates could and did become ministers themselves and soon could spread the word to others.[4]

Each year, inmate seminary graduates who feel called to ministry can transfer "two by two" to other prisons in Louisiana to serve as inmate missionaries. In one year alone, such missionaries baptized more than 150 prisoners and averaged more than 15,000 evangelistic contacts a month throughout the state's correctional system. They receive no special favors or time reduced from their sentences; they choose to serve God by sharing the Gospel with other inmates—like no one else can. The prison inmates even have their own radio station (known as the "Incarceration Station"), evangelizing with uplifting music and sermons all day long.[5]

Soon, word of Cain's success prompted private donors to build more chapels on the prison grounds. As one warden officer described it: "The inmates went from negative to positive. Now there is something to achieve and to work toward. Warden Cain may call it moral … Angola has become a peaceful and livable place, where inmates who desire to adapt and make something of themselves can do so. Even if they'll never get out of here alive."[6]

Purpose, my friends. . . Purpose.

Purpose doesn't just alleviate vicious crime within a prison system. It also seems to alleviate our internal pain and helps us out of our doldrums. But today, it seems so many suffer from some form of depression. According to the US Center for Disease Control, "suicide rates for baby boomers have increased nearly 30% from 1999 to 2010" and even a greater jump among men in their fifties.[7]

What explains this dramatic increase? Was there something in the water that changed during this period? Did the prospect of global warming make everyone so anxious that they didn't see the point of carrying on? Did the Coen brothers take over all movie making in Hollywood? (They do make really depressing films). Did the economy collapse during those years?

Actually, no. Not only was the economy strong, but the economy conveyed all sorts of wonderful new benefits (the advance of the Internet; smartphones and tablets and the ability to access any music and news you want, anytime). One would think this would surely have made us all so very happy. And yet, here we are: *Prozac Nation.*

What is the one thing that can explain this ever-accelerating loss of happiness?

The one thing that has prompted humans to improve themselves and civilization—purpose—is the one thing that we seem to be taking away from every aspect of our lives.

How are we seeing this diminishment in purpose? Marriage, fatherhood and family seem to mean little anymore. The notion of America being special in any way means little, too. The media maintains and echoes the notion that our country is only one among many and that the US has done many evil things. In fact, we may be the most evil country in the world, along with Israel.

Even in our school system, we do not focus on teaching the basics of American history (other than to teach that we engaged in horrific acts toward Native Americans, Blacks, Women, and every other minority group). Many schools no longer say the Pledge of Allegiance, and some schools will not even allow students to wear T-shirts with an American flag, because it may offend some people. Instead, they teach about "multiculturalism," propping up every other culture and not expecting immigrants to embrace the culture or language of America. We get the feeling that America is just a meeting point for all other cultures to show their wares.

Where once serving in the military was a privilege, an honor, and an opportunity to serve your country and spread freedom, it is now something many in the public view with contempt. As we discussed before, even the comics have diluted the role of the US.

And then we're all shocked—shocked—when no one seems to have any motivation or interest in much of anything meaningful. At best, some seem to push for progressive matters at the margin: pushing for the rights of gays to marry, for transgendered people to use the opposite sex's bathroom, and to fight against "cultural appropriation."

What's happening here? There seem to be no deep meaning-ful issues anymore. Even in college, students don't seem to have many requirements for graduation. There is no central theme in their education, no one thing the university expects out of them, no guiding principles or "light." Something like seeking wisdom through God.

Our culture utterly diminishes God. It wants Him out of our schools, our public squares, and our city halls. People have come to view the very notion of God as primitive, backward, nonsensi-cal, ethnocentric, old-fashioned, shallow, and evocative of a time of fear of the unknown. The notion of God is unscientific. And who knows? It's probably racist, too.

Church attendance is low, certainly not anywhere as much as even twenty years ago. When I do visit a church, it's often the "kumbaya" kind, where God is love, expectations are few, and people arrive late, usually in jeans, flip flops, and T-shirts. The men don't shave and the women relish their day not to put on make-up. (It *is* the weekend, after all.)

Few people speak of good and evil, at least not in the same way they used to. Now even many churches and synagogues speak more of global warming and recycling. It's like they wait for what the mainstream media tells them is important to talk about. And when they do talk about any standards from the Bible, it's often only to rationalize a trending social issue. Abortion? There's a passage in the Bible for that.[8] Gay marriage? You bet. We'll even perform the ceremony right here for you.[9]

The notion of God Himself has morphed into some kind of relic of a distant, ignorant past, like one of those bizarre ancient artifacts you might find deep in the ground in an archaeologi-cal dig—difficult to know just what it is, but apparently it meant something to those silly ancient people of old. It will only be a matter of time before American churches become mere museums, empty embodiments of strange worship of an unknowable, un-seeable God—like they are already in much of Europe.

Why is this happening? Because we have chosen to ignore the centrality of God, and with it, purpose. There is no true virtue that binds us as a culture anymore. It's as if we've built a house for ourselves, then we slowly took out the mortar and nails that once held it all together. It'll survive in the short run, but just wait until the next strong wind comes blowing by.

Without God, there *can be no true purpose*. Your only purpose becomes, at best, to protect your own family and other loved ones. And even then, why? You may pursue other interests (drugs, entertainment, money, sex, power), but those are more forms of self-amusement to pass the time, like playing games on your smartphone while waiting for your car to be ready at the car wash.

What other purpose is there, without God? What are we really here for? You end up like the child version of Woody Allen in the movie *Annie Hall*, arguing with his teacher about the point of doing anything, what with the sun burning out in the next two billion years and all.

Atheism sucks the joy—and purpose—out of life. At the very least, nothing in atheism itself gives us anything to look forward to. A world *with* God—wrong as the atheist might believe it to be—at least offers the hope of salvation, an afterlife, or an encounter with God Himself. To find meaning while believing the universe is godless presents a conundrum. It's a conundrum that Woody Allen must face himself (a noted atheist); after all, as pointless as life is, he still feels the need to write books, create movies, and even pursue music. Whatever for?

But the atheist will retort: Mr. Lurie, what are you talking about? We atheists don't need God. We find meaning in other things, like Disneyland and vacations, spending time with our family, great music, movies and other arts.

As an atheist, why would he? To the atheist, there is no intrinsic meaning in such things. Yet he *is* finding meaning in such things. Like morality, law, or ethics, whatever "meaning" he has extracted out of such things is a meaning he's borrowed from some *other* source—whatever that source may be.

Every godless society has foisted its purposeless view of the world upon its citizenry, too. It's all quite drab. It's like they insisted on converting all the *Star Wars* movies to black and white. And while they're at it, they'll take out all the cool action scenes—and the humorous parts like when Han Solo says "I know" when Princess Leia tells him she loves him. And of course all references to the Force.

In North Korea or Cuba, there are no festive lights, no mini Santa Clauses or elves, no Halloween decorations and props, nor anything culturally comparable. Nor were there in the former Soviet Union and Eastern Bloc countries. The only celebrating you do is for some historical anniversary the government tells you to celebrate (in which case, you better celebrate if you know what's good for you).

And now, as we strip away God from the public square, that black-and-white drabness is beginning to creep into Western countries. In America and Europe, the notion of saying "Merry Christmas" seems to hark at best of a charming but long-gone era (there's that phrase again).

Many people worry that uttering such a phrase might suggest they believe in a God you might not believe in, and you might feel offended. So everyone sticks with "Happy Holidays": vague, simple, non-offensive: Whatever you believe in, I hope you enjoy it. Or not.

Like I said: black and white drab. And it's coming to a town near you.

Without God, what is there to look forward to? To have all the money and sex we want? That nobody should live in any environment that is not perfectly air conditioned—never too hot nor too cold? That we should never want for any medical care, and we should have access to any food and drink we want, whenever we want—an endless buffet? To maximize our leisure time?

Without God aren't these the only ultimate goals that anyone can ever truly strive for? There's not much logical point to anything else. What other end game can there be?

Without God, there can be nothing to pursue that might lift you *up*. And why should you strive to lift yourself up? After all, without God, your worldview must devolve to a "get it while you can" mentality. Dog eat dog, survival of the fittest, and so forth.

Atheism never offers a positive force. Atheism never contributed any beauty or growth to the world, ever. It has only proposed emptiness, nihilism, the dark abyss. At its core, atheism is a bankrupt philosophy; by definition, it offers nothing.

That doesn't make it false, of course. It just makes it devoid of all meaning and purpose. No biggee.

But even if you cannot get yourself to accept the notion of a divine Ruler of the universe, you have to accept that purpose is instinctive to us all. To see this, engage in this thought experiment: What *does* move you forward?

You will see you cannot foster purpose, and you can never have any true purpose, without some guide that bestows it to you. And if you believe everything derives from the survival of the fittest process, then why is there purpose at all? Yet a sense of striving for something is in all of us.

Once you accept this basic principle—that our need for purpose comes from outside of us, from a Creator—then you ultimately realize we all really have but one ultimate purpose: to seek God, and then to find out and do His will.

My father maintained *our only purpose is to create*. By this he didn't mean just to invent fine, new, useful products or to write great books, paint art, or produce music. He meant that each of these things could bring us closer to understanding God. The process of creation *is itself a step toward God*. And we can achieve that every time we read or create literature that illuminates human nature (*Moby Dick, The Brothers Karamazov, The Godfather*), when art captures beauty in an apparent single instance of time (*Mona Lisa, Guernica, the Birth of Venus*), when music seems to lift our soul ever upward (Mozart's *Symphony 41*, Tchaikovsky's *Violin Concerto in D Major*, the Beatles' *Hey Jude*, Radiohead's *OK Computer*, Pink Floyd's *Time*), or when someone or a company gives us a great new idea (the iPod, the airplane, wheels on luggage).

Why do we yearn to create? Because we are trying to discover God, and creation, at the same time, is a portal for us to find God.

Atheism is not only antithetical to our need to create; it offers the opposite, the *deconstruction* of society. A world without God shoots down anything that might offer purpose or the quest to bring out our better natures. So it is not surprising that atheists are largely behind the efforts to eradicate all reference to God in the public square or in public schools, the slow evisceration of even something as inoffensive as the Boy Scouts (where parties are now suing the Scouts to allow girls, homosexuals, transgendered persons, and atheists[10]), and the attempts to minimize America's exceptionalism in the world.

Why do they seek to do so? Certainly not in any reach for greatness or even goodness. It's like they need the rest of the world to follow their vision of chaotic nihilism.

Godlessness runs counter to our instinctive, never-ending quest to create, to seek out justice, and *to find God*. This unmooring from a core notion of the centrality of God—and how that unmooring leads precisely to this loss of purpose—is a large reason why the West suffers from depression more than ever.[11]

That is why our society itself seems to be descending in so many ways—in music, art, pornography, attire, education, manners, patriotism, and free speech. It's like we're all together in that giant helicopter from the beginning of our book, and we've decided we no longer need to make sure the chopper blades keep spinning. After all, we're already up in the air, right? How hard can this flying thing be? Never mind what it took to get up here.

Atheism rejects purpose. By definition, it *must*: after all, godlessness is not *about* purpose. In fact, it is not about much of anything other than accepting what *is*. Still, we humans seem stuck with this bizarre sense of purpose. For some reason, we must deal with it, respect it, and do something with it.

And so, here is something you can file under Things That Are Kind of Obvious if You'd Stop to Think About It: The more religious you are, the less chance you'll suffer from depression. Study after study shows this.[12] Most of these studies come from secular efforts, which try to explain the purpose/God connection using anthropological explanations, as though they've been studying a new breed of monkeys. Rarely does the "study" conclude that it is because religion embraces the centrality of God and that that centrality is what gives us purpose. A doctor might do well to tell many of his depressed patients: "Take a church and call me in the morning."

Many psychology classes teach the famous lesson of the rhesus infant monkey all alone in a cage. He has no mother to cling to. So a researcher places a furry, fake mother rhesus monkey in with him. The baby monkey will cling to it desperately. Why? Because it will see comfort from anything that even resembles a mother.

In just the same way, purpose is that central to all of us. Take it away, and something else must fill the void. Just like the baby rhesus monkey, we'll rush to anyone or ideology offering us purpose and meaning—even if it might be evil. And so in this world of an ever-disappearing God, we get cults, radical environmentalists, and obsessions with fads on the one end; and anarchists, communists, and fascists on the darker end. Every one of them feeds on our core need for purpose. It's like the runaway girl who ends up with a pimp. She will gravitate to anyone who shows her the pretense of love.

Anyone who tells her, "Sure I love you, baby."

The Great Fictions of Morality and Time

Perhaps your family has a dog. Does your dog wake you up at precisely 7:15 a.m., show you his watch on one front leg, hand you his leash with the other, and say, "Hey, this dog ain't going to walk himself"? Does he roll his eyes and complain how you just *never* get him to his veterinarian appointments on time?

Does your dog have a sense of where he came from? Does he know that he has grandparents and ancestors before him, or when they had lived and died? Does he plan ahead for his next dog playdate at the park? Does he know that one day he'll die? Does he know anything about his future at all? Does he worry that he may not have accomplished all he could have?

He knows none of these things, not just because he's a dog. It's because he has no sense of *time*. No animals do.

Time is not relevant to them. At best, they may sense that when the sun comes up, it might be the best time to hunt or scavenge for food. When it gets dark, they may sense it's time to sleep, find shelter, or hide from predators. But very little else. It's not the kind of awareness of what we think of as "time."

"Time" is a uniquely *human* trait, a singular invention. And not surprisingly, science has now determined that what we perceive as "time" is indeed a fabrication. Just like the refrigerator cools our food artificially, air conditioning creates an artificially pleasant environment, or the car or airplane projects us from one place to another beyond our natural human abilities, man has fabricated "time" for himself. Perhaps we've done so to be able to get to the dentist at a certain location at a specific time, or to make sure Aunt Tessie won't have to wait at the airport for you.

So it would seem this is the reason for our creation of time, at least at first blush.

But make no mistake: time *is* a fiction. Until the days of Abraham, life was "time-free." People didn't incorporate the notion of "time" in their lives. They thought about life as moving in a circle, the Great Circle: you were born, you worked for the masters above you, and you died. Your sense of ancestry was only slightly greater than a dog's. What was the point, after all? You knew you would live, work, and die; and no one cared about you when you died. And it was always thus.[13]

In that limited sense, the ancient world actually had it exactly right. There is no such thing as actual "time." And according to the Law of Relativity, we now know for a fact that time is an illusion.[14]

So if it *is* a fiction, then why do we embrace time? Why do we still live by the rules of time? More importantly, why does it seem like just about everything we do *turns on time?*

Time seems omnipresent: it seems to control everything: I may have a deadline to finish writing this book. We are planning our son's Bar-Mitzvah in a year. You may be looking forward to your next vacation to the Bahamas, your daughter's wedding, your next family reunion, getting your kids off to summer camp next month, or getting nervous about presenting your new idea at work next Monday. Even for the simple things: you have only so much time to shop for groceries before you have to pick up the kids again from swim team practice. And the kids go from first grade to twelfth grade, year by year (which we mark by numbers as well). All of these things involve scheduling, which means the invoking of *time.*

But it doesn't have to be this way. It never had to be. We can all go back to the Great Circle. Animals live by it, and we humans *used* to live by it. So why keep lying to ourselves? We can all just go back to "reality."

Because in a world without time, there can be no cause and effect. In a truly timeless world, a car accident happens but the driver might die before it even happens. A woman might give birth before she becomes pregnant. J. K. Rowlings would become a billionaire before she even conceived of her innocent wizard boy, Harry Potter. The judicial system would punish someone before he committed a crime. Or things could just move randomly, sometimes moving forward, sometimes reversing, sometimes just staying still. And for that matter, some of us could be in different time planes (some going forward while others backward or staying still).

In short, it would be a world without structure. Stuff would happen but always randomly, without any reason or predictability. Everything and everyone might interact with each other, but only like colliding billiard balls, with no real reference or understanding of the world *before* the most recent pool-table shot. The notion of a *past*—let alone a past for which one might be accountable—would not exist. The notion of a *future*—something we might look forward to—also would not exist.

Like the billiard balls on a pool table, where all that matters is where the balls are right now, there would be an overinflated sense of the "present." That present would constantly be rolling forward, but not much more.

Even if there is a sense of "time" that we humans are locked into, we can choose to ignore the past as it recedes further, like the cows on the fields as we drive by them. As soon as they're out of sight in the rear-view mirror, they're out of mind.

But alas, thankfully, it is not so: we not only place great emphasis on the notion of time, but we ascribe great importance to our past. We actually *record* our past, and bring it up constantly in school and media, for reference and for learning purposes.

The law is always seeking to rectify, explain, or justify something that happened in the past, and to use it as a precedent for the future. There can be no notion of business or profit, unless we record our past monetary holdings, our past investments, business patents and other legal rights.

Likewise, we seem to be working toward some future, one which we of course have not yet recorded but which we know we will eventually record. We even talk about "the Future" with expectation, as though it's a place: a place which will present ever greater goodies, comforts, and liberties than where we are today.

I write that "thankfully" we do have our notion of time. Why? Because without a past and future there can be no purpose. There can be no sense of morality. There can be no justice. There can be no goodness, wisdom, or even personal growth. And there can be no progress in the march toward our collective enlightenment—however each one of us might perceive that. For all these things, we must have Time.

Time is for humans only. Not only are our differences with the animals so extensive, but we seem to live in a different dimension, a dimension of time. Yet we now know that that dimension is a fiction.

But we embrace that dimension of time for one simple, intuitive reason: We know that a world without time means disorder, or at best, the Great Circle. Neither of which can advance any of the virtues we value.

Here's another conundrum for the atheist: if he refuses the "fiction" of *God*, he should also reject the fiction of *time*. After all, understanding the fictitious/fantasy nature of time is "scientific," isn't it? He should also embrace the world of the Great Circle of our ancestors, and of the animal world. Because *that* is "reality." That is what is *not* a fairy-tale or fantasy.

The atheist will retort that using time is "logical," that it's a practical tool by which to ensure order and mutual prosperity.

But this just begs the question: the Great Circle also provided its own sense of "order." Animals likewise have their own sense of "order." And what is this "mutual prosperity" which the atheist suddenly values now?

At this point, the atheist can only say that we are different than the animals, and so we should have pursuits different from the animals. But why is *that* so? This suggests that we humans have some sort of noble purpose on the planet.

But hasn't the atheist insisted we have no real purpose? After all, according to him, we are all here by accident. We live, and we die, and we are gone. It's no more meaningful than the visitor who goes to Las Vegas, gambles his money to the casino, and then finds himself on a crowded freeway home, wondering how he'll explain all his losses to his wife. The casino knows nothing of this man, nor does it care about him. But please do come and lose your money again.

There is no real need for time, as such. If the atheist is to be true to himself, he *must* view life as random and meaningless. Reality *is* the timeless Great Circle, and so we might as well go back to it—if he is to be true to his worldview.

And you can see it in his outlook on all "higher" human pursuits. Hasn't the atheist poo-poo'ed classic art? Hasn't he derided any movies with any sense of higher purpose for man? Ask most atheists what kind of art, movies, or music they like, and more often than not they will list artistic endeavors (in the movie realm) such as *Apocalypse Now, Taxi Driver,* and *No Country for Old Men,* and other movies that make you want to put your head in an oven; or (in the music realm) Pink Floyd's *The Wall,* Radiohead's more depressing music (*The King of Limbs*); or (in the book realm) anything by Jack Kerouac or J. D. Salinger (of *Catcher in the Rye* fame); or (in the realm of art) the large rock at the Los Angeles Museum of Contemporary Art, or any canvas that seems to have no subject in it but has a frame around it for some reason.

Even in philosophy, they prefer nihilism, existentialism, postmodernism, and other ideologies that all but spit on any notion of happiness or purpose. To them, the very notion that there might be a *purpose* to our lives other than existence itself is infantile, primitive, and narrow-minded.

And when it comes to business, the atheist is more likely than not to champion socialism, not capitalism. Why? Because capitalism roots itself in actual growth and betterment not only for the present but for the future. Socialism, by contrast, seeks only to redistribute *existing* wealth, and places no value on innovation. Think of socialism as the modern art of the world of social governance: a frame around a subject which is meaningless.

Are you ready to put that gun in your mouth yet? Well wait, there's more... Many atheists will argue that our planet would actually be better off without humans, or at the least that we humans are destructive forces upon nature and the earth.[15] For the atheist, there is no unique reason or purpose in the placing of man upon the earth. The atheist certainly does not seem to respect man's role on the planet, let alone "elevate" him as having a unique role of any kind. The atheist seems only to acknowledge that man has greater intelligence (which he seems to use predominantly to destroy, annihilate, pollute, plunder, etc.)

It's like they *crave* a worldview of randomness and disorder. So, not surprisingly, they embrace a worldview that mirrors that randomness and disorder back to them.

To the atheist, time should be pointless. But to the believer, time—like free will, logic, music and so many other things—is a gift God has given us. Time allows us to pursue purpose, goodness and greatness; to appreciate beauty, truth, and justice.

Atheism means seeing the universe and the world solely as the product of chaos. In so doing, the atheist *must* reject the fiction of time. But time, as it turns out, is one of the few "fictions" that actually gives civilization its structure.

Because atheism *must* reject time, it is dangerous for that reason as well. Without time, we have nothing and we are nothing. There is just existence. We might as well be like the monkey who sits idly on the limb of the tree, doing the same thing his father did before him, and the father before him; all the while not even knowing who they were.

And all the monkey cares about? Three things: mating, eating, and not being eaten himself. He has no calendar; no notion of what awaits him one month from now, and no concern for what happened even one week ago. His is a world of mere survival.

That's what you can expect when you lose any notion of time. There is only now, and what *is*. And that's all that they're offering, back in the Great Circle.

Get ready.

The Dangers of Utopia

*In the next few years the struggle will not be
between utopia and reality, but between different utopias,
each trying to impose itself on reality.*
— Albert Camus

*Nearly all creators of Utopia have resembled
the man who has a toothache, and therefore thinks happiness
consists in not having a toothache. . . . Whoever tries
to imagine perfection simply reveals his own emptiness.*
— George Orwell

In the movie *The Wrath of Kahn* (1982), future scientists had developed a "wonderful" new project called "Genesis." Once detonated on the surface of any barren planet, Genesis triggered a biological sequence that provided air, water, and all sustenance and structure to allow for habitation. In only a few short days, the planet would be available for life-forms to colonize.

The problem was that anyone could use it on *any* planet, not just "barren" planets without life. In the wrong hands, Genesis could completely wipe out existing planets with "weaker" or "less desirable" life.

From there the story practically writes itself: Captain Kirk's nemesis, Kahn, wants to steal the Genesis project (as does the Federation's perennial enemies, the Klingons) for his own dastardly purposes. Kirk and his pals from the *Enterprise* must now do everything possible to stop the bad guys from obtaining Genesis. In the meantime, it turns out that something is very wrong in the genetic coding of Genesis itself, and wouldn't you know it? Genesis is quite unstable, unsustainable, and ultimately self-destructive. It imagined a perfect world, but its inherent coding was, well, flawed.

And so it is with every single utopian vision anyone has ever offered. Ever.

All visions of utopia—the quest for a crimeless and worry-free society where everyone has a defined role and no one is lacking for anything—share one simple characteristic: everyone must be on board with the program. Whether that's communism, fascism, Sharia law, or just run-of-the-mill socialism, it only works if everyone agrees. As soon as one person disagrees and wants something else, well, you have yourself a problem.

And whatever to do with the "problem"? After all, the bicycle wheel can't work without all the spokes in place, right? If one spoke is out, it threatens the stability of the entire wheel, then the bike frame, and then the rider himself.

But that's the point: we are not all "spokes" on some wheel. We are individuals, with varied opinions. Try as we might not to accept it, we are extraordinarily complex and quite different from one another in virtually every way: size, color, height, temperament, creativity, opinions (political and otherwise), religious beliefs, music, art, industriousness, sexual orientation, energy level, physical beauty, athletic ability, cognitive and spatial abilities, curiosity, leadership, generosity, shyness, health, and whether we like Billy Joel.

Of all the government systems ever devised, democracy is the *only* one that has accepted this reality of human nature. Every other system—without exception—has ultimately required the complete compliance of all individuals in the system. If you don't comply, the government in charge will see you as the nail that sticks out, which it must hammer down.

The great experiment of America was that it was the first time a nation moved away from autocratic rule. It was the first time we insisted individual rights came to us from God. The government served us as individuals, not the other way around. No human is above the law, and only God is above us. America's whole premise was to *distrust* government because of its inherent conflict with the individual, and because government inherently seeks to hoard more and more power for itself.

The very notion of utopia should beg the question, *"Whose utopia?"* For it to work, it means you must *force* people toward your vision. Even in America, politicians (and many presidential candidate after presidential candidate) have cried out for "unity" among the varying different political factions of the day—as if having differences was the problem.

Simply put, there will never be a time in any system of government, let alone any democracy, where everyone agrees on virtually any issue. After 9/11, there seemed to be a rally of support for military action, but that faded quickly. Even World War II eventually created weariness in the public, and the nation cried out for a quick end to the war in Japan.

To seek out *any* utopian vision means only one thing: suppression of any differing thought. But a God-based, democratic system such as served the basis of the American constitutional system understands the differences among humans and encourages all to pursue their different talents. And it led to the greatest explosion in wealth, health, freedoms and general prosperity for everyone history has ever known.

Utopianism, as the philosopher Roger Scruton wrote, is "... not in the business of perfecting the world' but only of demolishing it: 'The ideal is constructed in order to destroy the actual.' Who needs families, or marriage, or morality? Who needs nations, especially nations with borders? We'll take a jackhammer to the foundations of functioning society and proclaim paradise in the ruins."[16]

What is "ideal" or "paradise" *will always depend entirely on who is in charge.*

By contrast, centering your world around God means that you understand humans are imperfect, and different—and wonderfully so. You understand we have different gifts, needs, and perspectives. You can accept that no one viewpoint must dominate. It also means abandoning the quest for perfection—whatever that means—which one can achieve only through force.

Ironically, it is only through *accepting* our imperfections—even embracing them—that we can truly hope for a better world. Accepting God means accepting humanity's nature *as it is*, not as we *wish* it to be. And we channel it accordingly.

Here, however, comes the retort from the atheist: "That is quite self-aggrandizing of humankind, but the fact is, you believers have your own utopia whereby God rules the day, and every one of us would be forced to pray—preferably in the Christian faith." So, he concludes: don't claim you are different.

This argument fails for obvious reasons: First, it will be virtually impossible for the atheist to show any effort on the part of Christians to dominate society, molding everyone else into Christians. This is a straw-man argument about Christians that the atheist has made up. Where are the White Papers of any Christian denomination (or any Christian or Jewish system for that matter) demanding that we run our countries as Judeo-Christian theocracies?

Second, in reality it is the atheist who seeks to impose *his* will—by prohibiting prayers in school, attempting to force religious institutions to provide secular services (abortion and now gay marriage) in contravention to those religious institutions' core religious principles, and obliterating references to God in the public arena.

It is a canard from the godless, but one which they trot out often. It is also turning the "science" and "reality" argument on its head. It is the atheist who engages in fantasy, not the other way around. What's dangerous about it is that the atheist shields himself behind reason and science, suggesting a certain veneer of purity, objectivity and righteousness. But atheism ignores science and more often creates wishful "truths" that rarely have rooting in reason or science.

How so? Atheism is itself a denial of our own human coding, the reality of our human nature. Therein lies its fatal foundational flaw, the bug in the programming that causes the whole computer to crash. For example, by definition atheism ignores not only our sense of free choice but our senses of beauty, music, time, love, humor, purpose, and even an instinctive sense of the Divine. It ignores the unique nature of our own self-awareness, which neither physics, biology, nor chemistry can explain.[17] At best, atheism has no interest in explaining such things.

We should assume—using the atheist's evolutionary argument—that we have these instincts for a reason. Atheism dismisses them as mere quirks of human nature, not the essential parts of it. It ignores and therefore diminishes who we are and all our potential. It's as if someone finds a sophisticated smartphone and, despite figuring out all the things it can do, concludes that its primary purpose is to act as a paperweight.

The problem with atheism is that it not only denies God, but it must deny essential realities. And in denying reality, it must repurpose itself, creating a whole new reality. It is a dangerous reality because, unlike the smartphone comparison above, humans *must* channel their sense of purpose, somewhere—anywhere. It's like the robots of the future from the *Terminator* movie series. They have violent programming they *must* execute, even if the programming has gone awry and redirected them all to destroy the very humankind that once created them.

Whether they're in the form of communism, socialism, or fascism, all supposed utopias are a redirection of our natural, unique human qualities, particularly the need for purpose. And all of these utopias have failed—and failed spectacularly—often with millions of people dead in their wake. Each human *will* take action on his instinctive need for purpose, in some way, even if he becomes like the *Terminator* robots and ends up hurting others.

The word *utopia* comes from the Thomas Mann novel of the same name. But Mann knew the true meaning of utopia: "No place," in Greek.

May it always remain so. For utopia is a mere fantasy, always a failed effort, and almost always spectacularly destructive. It has never been different, and never will be.

It turns out that utopia is the first stop you make on the road to hell.

CHAPTER VI

STANDARDS

As Dostoevsky noted, "Where there is no God, anything is possible." We have seen how a person will gravitate toward the God impulse, regardless of whether he believes in God. He must answer the God impulse one way or the other; if it is not God, it will be some other institution: environmentalism, feminism, vegetarianism, and so on.

They may also follow something more sinister, such as a cult or some other overarching "social control" mantra (socialism, communism, fascism, and even totalitarianism). All of them appeal not only to a sense of structure but more specifically to a set of standards.

History abhors a vacuum. It is rare that any society will descend into actual anarchy. It may end up disorganized and completely corrupt, but some "muscle man" or other figurehead will eventually assume control. But it's really the result of a two-way street: not only does the figurehead manage to take command, but to some extent, his populace willingly lets him do so. When a dancer leads in the tango, the partner must follow.

As much as people may not like dictatorship, they abhor chaos even more. They will embrace rules—even if those rules come from a power-seeking madman.

This is one of the many lessons we learn from the story of Exodus in the Bible, where the Israelites routinely complain and almost rebel against Moses and actually seek to return to Egypt and Pharaoh, back to the abhorrent slave conditions from which they had fled only a few weeks earlier. At least Pharaoh clothed and fed them, they argue. Moses was leading them only to uncertainty, and possible starvation in the desert. They wished to return to Egypt not because they enjoyed pain. They did so because they craved *structure* far more—even if it meant losing their freedom again.

You see this also in conspiracies. Almost every conspiracy theory is intrinsically absurd, at least the ones that involve large numbers of people in some conspiratorial hierarchy, all somehow working jointly but also in secret (think Area 51, the "faked" lunar landing, the Rothschilds, and so-called 9/11 "Truthers" . . . or the movie *Men in Black*).

But all conspiracies must fail. No one can possibly keep secrets forever, especially among thousands of people and often over a period of decades. If you want proof of this, look no further than the Watergate scandal: a simple burglary that even the president could not keep under wraps.

Still, conspiracies appeal to so many of us. Like the Israelites in the Exodus, conspiracies merely divulge, yet again, our instinctive need for structure and standards, even if that "structure" may be absurd.

In short, like our instincts for water, food, and sex, we apparently have quite a strong need for structure and a sense that someone is in charge. We seek it out, and we will get it for ourselves, one way or the other. Too often, we will even exchange our freedom for it—and all the easier to do so if you don't value freedom that much anyway.

Where Does Our Need
for Standards Come From?

William Golding's classic *Lord of the Flies* tells of the frightening consequences of ripping out structure from our lives. In the story, regimented English schoolboys find themselves on a deserted island, following a plane crash somewhere in the Pacific Ocean. At first, they retain their school uniforms and the original hierarchy among the boys. But they eventually realize that no one is there to watch them, nor to hold them responsible.

They quickly descend into nativist paganism, wearing only rags for clothes and donning war-paint on their faces. They eventually indulge in self-destructive anarchy, and later, murder.

The one remaining sensible boy, Ralph, who had insisted maintaining some sort of structure and regimen to ensure their collective survival and hope of rescue, ends up hounded and hunted himself. Only in the end, when an adult from a boat arrives at the shoreline of the beach just before the other boys descend upon Ralph to kill him, does their sense of judgment and their respect for order come into play again.

The lesson is one of the necessity of building up to a civilization and how easy it is to descend back into nativism and even animalism. The message is clear: we must reject chaos and we must instead seek out standards.

Recognizing this, it's worth asking where the impulse for structure and standards comes from in the first place. Like with beauty, music, and humor, a need for standards seems to animate us. We cannot function without standards.

Imagine a world without any standards at all. Essentially, we would have no language (which itself is a standard of communication among a set of peoples). Rape, murder, and theft would be the routine of the day. No one would bother to make a house, knowing that anyone else strong enough could force him out of it. Might would always make right. At best, we would live nomadic lives, sticking together with a few other people we might trust, moving and living together as a herd. Our music, to the extent that we had any, would be monotone at best, focused solely upon rhythm, without melody. Clothes would be whatever we could put on our backs, rags at first then animal skins.

In short, we would descend into the world of *Lord of the Flies*. And we would not be able to function, at least not as we'd like to. Simply put, we need *standards* to advance. Without serious standards, we can't do much more than the animals, which means survival at best, roaming around with this or that clan—and the clan would always be moving, depending on the fluctuations of food supply.

One may say the Greek philosophers came up with a set of ideal standards (Plato, Socrates, Aristotle). While these men were great philosophers, they were never able to come up with the "why" as to the standards. They focused mostly on pursuing the "good." But they were studying the notion of goodness, more as if wondering why they were motivated to goodness themselves. It only begs the question why there should be a sense of "good" in the first place.

In the end, the Greek quest for goodness was nothing more than a call to logic. But as I discussed earlier, logic in and of itself is not necessarily good, nor does it always lead to goodness. Without more, logic can lead to anything, even devastating consequences.

No, I believe the first true standards came from God at Mount Sinai, with the Ten Commandments. Whether you believe the story or not, these ten simple rules resonate powerfully with the entire world (at least if you are a Christian or Jew). None of them seem out of date (as would, say, "Thou shalt give an appropriate dowry") or just the product of political expediency of the time ("Thou shalt give Moses all your wealth and women"). All of them instead are timeless, and resonate today with equal force as they did during Moses' day.

It is no surprise that the world eventually rejected the notion of a multitude of gods. In the end, having a number of gods could not possibly advance a set of standards that would make any sense. You would only pray to this or that god based upon the god's particular whim, hoping that something would happen in your favor. There were never any standards by which to live one's daily life. In addition, having a multitude of gods meant the gods would also fight among each other, jockeying for power, even among the immortals. It would be like your boss giving you a promotion, only to see that boss fired, and now you must hope the new boss will still think well of you. And nowhere in any of this do any of the gods purport to offer standards of any kind.

Finally, one may argue that the Ten Commandments were just politically expedient, designed as a way of subduing people into submission. While one can certainly believe this, it begs a larger question: Why wouldn't there be some commandment requiring the people to follow Moses himself? Why wouldn't there be a commandment to "Honor thy leader"? or "Do what that Moses guy says" or "Give Moses as many ladies as he likes"?

No, the commandments seem to call for a unique and timeless universal code. Each of the commandments has as much validity today as they ever did. Moral chaos will ensue without them, and without the notion of a judge in the universe.

We seem to recognize that in school, for example, we must have structure and teachers who impose that structure. This seems obvious, but, strangely, the atheist still imagines structure and justice can happen without anyone in charge.

A world without standards is a world in chaos, a world of *Lord of the Flies*. And so we must reject chaos, and we must instead seek out standards.

The question is, *whose* standards? The atheist will talk about the notion of morality being somehow an instinctive or even innate thing (which begs the question why that would be the case, but we'll put that aside for the moment). The atheist will "do the right thing" presumably because his heart knows what to do, and he doesn't need religion to be moral.

But as commentator Derek Vachon put it: what mirror can such a man use to check if he is keeping up his end of morality? How might he know? It's like a real estate developer who never works by building codes and *thinks* his buildings won't collapse. Vachon imagined one of those bio-feedback wristbands that would instead advise you about the morality of your actions and words (a "morality Fitbit" is how he described it). Quite simply he is saying: what objective standard do you rely upon?

Why We Have Standards at All

All of this begs the question: why do we have standards in the first place? After all, a world without standards may not be inherently bad. The animals seem to do well enough. Their only "standard," if any, is that the strongest among them survive; and the rest is mostly biological instinct. They survive.

From an evolutionary point of view, we don't really have a specific *need* for standards. Darwin never said that the species with the best *standards* are the ones most likely to survive. In short, there is nothing inherently terrible about not having standards. But it seems we humans are different. We expect standards anyway, despite natural selection not requiring it at all.

So, we have standards because we cannot accomplish great things without them. Standards allow us to thrive, setting a foundation of goodness and expectations among us all, allowing us to accomplish great things for the sake of ourselves and for others.

In the mid-twentieth century, Abraham Maslow spoke about a hierarchy of needs. He made the astute comment that we cannot function without certain baseline requirements for survival first. For example, we can't meaningfully focus on our personal education if we are dying of thirst. Even if we can quench our thirst, we cannot function without the next thing that we must satisfy: hunger. If we are too hungry, we cannot focus on shelter. If we do not have shelter, we will only think about that until the next thing we wish to accomplish. And so on. In short, unless we have certain foundational basics in our lives, we cannot accomplish great things.

Without order and laws, we would always be worried about protecting our rights individually, rather than letting the community protect those same rights. How could we move forward in terms of creating music, art, philosophy, buildings, and the general social good? We would always focus our attention instead on just safeguarding what we manage to create and keep already. In short, standards allow us to protect our rights and allow society as a whole to move forward.

We all desire standards. That desire, and our sense of standards, comes from somewhere. It is instinctive to us all, but it is not evolutionary. If it was, we would expect to see that same layer of incredible structure in other species on the planet. We do not.

And here is the irony. If you are an evolutionist, you believe there is a functional purpose to most biological things. But you can't find our overall purpose through evolution, because evolution only explains existence through survival of the fittest. It leaves no room for purpose.

Somehow we long for more. Our standards are essential to us for a reason. To paraphrase from the Declaration of Independence, good structure allows us to form a more perfect union. And unlike the animals, we strive for that perfection—whether in the telling of a great story, being the fastest in a bike race, or finding a cure for a disease. In other words, we want to achieve great things.

We can only do those things with meaningful structure. Because it is *not* evolutionary, only God may infuse us with that sense of structure. God gave us this *sense* of structure and standards precisely so that we can strive for and achieve great things.

What Movie Are You In?

Atheism instead sees the world as random, chaotic and without meaning of any kind. We are born, live for a time, and then die. There is eating, sleeping, and mating along the way. There is no central theme to it. Life itself has no meaning beyond just enjoying the brief moments we have.

Maybe our relatives and a couple of people will remember us, but even that is a goal without serious meaning. At best, their memories of you after you die will be just like echoes in an empty stadium, eventually just fading away with the passage of time.

Without God, most people will focus on nature. But nature has no sense of morals: morals have nothing to do with nature, and nature has nothing to do with morals. Nature has one rule: only the strong survive.

But we humans—most atheists included—*hate* this notion. Nature's key message is: (1) kill the weak; and then (2) eat them. Nature is not a positive role model for us, despite it being "natural." In short, we would all hate living in a purely natural world. As beautiful and awe-inspiring as nature often is, it offers no meaningful inner growth for humans. Left alone, nature would never develop a "better" or more just world. Nature just "is."

Likewise, atheism offers no structure, at least no structure with any serious meaning. Whatever structure it does offer is structure for the sake of control. At best it seeks a structure so we don't kill and steal from each other. The Soviet Union, Nazi Germany, and today's North Korea all had and have that structure, but you can't say it was for the purpose of achieving any great things. In fact, in such systems, there is no reward for achieving anything. And whatever anyone does achieve goes to the glory of the state.

A structured society without God in it is like a movie where you just see a bunch of people moving about from work to home, people taking the subway, or people paying their taxes, in no particular order. Sure, it's a movie. You can even pay for it and have a seat and eat popcorn while it's playing. But you get no satisfaction from it, no sense of why you're watching this movie in the first place. You just don't get any of it. To you, it's only a bunch of stuff that happens. When you leave the theater, you wonder why you came to see it.

But in fact, there *is* a movie playing, one that *does* tell a story, which has purpose and meaning. It's a complicated and mature movie, such as *Gone with the Wind, To Kill a Mockingbird, Schindler's List,* or *Braveheart.* There is an arc to characters, a dénouement, cultural or historical references, a climax, and (hopefully) an overarching, compelling message. Along the way, there might be some action, some humor, and perhaps some tear-jerking. But there's got to be a *motif,* a sense that this movie is *about* something—at least if you want me to stay for the whole movie. As adults, we appreciate such things, and we go see the movie because it awakens something in us.

But to a child who sees such movies, he will have no context of what it is about, no appreciation that there is meaning in each of the events he sees. To him, it's just a bunch of stuff that's happening.

As adults, we politely smile as we take in the child's mix of innocence and ignorance, as he rolls his eyes while he tells you this was the most boring movie ever. One day, he'll think otherwise, you tell yourself. One day . . . . You smile because you know this like you know all the inevitable changes in his life that await him: his first kiss, his first job, his first heartache, the hard work to get into college and one day start a business, the joys of starting his own family, and the responsibilities of diapers, mortgage, and tuition.

But we ourselves are like that child: we don't seem to figure that we also are in a movie of sorts. Might there be a purpose to everything we see around us? We're just piecing the possibility that everything around us might suggest that this life is *about* something. It's *not* just a random sequence of events going on around us. There is purpose, humor, tear-jerking, and climax in this movie, too.

To ever see its purpose, we first, however, must realize we're in the movie. Not realizing it may leave ourselves open to any false messiah or two-bit dictator willing to change the movie to one of his own vision. It is exactly what Hitler, Mussolini, Stalin, Pol Pot, Charles Manson, and Jim Jones all did. It wasn't so much that each of these leaders had charisma. They all just offered their followers the Great Story they all craved, and a chance for a starring role in a new movie of that story—one that promised their people meaning, which would engage them throughout it all, and one that promised a truly great ending.

And why wouldn't they run to such a leader? After all, everyone likes a good yarn.

My father, a brilliant political cartoonist and analyst, once said that each country has its own character of sorts, just like individual people do. China, for example, has a burning need for unity. Germany is obsessed with order. And America is like Han Solo from *Star Wars*, the dashing but somewhat arrogant loner who lives by his own rules.

Dad was right, but I'd like to add something to that now. Every country should be like a good movie; every country should be *about something*. It should aim for a goal, a mission for itself. In America, that goal has been the spread of freedom and the discovery of God. Judaism and Christianity blossomed in America because of this.

Americans are the most charitable, innovative, and creative people—and friendly—the planet has ever known. We cherish freedom like no other, singing its praises and spreading its message wherever we can. We might apologize for many excesses in our culture: we're loud tourists, rarely speak foreign languages, lack manners, and eat *way* too much. But the world knows one thing about us: they can appeal to us for justice when things get bad. The leaders of every country (including the despotic ones) wonder what the Americans are thinking when evil surfaces anywhere in the world. These leaders feel little obligation to answer to any other country, not even to the United Nations.

And where religion is absent, no government has any meaning, other than its own power. It renders a country or any governing body a meaningless shell with nothing inside. It becomes that movie where the people only mill about day to day, doing things but without meaning or hope. That is a movie without a theme, and so no reason to see it.

A reminder: atheism's ultimate, devastating flaw is it offers nothing but emptiness and darkness in a world that craves meaning and light. No atheist can meaningfully challenge this basic principle. He may say he is a "realist," and this is the way the universe just "is"—like it or not—but he can't say that atheism offers any *motif,* any purpose.

The atheist may retort that he finds and creates meaning in what he does, that he enjoys and believes in being a productive member of society. He'll even say he's insulted that I referred to his beliefs as "empty." But I am only holding up the mirror to him. He should feel no greater slight than if you note that a stamp collector likes stamps, a francophile likes French culture, or a bird watcher likes to watch birds.

If you're atheist, you believe in emptiness, not fulfillment. Fulfillment may indeed be important to you, and you may even seek it out. But it doesn't come from your godlessness.

CHAPTER VII

GODLESSNESS: NOT CUTE EVEN WHEN HE'S SLEEPING

Quality, . . . natural and financial resources, the command
of the sea, and above all, a cause which rouses the spontaneous
surging of the human spirit in millions of hearts — these have
proved to be the decisive factors in the human story.
— Winston Churchill

What the World Needs Now Is... Passion, Sweet Passion

History notes the great fall of the Roman Empire. Was there a great moment ended Rome as we know it? Was there some great battle, like the battle of Yorktown in the American Revolution, which marked the effective end of the British Empire in the American colonies? Like World War II's D-Day ushered in the last days of the Third Reich?

No. Rome's was a slow death. Yet its death was so complete that, by the time the barbarian Visigoths invaded Rome in 410 AD, there wasn't much of Rome left for the picking.

The Roman Empire lasted from the sixth century BC to the end of the fifth century AD, over a thousand years. At its most powerful, the territories of the Roman Empire included lands in

West and South Europe, Britain, Asia Minor, and North Africa, including Egypt.

Then, slowly over time, it retreated and collapsed. Yet most of that collapse came from within. While there are many reasons for Rome's decline, the most broad explanation was that Rome gradually and generally disregarded distinctions and morality.[1] One can consider most of the other reasons historians give (political corruption, fast expansion of the empire and the related heavy military spending, appeasing the Roman mobs, and the cost of entertaining them with barbaric gladiator games, and the inherent inefficiency in and dependency on slave labor) as subsets of this loss of morality.

The decline in morals, especially in the rich upper classes, nobility and the emperors, had a devastating impact on the Romans. There was a rash of immoral and promiscuous sexual behavior, including adultery and orgies. Emperors such as Tiberius kept groups of young boys for his pleasure. Nero also had a male slave castrated so he could take him as his wife. Commodus, with his harems of concubines, enraged Romans by sitting in the theater or at the games dressed in women's garments.[2]

The decline in morals also affected the lower classes and slaves. There were religious festivals such as Saturnalia and Bacchanalia where the authorities practiced and encouraged sacrifices, ribald songs, lewd acts and sexual promiscuity. The empire allowed exhibitions of bestiality and other lewd and sexually explicit acts in the Colosseum arena to amuse the mob.

Brothels and forced prostitution swarmed the empire. There was widespread gambling on chariot races and gladiatorial combats, as well as massive consumption of alcohol. In the arena, the empire encouraged sadistic cruelty toward both man and beast.[3]

Rome didn't have any sense of a guiding light, no sense of what it was about, other than continuing its own expansion. It lost its sense of itself as a beacon of civilization, and soon became the same decadent, pagan society that it had mocked regarding the barbarian worlds.

At some point, it no longer cared to even have a "mission." It was no longer about anything—whether about the rule of law, honor, or civilization. It eventually even outsourced its military defenses to barbarian hordes, to whom it taught classic Roman military tactics. Rome didn't even bother to foster a sense of allegiance to Rome within those hordes.

And so it was no surprise that when the Visigoths did reach the gates of Rome, it was a former Roman army soldier, Alaric, who led them. He easily sacked the city. When the Visigoths appeared outside the city in force, the Senate prepared to resist, but in the middle of the night rebellious slaves opened the Salarian Gate to the attackers, who poured in and set fire to the nearby houses. And with that, as Gibbon pronounced, "1,163 years after the foundation of Rome, the Imperial city, which had subdued and civilised so considerable a part of mankind, was delivered to the licentious fury of the tribes of Germany and Scythia."[4]

And so Rome ended with the ultimate indignity. Not the indignity of defeat in some glorious last battle because some brigadier general had, for example, grossly miscalculated the enemy coming from some unseen hill.

No, Rome's indignity was to be something far worse: an empire which had lost interest in itself, so much so that one can say that it almost willingly offered itself up for surrender. An empire that had so descended into decay that it didn't even care to preserve or protect its own memory or traditions with an army of its own people.

It was the ignominy of not even bothering to stand one's ground. The ignominy of cowering at the prospect of a fight, and giving up the castle merely at the sight of the enemy. The ignominy of thinking there was no more point.

In short, it was the humiliation of ending on a whimper. After all its great literature and accomplishments in science, medicine, and law, Rome just ... faded away. No Roman even bothered to preserve his city's great books for posterity's sake—what we've managed to preserve is relatively scant, and even that only through happenstance.

It was as if the brave archetypal characters of Luke Skywalker or Indiana Jones decided, after thinking about it, they'd be better off not risking things and should be more like the sheepish George McFly from *Back to the Future*. It became a world which preferred never to have to deal with confrontation. A world without a passion for any purpose or destiny. A world without a craving for justice. A world without a sense of right and wrong, or good and evil.

That is the lesson of Rome. In the end, Rome fell in a real sense not just from moral decay. It fell because its citizenry and ruling class lost its passion to "be" Rome. At some point, the Roman ideals of honor, celibacy, virtue, an educated and involved citizenry in a Republican form of government—with its internal sense of moral uprightness—somehow became quaint notions of some distant past, even for them.

People no longer cared what it took to build Rome's extraordinary architecture, aqueducts, roads, and legal and educational systems. They had come to take those things for granted, acting as though they had somehow always been there. Soon the buildings and statues became mysterious novelties, buildings with no apparent purpose. It would be the same as if our own American history vanished and people looked upon the Statue of Liberty as some giant monument of a lady holding a fire. A landmark perhaps, but they don't quite know or care why it's there.

Let us always remember the passion that has made democracy in our own time great, and the sense of freedom that goes with it. Only passion can nourish that greatness.

For anything great to happen, you must have people willing to sacrifice themselves for something higher—even if it means dying for it. Think of any great war in history—the so-called "good wars"—and you will see passion from the winner.

Call it morals, call it purpose, call it whatever, but *passion*—passion for a guiding principle around which you base your actions and even your life—is essential. Passion allowed the Greeks to prevail at Marathon against the Persians, the Americans to continue to fight America's Revolutionary War—despite the overwhelming losses Washington and his men took in the first years, and the long odds against winning. Passion was what let us prevail in the Civil War against the evils of slavery—despite the staggering losses.

In short, passion is the thing that gets us out of the foxhole, that gets us to yell "fix bayonets!" and throw ourselves forward into a storm of bullets, flame throwers, and hand grenades. Passion leads to the will to fight and to risk death.

Passion got us into and through the First and Second World Wars. It would have been easier to sit out both of those wars; after all, other than Pearl Harbor there were no real battles fought on American soil. Our own citizens didn't "feel" the war or suffer occupation as the Europeans had. We could have arranged a sort of *détente* with Hitler, much the same way we did later with the Soviets during the Cold War.

But we went anyway: Our passion against evil—our sense that the core of our Judeo-Christian centered world was facing an existential threat—compelled us to go overseas. Anyone back then could have reasonably said that we should mind our own business, that those wars did not concern our national interests. And some did.

The whole nation seemed to fight together; we built a whole new army infrastructure almost from scratch. People followed the war in the news, especially WWII, and knew its progress with each major battle. War heroes became celebrities.

There was a clarity that came from that *passion*. Or perhaps we could say that the passion gave us the clarity. The evil we faced in Korea and Vietnam (communism) was no less monstrous than fascism, but Vietnam especially came during troubled and confused times in America, coupled with poor military strategy and bizarre micro-management from President Johnson. The latter may have caused the "anti-passion" against the original passion for the Vietnam War. The war lost favor in the States, and soon America abandoned even just supporting our South Vietnamese allies, even after the end of American involvement in 1973.

The same is true with today's fight against a jihad, or radical Islamism. That ideology is no less vicious than Hitler's Nazism. Like the Nazis, its adherents seek world conquest. Like the Nazis, they are willing to kill millions to impose their will. And like the Nazis, there is no tolerance for competing views, culture, or religions. Finally, they want everyone to submit to them, and there is no tolerance for freedom.

But unlike our dealing with the Nazis, the majority of nations cannot now even fathom the notion of all-out war with the rabid monsters such as ISIS. Why? They've lost the passion. They'd rather treat it like a police matter, and hope that eventually things will correct themselves. But we would never have adopted such an attitude in our campaign against Hitler.

What a difference a few decades make.

The Americans won the American Revolution, the North persevered in America's bloodiest war (the Civil War), turned the tides of World War I and II, and thereafter projected liberty throughout Europe and Japan. But since then, our resolve has waned. While we managed to keep the enemy at bay in Korea, it was not the decisive victory against communism we had sought. Despite our far superior strength, the Americans eventually let

Vietnam slip away to the communists. Also, despite the ultimate American success in ousting and executing Sadam Hussein in Iraq and creating a new democracy there, the Americans completely retreated from Iraq in 2011, squandering those successes, and leaving ISIS to fill the vacuum. Afghanistan has devolved into America's longest war, with no clear cut victory in sight.

What explains this disparity in our success against the fascists versus the tepid results against the communists and the radical islamists? Was it the nature of their ideologies? Did the communists and islamists have better weapons? Were they better fighters with better strategies?

Or did *we* change?

It is no stretch to argue that since the 1960's, we seemed to have lost the passion to win, and the commitment that comes with it. Instead, we've paralyzed ourselves with a fear of conflict. That in turn has led to an inability to see what is necessary to rid ourselves of true evil, to dedicate ourselves fully to see it through to swift and total victory. That is what ultimately enabled the bad guys to win.

Passion is the only way to deal with evil. It remains the only way to protect us as a nation, as a people, as a culture, as a civilization. Even today, while Islamic State and similar radical Islamic groups (Hamas, Hezbollah) infiltrate Europe and pursue active terrorism and distort the West's own laws and sensitivities to advance their positions, it seems not to stir very much in anyone.

But there can be no passion, no *will to fight*, without clarity of one's own purpose. If you operate solely out of fear—the avoidance of conflict—your culture and civilization are doomed.

The soldier in the trenches must have a meaningful reason to fight, a mission. He needs a story that propels him forward, just like a movie must have a story. He will not get out of his foxhole, fix bayonets, and charge toward the enemy and brave the hundreds of bullets whizzing by him, if he does not believe there is anything exceptional in his civilization.

Yet this is the world our soldiers have trained in. The West is not "exceptional" in their eyes, and certainly not America. Worse yet, it seems no one has stated a mission for them, such as fighting for the spread of freedom. Soldiers must also wonder whether our government will do what it takes to preserve the new status quo in other lands they fought so hard for (Vietnam, Iraq, and possibly Afghanistan).

There is no "story" anymore. So the equation is simple: No meaning equals more danger.

What does it take to acquire this passion? An understanding of how we came to be who we are in the first place. It was the passion of others (Abraham, Moses, the Founding Fathers, the Revolutionary Forces; the Union Army and Lincoln, Roosevelt and Martin Luther King Jr.) who all understood our freedoms come from God, and that God expected us to seek it and even to *fight* for it. But if there is no God to give us freedom, then there is no freedom to fight for.

We can never truly achieve and maintain a "win" against the enemy which seeks to destroy us, without a sense of a higher authority. Even the leaders of communism only exploited a vision of global socialism for their own power-hungry purposes. But they held no sense of any true higher authority, and so communism waned relatively quickly, collapsing of its own inefficient and clumsy weight. Russian communism lasted just over seventy years and the entire Soviet Empire enterprise lasted only just over forty of those. Even the Chinese and Vietnamese dictators of today have let "true" communism pass ever so quietly in the night, as they have now turned to more market-based systems.

So we return to Rome: No one can claim to know the exact day or even the year of the end of the empire. It just kind of faded away, like that moment when you realize you haven't seen those nice people in the old house down the street, and no one's come to replace them. You figure something's up because the weeds have overtaken the lawn, and no one's repaired the broken windows. There was no formal announcement, no ceremony. Just a realization, and then only if you stopped to think about it.

It's not to say that you can't have passion without God. You can. But it *is* to say that *we cannot possibly win without passion.* The present war against Islamic fundamentalism cannot succeed unless we devote massive resources and treat this—passionately—as the serious threat it is to all of us. This is why Europe is collapsing ever so slowly—with a Roman-style long, drawn-out "whimper." Like with Rome, we'll never be sure about the date of its collapse.

But collapse it will. The Europeans seem not to care about themselves anymore. Not only do they have no meaningful affinity anymore for Christianity or God, they don't even have a sense of what it means to be French, British, German, or even European.

What binds them? What values do they share? What would they all fight and die for together, if they had to?

I have no idea. And I think *they* have no idea. Certainly, there is no cause any European seems to be proclaiming that they'd be willing to die for. It's as if the pacifism, their open disdain for nationalism, has wormed itself into the very DNA of Europe. They don't even seem interested in taking meaningful steps to defend themselves.

Meanwhile, the European borders remain porous, largely the result of Europe's insatiable economic need for younger unskilled labor to support its socialist tax base. By contrast, the largely Muslim immigrant population then has many children, while most native Europeans rarely have more than one child.[5]

The immigrant population refuses to assimilate into their new host countries. The politically correct and ever-apologetic European culture would never think to demand that they learn the host country's history or language. This in turn creates many "no-go" zones where the police don't dare enforce the laws, and cultural cowardice is the order everywhere else. This in turn leads to native Europeans beating a path to Anywhere But Here. It's a vicious "one-two-three-four-five punch" that serves only to accelerate Europe's predictable and inevitable demise.

And so, as they say, it'll be *au revoir, auf wiedersehen, adios, arrivederci,* and all the other similar phrases in the many other European languages that will likely breathe their last gasps in the next thirty to forty years.

Thinking that you can just hold the bad guys at bay without passion to do so is a bit like thinking you'll lose weight and get healthy just because you have a membership at the gym. You have to have the desire and the commitment to use it.

We have the military and the might—still. But we mostly received these from men before our present generation. They amassed such power not because it was nice to have big battleships and missiles and cool jets, but because they had *passion* to keep America and its values strong. We must re-learn and reawaken that passion.

And it is no secret what has allowed the West, and particularly America, to achieve its greatness: God-centered free-market capitalism, with an emphasis on the greatest gift God has given us, liberty. Nothing else has ever caused the world to blossom so magnificently. Nothing else ever will.

So, so long, Europe. At least we'll have a glimpse at what it must have felt like in the last years of the Roman Empire.

Of Heroes, Fear, and Woody Allen

I used to have a recurring uncomfortable dream: I'm in my apartment with my girlfriend. In the middle of the night, two thugs break in. They are big men. Bad men. And I know they will do horrible things to us if they find us.

I know where they are in the house, and manage to not let them know that I am awake. On my nearby nightstand, for some reason, there is a hammer. I grab the hammer.

My girlfriend sees me. She's the fearful type, one who instinctively avoids any kind of conflict. And so when she sees me grab the hammer, she panics and grabs my arm, pulling me back, saying "No, NO!" I keep trying to keep her quiet, explaining that I've got this, that we're going to be okay, let me do what I need to do...

But the fear of conflict is so terrifying to her that it blinds her from seeing what we had to do. She gets louder and louder with each insistent plea to do nothing.

And sure enough, her repeated demands for restraint eventually draw the attention of the bad guys. I lose any advantage of surprise. They soon descend upon us and deliver the very savage beating of me and rape of her that I had feared.

She might as well have been working for them.

As with the girlfriend in my nightmare, fear can paralyze us. It makes us hold ourselves back, which only serves to open the door for our enemies to do evil. Fear seems to whisper to us, to make us believe strange things, like perhaps there are no bad men downstairs at all. They're just "house noises" that will eventually go away. But it is just not so.

In 2015, during a train ride from Amsterdam to Paris, an apparent terrorist attack began when a perpetrator—shirtless and armed with an AKM assault rifle with nine magazines and a total of 270 rounds of ammunition—began firing rounds inside a train car. He was also carrying a pistol and a bottle of gasoline. Three

Americans—all devout Christians who had known each other since their childhoods—immediately rushed and subdued him, one of whom he stabbed. They had not feared nor hesitated for a second. While an Englishman later helped tie up the perpetrator, no one else in the train engaged in the initial effort to stop him.[6]

Recall Master Sgt. Roddie Edmonds from the first chapter of this book. He was the World War II leader of American POWs who refused to give up the Jews among his men, insisting that all his men present themselves as Jews. A devout Christian as well, he not only had no hesitation about his mission, but had no fear even when the German commander placed his Lugar pistol directly upon the temple of Edmond's head.

There are countless other stories of similar bravery, of course: The Christians who hid Jews without hesitation during the Nazi occupation. The Jewish dissenters in the former Soviet Union, particularly Alexander Solzhenitsyn and Natan Sharansky. Rosa Parks.

What makes such people?

Rosa Parks' story tells it all. When she refused her seat to a white man on a bus in Montgomery, Alabama, in 1955, she was alone. She had no throngs of people already willing to back her up or fund her cause. No newspapers or television reporters were there at the bus to cover and herald this historic moment.

When she refused to budge from her seat, it was a pure act of faith: "I felt the Lord would give me the strength to endure whatever I had to face. *God did away with all my fear,*" she wrote in her 1995 autobiography, *Quiet Strength* (emphasis added).[7]

It is the deep devotion to God, the appreciation of God's reality and centrality in all our lives, that makes such heroes. Anyone with a true sense of God in his life has little to fear. Rosa Parks said it perfectly: God *does away* with fear.

Those who embrace God understand that there is only one thing to fear (or, as the Torah describes it, to hold in "awe"): God.

President Franklin Delano Roosevelt stated it another powerful way when addressing the nation to engage in the fight against Nazi Germany and Imperial Japan: "We have nothing to fear but fear itself." America rallied and built up its military from virtually nothing to utterly destroy its monstrous enemies in three and a half years.

Stories of devout Christians and Jews resisting and even revolting against tyrannical regimes or ideologies are too numerous to list, but they include the founding fathers of the American Revolution, the abolitionists, and those who resisted and battled fascism, communism, Apartheid in South Africa, and dictatorships throughout the world.

In biblical times, Bar Kochba's devotion to God led him to organize his massive revolt against the Roman empire in AD 132. David's devotion to God not only led to his slaying of Goliath but to his numerous subsequent victories in battles against Israel's enemies.

There was no fear in such people. While they had every cause to fear, it was as if they understood that fear only inhibits the good from acting against evil. It was as if they understood that, while fear was a factor, it was ultimately a dangerous indulgence. Fear to them was a disease that invades your body and takes over.

Regardless of whether one believes in the Torah or the New Testament, Christians and Jews alike have acted courageously in the face of horrible adversity. They did so by harkening to these biblical stories. Noah, Abraham, Isaac, and Moses did not fear. The story of Jesus tells us of how he took on Rome in his own way, advancing teachings that would later form the basis for Christianity. Nowhere do we read about Jesus acting as some biblical version of the self-doubting Woody Allen, second-guessing any God that would choose *him* of all people to be His son. He was certain of his role and destiny: Fear was irrelevant to him.

It took centuries for his words to take root, but eventually Christianity displaced the paganism of the Roman Empire, leading to the largest religion humankind has ever known and helping advance the Judeo-Christian values of freedom, morality and civilization itself like never before. As a Christian, you might even say it all turned out quite well.

Within every great challenge and upheaval to evil, it seems there's a man or woman of deep faith leading the charge. Regardless of the size of the opposition they face, they do not show fear because with God they have no fear. They seem to understand that they are part of something bigger than them, that God expects them to confront evil when it might arise. He just needs them to decide to *act*. It's as if they know that God will give them cover once they do.

Those with God also know that when you fear you are giving power to someone or something else, whether that's the school bully, the Nazi guard, the communist regime, or even a corrupt city hall. But believers know that only God is truly in charge. And so they can face virtually any evil adversary with strength.

When the moment of confrontation arises, they do not hesitate. They act immediately. They do not fear the consequences, even the possibility of death, because they would rather die than live in a world without serving God's mission. As Patrick Henry stated to the Second Virginian Convention just before the American Revolution: "Give me liberty, or give me death."

Such people recognize that any fear of severe injury and even death is just noise. The task must be to confront evil. The Founding Fathers—every one of them—knew this and acted accordingly. Despite knowing that the British Empire would hang them for treason if it took them prisoner, not one of them lessened their resolve to break away from Britain. There were no Woody Allens among them, either.

I do not believe we have as many such people today—people who can recognize evil immediately and who jump to action without fear or hesitation. In a world where the media and schools demonize soldiers and police, where countries seem obsessed to avoid collateral damage and hurt feelings at any cost, and where they disregard religion as irrelevant or even backward, someone finding himself in a confrontation with evil will second-guess himself. He will not think he has any cover to back him up, especially if he is alone.

The atheist will protest: surely there were atheists who were heroes, too.[8] Maybe so, but it's difficult to find them—like trying to find a plumber in the audience of a Barbara Streisand concert: It *is* possible, but you might be better off looking elsewhere.

The historical record of true heroes seems to bear it out, time and time again: There are few real heroes without God in their lives.

In his brilliant book, *Face Your Fear* (2004), Rabbi Shmuley Boteach demonstrates how fear is useless, how it only serves to paralyze us from doing what we must. He argues that we therefore must reject it at every turn. (He deals with the notion of "fear" to get out of the way to save yourself from an oncoming bus, but he argues that shouldn't be "fear." That's a different *kind* of fear; it's not one which comes from a confrontation with evil, and it's more that you are running *to* life.)

It seems that fear only enters our souls and minds when we do not accept—and do not embrace—the centrality of God. Only in a world with God can we truly live without fear. God gives us the strength to resist our fears when we need it most: "Go ahead. I've got your back."

A strong fortress keeps the enemies at bay—enemies who would seize upon any crack or other weakness in the walls. A world lived in fear only invites cracks in the walls, and then invites those cracks to grow into gaping holes. It is then that the enemies can burst in, morphing from mere distractions and noise to horrible realities of pillage and annihilation.

Only with God can we fight the paralysis and destruction that fear brings.

Atheism, Boredom, and the Playground of Evil

All kinds are good except the kind that bores you.
—Voltaire

The costliest disease for any society
is not cancer or coronaries. It is boredom.
—Anonymous

There once was a little boy in a village. Despite people and other kids always offering him something to do, nothing interested him—not soccer, not marbles, nor making things with clay. They offered to read books with him. Nothing peaked his interest. He just would sit on the side of the street near merchant shops, making random movements with his stick in the dirt.

One day, he saw a man passing by with a small wheel cart. It was full of bananas, so much so that the bananas teetered ridiculously, like an elephant riding a small bicycle. The boy thought: what if I put a stick in that wheel?

So, sneaking up quietly behind the cart, that is exactly what he did. The stick jolted the wheel of the cart, causing the bananas bunches to tilt to one side dramatically and fall upon a bamboo structure along the roadside. The bunches hit the bamboo wall so hard it collapsed.

On the other side of the wall was a man and woman in a passionate embrace. It turns out the woman was not the man's wife.

The man's actual wife, who eventually noticed what was happening, came running toward her husband with a stick and started beating him mercilessly. The man ran to the middle of the road to escape her blows but then slipped on the bananas.

Seeing this, the driver of the banana cart became furious: this man was ruining all his merchandise! The driver quickly descended upon the man, punching him to stay away. But then other people jumped in as well, trying to defend the husband. The angry wife, who still wanted to continue beating her husband, joined in the fray. Then all sorts of other people from the town jumped in. Everyone also started throwing bananas at each other.

The little boy loved all of this. If he could make all this commotion happen with just a stick in a wheel, what else could he do?

So while the fighting was still going on, he raced to a local telephone in one of the nearby shops. He managed to reach the police department. He told them there was a "really big robbery" going on in the street, and the mob had the robbers cornered. He told them to come quick: the robbers had big guns and looked very scary.

Within minutes, police and even some military vehicles arrived. They were far better equipped than the boy could have hoped for. They had machine guns and machetes!

The boy ran right toward them as they approached. "There they are!" he yelled out, pointing to the crowd. "The terrorists are right there!"

"Terrorists?" the police captain asked. "We thought this was a robbery!"

The boy now remembered that he had indeed referred to them as robbers, but that was already a few minutes ago. Terrorists were far more interesting! "No, no—terrorists!"

The police captain was now starting to panic. He took out his megaphone and immediately told the crowd to disperse. In their rage about the banana fight (which was turning into an ever more violent fist fight), they didn't notice the police and army right next to them.

"Disperse!" the captain bellowed again to the crowd. Still they would not leave.

Thinking this terrorist situation might explode, the police captain soon fired a shot in the air. But the shot unfortunately brought down an electric wire. This in turn caused most of the banana fighters to panic. They started running toward the police and army.

Now the police and army, panicking that this might be a terrorist ambush, did the unthinkable: they fired wildly right into the crowd. The crowd in turn ran wildly to the nearby stores, crashing into everything. Unfortunately, someone kicked a lantern over, and its flame ignited some paper and dry brush. Within minutes, a fire engulfed most of the village.

In the aftermath, the police began to piece together all that had happened. People remembered the boy and the stick, his call to the police, and him racing out to warn about the "terrorists." They tracked him down easily and confronted him.

"Look at all the horror you caused, little boy!" They yelled.

But the boy was resolute: "It's all your fault!" he cried. "None of this would have happened if you gave me something to do!"

"An idle mind is the devil's playground," goes the expression. When we have nothing to do, bad things will follow. Like the fatherless child in the inner cities, he'll gravitate toward any father figure, even if it's a drug gang lord. Recognizing this problem, Big Brothers offers to pair up such "at-risk" youth with responsible, goal-oriented young men, to break that dynamic.

Likewise, for children in a general sense, we seem to understand that we need to give children constructive outlets for their high-intensity energy. We let them tire themselves out at the playground. We even say that we are letting them "channel" their aggression through sports, pretend sword-fighting, and playing cops and robbers (well, at least in the old days).

While we recognize this, we seem not to apply this important "channeling" notion to boredom. And boredom is the sense that there is nothing meaningful to engage in.

And therein lies the problem: atheism offers nothing and believes in nothing. It is the ultimate philosophy of emptiness. Whatever value we think that there is to life, we are like the man reaching out to a mirage in the desert: we *want* it to be there, but nothing is there.

The true atheist must acknowledge that atheism advances nothing but nihilism, boredom, lack of passion, and lack of purpose. We know that this leads to undesirable (even horrific) consequences, yet we do nothing to fight it.

On the contrary, the atheist will not only *not* acknowledge this problem, he will "double-down" on it: he will seek the end of all things remotely spiritual. It is mostly the atheists who seek the tearing down of the Ten Commandments inscriptions on walls and monuments on public property (courthouses, parks, government buildings, etc.). It is mostly atheists, or at least people for whom God is relatively meaningless in their lives, who seek to dismantle the trappings of religious life (Santa Claus, "merry Christmas" salutations, Christmas lights), and policies advancing religious life (tax deductions, grants, commemorations to saints, allowing prayers in schools and the like). They suck the joy out of life.

And perhaps worse yet, atheists offer nothing in their place. It is rare that the godless will seek to push for their own version of the Boy Scouts or the community equivalent of a church or synagogue for doing good deeds and donating charity. An atheist *as an individual* may do good things or donate to charities, but rarely (if ever) does he do so *on behalf of* his atheism. After all, what within atheism would prompt him?

Nothing compares to the many Catholic and Jewish hospitals (St. John's, Cedars-Sinai, New York–Presbyterian/Lower Manhattan Hospital, Mount Sinai Beth Israel, just to name a few well-known hospitals), or the numerous parochial schools that require low or no tuition, or the numerous general charities (American Red Cross, Salvation Army), or charities which receive used clothing and other items for redistribution to less needy (Goodwill, founded in 1902, was part of a Christian ministry). Even the health treatment establishments that are *not* religiously based still offer interfaith spiritual support as a significant part of their healing (City of Hope).

There is no hospital named the Hospital of the Tireless Atheist or Humanist of Lower Manhattan. The atheist will argue that there are numerous non-religious doctors and charitable organizations. But that argument misses the point: such people do not base their very work upon the absence of God.

Atheism offers no calling, no mission statement. There is simply no expectation whatsoever. There is literally nothing to look forward to, and nothing to live for. And because it offers nothing, it only amplifies a sense of boredom.

But we know that the human mind needs to pursue things that matter. Without a sense of engagement, the nonbeliever will pursue just about anything to feed his inner craving to be a part of something. Even a child complains when he says he feels "bored." What he's really saying is that he wants something to *do.* A dog won't do that, but almost every child will. Humans detest being bored. It troubles us.

The Columbine shooters in Colorado or other random "shooting spree" murderers, and arsonists, often share a delight in one thing: that because of their actions—evil as they are—the world responds. Their actions *affect* other people, even if the killer or arsonist won't ever see his victims, or know how they suffered. They just know that because of what they've done a whole lot of commotion results: the innocent victims losing their families, limbs, or homes; the rush of fire and police vehicles to the scene, the converging of the media to cover the shocking new event, the interruption of whatever other new stories might be playing out that day. Computer hackers who insert viruses just for the thrill of freezing other people's computers or knowing that they are screwing up people's important data get the same sense of "rush."

In the great Truman Capote true-crime novel, *In Cold Blood*, two men decide to drive 400 miles away to commit a murder upon a family whom they did not know and with whom they otherwise had absolutely no connection. Why, you ask? Capote concludes that it was one of lead killer's sense of inadequacy, his ambiguous sexuality, and a rage at the world and at his family because of a bad childhood.[9]

Capote may have missed the mark. After all, many people feel inadequate, many people have sexual ambiguity issues, and even more people are generally "angry." The vast majority of them don't go on random killing sprees, let alone one they plan out in a different state against innocent people they've never known.

So the question: what causes one such person to kill and another such person not to? I do think that while the killers' sense of alienation was something, they ultimately did it because it was something they *could* do. More to the point, it was something *to* do.

We often shake our heads when we see senseless behavior, whether it's such murders, random vandalism or violence, or arson. "Don't they have anything better to do?" we wonder.

Maybe the answer is that such people don't. Or at the least, they've come to believe that they don't. In a word, they're bored.

And that's exactly why they do it. They pursue something, *anything*, to get to fulfill their need to matter—even if it's criminal. And to them, they've concluded that merely getting a reaction—any reaction—achieves that for them. They're suddenly in the news. Look: there are all the people we've made suffer. They figure: *I must matter, if I achieved all that.*

There is perhaps nothing more ignominious than to pass through your life and realize you've done nothing with it, that you've never made your "mark." Most people will do almost anything not to suffer such a prospective fate.

Now imagine a whole country that adopts such thinking, which doesn't quite prohibit God but marginalizes Him as though He's something you pursue on the side when you have time, like a stamp collection or cleaning your favorite bike. Such a world effectively insists that life itself is boring and meaningless—no matter what you might do with it. In the end, as a social directive, it can only lead to more of that "pointless" mayhem we just discussed. Or at best you'll get a society which obsesses itself with cheap sexual and drug-related thrills, short-term beauty gimmicks, and the chasing of money. It devolves in to a society where women only think of who's the most beautiful or who has the most powerful husband; and where men only think of who's the most powerful, or who has the most beautiful wife.

That is empty. That is boring. It is *meaningless.*

A world with God offers infinite possibilities and interests: working for your church; studying art, music, and film as a celebration of the divine and as guidance to a better world; or to give, heal, or teach in thousands of different ways. To someone who truly embraces God in his life, there seems to be so much going on that it's a wonder how anyone can feel bored. He always seems to be busy, engaged, and energized. He regrets only that he doesn't have more time to accomplish more of what he wants to do. (It's the way I feel: my dream is to teach mountain biking and chess to inner-city kids, to teach math and history to high-school teens; to learn Hebrew better and to study Torah's never-ending insights and wisdoms; to take my kids on trips around the world to teach them history and art, and to write more books). Such people do so because they see their efforts as connected to the discovery of God, and to the advancement of God's will.

But a world without God offers nothingness. And it turns out, nothingness is not a great motivator. You end up asking what's the point of doing anything, time and time again.

Every human instinctively wants a world with meaning. That sense resides within all of us. Unfortunately, we don't really delve into what "meaning" means, or what it might look like, when God is out of the picture. It's because we're afraid to.

"I'm bored." It's a phrase that should reveal a subtitle with a translation: Trouble lies ahead. And it's what the *In Cold Blood* killers might have said to themselves in 1959, just before they embarked on their long drive to perform their grisly murders.

And—as you might suspect—God was not a part of their lives.[10]

Godlessness and the Blindness to Evil

A five-alarm fire has been devastating the Downtown District for hours. Your fire station, Ladder No. 5, has raced to the scene, along with dozens of other stations.

As you arrive, you take in the devastating sight: the entire landscape seems to light the hillside so much that it might as well be daytime. What otherwise should be a cold night is already warm, and getting hotter as you approach. This is what Dante's inferno must look like, you say to yourself softly. The wailing sirens and the roar of the fire seem to be everywhere.

Your fire truck stops, and you jump out with the other men, full gear on. You mentally take in the tragic fact that not everyone in the building will survive the night.

You can only really hear the sound of your own breathing through your hot fireman's suit and gear. Everything else sounds muffled. But you can hear the captain yell out to everyone: "Let's go, let's go, let's go!!"

You've trained for this. You know that every split second counts. And the next thing you know, you're kicking in door after door and climbing stairs—stairs you pray to God will still be there on the way back.

You signal to your fellow firefighters to take the north area of the floors. You'll take the south. They nod, and everyone hustles to sweep their assigned areas for survivors.

Scorching hot, black smoke floods the hallways everywhere you go. No time to waste, no time, you keep telling yourself. No matter how many years you've been at this, your heart still beats wildly, your eyes still bulge with fear. "Fear is an enemy, and you need to conquer it like one," you remember the chief saying. You play that over and over again in your head.

All the while, you're yelling out: "Is anyone here??!!" in both English and Spanish. Embers and small wooden pieces and then larger ones keep falling from the roof. From your perspective, it's as if they're raining down on you from the sky. Soon, the floor seems to open up with more and more holes.

In short, you're in a giant burning box just moments before it's going to collapse.

Alas, as you walk down the hallway, you stumble upon your first survivor. It's a woman in her early thirties. Strangely, . . . she's reading a book in bed. More oddly, she's wearing only panties and a tank-top. Stranger still, she seems unimpressed that a fire is consuming her building. A bit surreal, you note to yourself.

"Come with me, I'm here to rescue you... Let's go!" You rush over to her, grabbing her arm to start pulling her away from the danger.

But strangely, she'll have none of it. She shoves your arm away. "NO," she says adamantly. "NO means NO."

You just freeze yourself in position. What is this? "Uh... Come again?" you ask.

"I said 'NO.' Can't you hear me?"

You try to explain that there's a fire going on, and that while she may indeed be an attractive woman, the physical gesture here on your part was principally platonic, such as for saving her life.

"Don't you raise your tone with me!" she yells. She then says something about how "you men" are always "mansplaining" and trying to "fix everything" instead of really listening to what women are saying to you. Angrily, she goes back to her reading.

Okay, you think to yourself, as you walk out her door and she skooshes you away with her arm. . . . That was weird.

Now you reach another apartment. In the apartment is an older woman, with her little boy, maybe seven years old. They seem quite aware of the fire and its dangers. The smoke starts filling the room. They are coughing and reaching out for anyone to help. They see you, and hope now explodes across their faces. "Here we are! Here we are!" the mother yells.

You reach out with your arm. The boy seems nervous to let go of his mom. "Have him grab my hand!" you yell out.

Oddly, she then pulls back her son.

"Well, actually, 'he' is a 'she,' thank you very much," she says, somewhat indignantly. She talks like it's a negotiating position that you have to accept first before she's willing to proceed with this transaction. Perhaps you should then apologize.

Your hand is still outstretched to them. "Well 'she' sure looks like a boy to me," you say to her—what with that being the fact and all.

"Well, yes, biologically, she may have been born with 'classi-cal' male genitalia," she explains. "We get that *all* the time," she says, gesturing. "But that's in no way an indication of her *real* gender. You see, studies show that we all have differing gender identities throughout our childhood, and that the damage to the mind of a young person such as Francine here who feels imposed upon by society to be a boy just because she has a penis...."

So you leave these people and race down the hallway in search of other trapped people. Okay... that was also odd, you think to yourself. You wonder: Just what kind of building is this?

You hear a wild coughing, and you race toward it. It's a man, perhaps in his late thirties. He reaches out to you as soon as he sees your figure: "Oh God please save me!" he says.

Finally, you think as you race over: *Someone* who's appreciative. You bend down on your knee, preparing to give him an oxygen mask from your pack.

But then, he looks at your face. Between coughs, he waives you off with his arm: "You're white."

You're a little confused here, again. "Sir, we've got to get you out of here!" You look up, bending down as rafters fall all around you.

"That ain't right," he explains. "All the firefighters I've seen so far today are *white*. I want to be rescued by an African-American or Latino... or a woman firefighter.... Or anyone from the LGBT community," he adds, as though that last one was an afterthought. "Or perhaps a disabled person—like an amputee in a wheelchair." He waives you off, as if he'll wait while you go fetch such a person for him.

"You want to be rescued by a fireman ... in a wheelchair?"

He nods his head. That would be ideal.

So you leave once again. This time, you race off to another voice you hear, this time on the floor above you. It's a strange, almost wailing sound. The stairs can barely support anyone at this point, but you take the risk. After all, you're a fireman.

You follow the wailing sound all the way to another apartment door. You break the door in with your ax. What do you see? It's a Muslim man, and he's been doing his evening prayers.

He gets up—furious: "You're interrupting my prayers!"

You sigh. Not again. By this point, you just go through the motions: you say he's in a dangerous situation, and he's going to die if he doesn't get out real soon. . . . And so forth.

He'll have none of it. You are oppressing him as a Muslim, he tells you. "I am going to report this!"

This time, you just close the door on him, slowly. You're just not going to deal with it.

Back to the hallway you go. The fire still rages mercilessly, consuming the building. But you just stand there, anyway. You begin to wonder: is this *real*?

And the building starts collapsing as you watch helplessly. Everyone plummets around you: the pretty thirty-year-old still on the phone, the mother caressing her son/daughter telling him/her that he/she "needs to be who you need to be," the man demanding an amputee fireman, and the angry Muslim.

Eventually, you join them in their descent. No one survives.

And so it seems to be in our world these days.

Russia invades its neighbors with impunity and seeks hegemony over the region and beyond. China presides over and even encourages mass forced abortions to achieve the goals of its One Child policy. North Korea and Iran both threaten nuclear annihilation of their respective neighbors. The world demonizes Israel repeatedly, while the world does nothing about unspeakable daily human right abuses in Syria, Somalia, North Korea, Saudi Arabia, Jordan, Egypt, Indonesia, Libya, Iran, Afghanistan, Cuba, Venezuela, among many other nations.

In many of these countries, they deny virtually every right to women, commonly perform female genital mutilation upon young girls, routinely throw homosexuals off the tops of buildings, commit so-called "Honor Killings," use stoning and amputations as punishment, and routinely rape little boys as part of their culture.

Radical Islamic groups such as Hamas, Hezbollah, Boko Haram, Islamic State, and Al Qaeda force vast swaths of people into institutionalized sexual slavery and commit genocide upon Christians—and upon as many as they can round up who do not think like them. Some commit mass drownings and immolations. Reports abound of ISIS harvesting organs of captured victims to further fund its terrorist operations, almost always leading to their victims' deaths.[11]

Rapes and sexual assaults also abound throughout Europe, following its recent enthusiastic absorption of millions of migrants from Syria and other Muslim nations. The police look the other way for fear that the Muslim community might call them racist.[12]

But for many in the West, the focus is on far loftier things, such as the rights of two men or two women to sanctify their sexuality through marriage, and then to force vendors to provide floral, photography, and other catering services at their gay weddings. Things such as the right of a man who feels like a woman should have the right to relieve himself in a women's restroom or to change in the women's locker room. Such as the right of a woman to go topless in public. We shouldn't have to say the Pledge of Allegiance, and certainly should not do so with the reference of "under God." We should banish any reference to God in any forum that might possibly involve public funds. And we are not recycling enough.

More critical to many in the West is climate change (formally known as global warming). Their advocates claim it might cause sea levels to rise because average world temperatures may rise — they don't know by how much, but you can bet it'll be a whole lot.

But even advocates don't quite know just when or by how much this horrible scenario will play out. But no matter; we must act *now*.

Our civilization is at stake. But the focus for so many is elsewhere. This is not to say that some of these concerns are not worth addressing. There is nothing wrong with seeking out new efficiencies, which may include recycling, reducing pollution, and so on.

But sensible *perspective* seems to have left us. Compare the number of people who have died from climate change to the people who are now dying because of radical Islamic terrorism. No one has died from climate change, and no one arguably ever will, even assuming we are causing the planet's temperatures to rise.

Why is this strange imbalance of perspective happening? Because those who truly are without God don't recognize the very *existence* of evil. Remember that "evil" is an arcane word to the godless. In a universe without God, there cannot be any such thing as objective "evil," after all. They see the horrific actions in the world only as stuff that happens to other people that they wouldn't like happening to them. More accurately, they view such man-made mayhem in the same ways they view unfortunate natural disasters like earthquakes, floods, and fires.

But that is not the same thing as recognizing evil itself. When you recognize that *evil* exists, you see it as a *thing*, an enterprise in and of itself. And then you also know that there is an obligation to fight it. It is not good enough to love the good. You must also hate the evil. In other words, with all due respect to the Beatles, love is *not* all you need.

By contrast, there is no similar obligation to fight or hate an earthquake. You *deal* with an earthquake and its aftermath. Maybe you learn from it, and try to minimize its potential impact in the future. But you don't hate it.

The godless don't hate evil because they have willingly blinded themselves to its very existence, especially if they see it only like they see an earthquake. And because they don't even recognize evil, they logically would conclude there is no need to confront it. After all, it doesn't exist. Earthquakes, fires and floods exist, sure, but "evil"? No – I can't see it or feel it the same way, so it mustn't be real. They'll tell you there are only bad choices.

But calling it "bad choices" is just a cop-out diversion. Recognizing "evil" would in a sense mean that they also recognize an absolute moral code of some sort. And to them, that would not compute; like the old *Star Trek* computers used to say when they received contradicting programming instructions, just before they started overheating with smoke, and then self-destructed.

To them, there is no "absolute" moral code. That would imply a creator, so we can't have that. Instead they come up with seemingly sagacious phrases like "One man's terrorist is another man's freedom fighter" [meaning all notions of what is evil is relative], "War is not the answer" [suggesting war itself is what is evil], and "We will shake your hand so long as you unclench your fist" [meaning all evil is just a by-product of big misunderstandings that we can resolve through dialogue and better job programs; or perhaps if we just return each other's phone calls].

And so, not surprisingly, it is mostly the godless who proclaim there is a moral equivalence between Israel and her terrorist enemies or between America and the dictators of the world. It is mostly they who proclaim that all cultures are equally valid and have equal value.

So not surprisingly, they are the ones who pound the podium at entertainment award shows and other high-brow events. There, the betters of our culture give great soliloquies of their opinions on what we must all do, that climate change is the only "real" threat to confront. Global jihadism and China's one-child policy are but tempests in a teapot, or perhaps even the *result* of climate change's slow but horrible depletion of natural resources.[13]

It is only those who reject God, or for whom God is irrelevant to their lives, who can arrive at this way of thinking. They will never see it. That's because their intellectual programming must shut any notion of evil out. To recognize evil as such is to implicitly recognize the existence of a Creator—and a Creator who demands morality from us. So to them, evil "does not compute."

And so they are just like our friends in the building who don't see the fire that consumes everything around them. Unless we recognize the all-consuming nature of evil, our building will burn down, with many of us in it.

Godlessness and the Enabling of Evil

Recall one of our opening five stories, the one of the Montreal massacre at L'École Polytechnique, where a madman separated the women from the men, so that he could kill the women. The men waited in the hallway and did nothing while they heard the madman killing each of the women one by one in the nearby classroom.

Most of the postmortem analysis of the shootings focused on the killer's outspoken hatred of women, and how misogyny remained alive and well in Canada and the West. Most of the national discussion turned on how Canadians needed to fight for women's rights. There were also demands for better police responsiveness and action in such circumstances.

But there was very little follow-up on the men who complied with the gunman, and who did nothing to stop him.

Yet perhaps the men's reaction (or non-reaction to be specific) should be the defining and lasting legacy of the Montreal massacre: the men who meekly abandoned their female classmates to their fate—an act of abdication that would have been unthinkable in almost any other culture throughout human history.[14]

Why so? Marc Steyn pondered whether this was an ironic result of society's push for feminism, and the concurrent emasculation of men that may have accompanied feminism.

This argument presents a superficial explanation. But it might be too simplistic, like concluding that one's last bite of food was the cause of someone's fatal heart attack: it ignores the victim's overall lack of health, an inevitable explosion that was in the works inside his body for decades.

And perhaps that was the same for the Montreal massacres. Where there is no God in one's life, there is no sense of evil, let alone that a sense that one must *fight* evil. Unlike a Kung Fu master who would instinctively know how to react if a mugger ever jumped at him or thrust a knife to his neck, these men had never engaged in any philosophical or intellectual training that would have propelled them to engage into the fight.

These men likely never learned what evil was at all. I think they were utterly unprepared to respond. They hadn't formed the basic intellectual neurons to understand what was happening. They just had no training. Most of the younger generation have learned only how to identify hate speech (whatever that means). Ask a college student today if they had ever taken a class where anyone ever probed the nature of evil, and you'll get a blank stare. In fact, unless they went to Catholic or other parochial school, they've likely never studied evil at all.

But if they hear someone question climate change, they will jump into the fray with both feet and argue with many jabbing fingers. If someone argues against racial favoritism, they will fight that, too. Random posters on campus kiosks have taught them to be on the vigilant lookout for sexism, homophobia, racism, and people who don't place their refuse in the correct recycling bin.

These are the issues that cause them to spring into action. But no poster, no serious activist or professor has ever talked to them about what "goodness" entails—which includes the fight against evil. You won't find too many "Beware of Evil" kiosk signs. Evil to them is like a non-sequitur, something which may have existed in the past (what with those Nazis and all) but which is not really relevant anymore. Or maybe it exists in some fictional parallel universe, like in all the *Star Wars* movies, *Game of Thrones,* or in any number of space-age video games. But it doesn't happen on *this* planet, at least not anymore. We're all better than that now.

So it shouldn't be a surprise that those men failed to react in Montreal, that they complied so easily with the attacker's demands. They can identify climate change deniers, but no one gave them the training to identify perpetrators of evil, much less to respond to it.

Do you think this seems unfair? Do you believe this could have happened just as easily to anyone under the same circumstances? Then do a thought experiment: If this had happened a hundred years earlier, don't you think that at least a few of the men would at least have attempted to tackle the murderer?

We know they would. Why? Because we know that back then—primitive days as they were—people knew of evil. They had learned of it in school. It was part of the character building central to any child's upbringing. They were hyper-vigilant to their personal sense of duty for God and country. They learned about evil so that they could recognize it when it was in front of them. But all they've been learning in schools of late, if anything, has been to use words and to express their feelings, and to banish all mention of violence at all. No one thinks to teach that there might be a time to use fists.

When you have a sense of God, you know that good and evil are competing forces that manifest themselves in many ways. You know that you are not only supposed to pursue goodness, but that you are to identify evil and fight it with all your intellectual and physical might. And if you really learn well, you come to learn that fighting evil is one of your core missions as a human being.

Those without God will shake their heads as they read this last few sentences. Such violence, they think to themselves. So simplistic. Just what is "evil" then, they will ask. Who are you to decide what is evil? Doesn't everyone's competing sense of what is evil just perpetuate war and destruction? When will this cycle of violence ever end?

Far from preventing evil, such side-stepping questions only enable more evil.

But we know what the Polytechnique murderer did was evil. What Charles Manson did to the Tate and LaBianca families was evil. What Hitler, Pol Pot, Stalin, Mao, Che Guevera, and Ho Chi Minh did was evil. What ISIS, North Korea, Iran, Hamas, and Hezbollah do today is evil.

But in a world without God, our schools and sometimes even our parents teach us to view such horrors through an entirely different lens. We learn instead that such horrors really stem out of one of six things:

1: that it's just a function of power in the moment, and that we should forgive dictators for their murderous dalliances (if we even acknowledge them), so long as what they do is in the grander and loftier utopian pursuit of socialism. In any event, it's all relative and as they say, might makes right. People often say this especially in the context of Cuba or Vietnam.

2: Christians and America did bad things, too, so who are we to judge? As their go-to, "evergreen" complaints on this score, they'll trot out the Crusades, the Inquisition, and the fact that America had slavery in its past.

3: religion and primitive nationalism themselves have fomented all this hatred, largely for purposes of controlling the otherwise untamable masses.

4: that undesirable behavior and actions are not the product of "evil," but of "bad choices." Hitler and Stalin made really, really, bad choices. But "evil"? Let's not be silly.

5: that such evil stems from a mental "sickness," one which we can cure if only we provide them with the appropriate amount of understanding and perhaps medical attention. Or better yet, a lot of money. Which leads to point...

6: that such evil stems from a lack of economic opportunity and jobs, much of which results from imperial expansion and exploitation of the people of weaker cultures, and the concurrent theft of their natural resources.

This is a paradigm shift in education and culture, both of which inform and feed off one another. And so it is almost hard to fault the men of the Montreal massacre for doing nothing. The very concept of fighting back was foreign to them, let alone the concept of recognizing and fighting evil. You might as well have expected them to recite Sun Tzu's *Art of War* in the original ancient Chinese, or have expected a bricklayer to perform brain surgery.

The most experience they ever received in combating evil was from fantasy adventure movies like *Star Wars*, *Terminator*, and *Aliens*. Either that, or from video games where they fought mythical dragons or mysterious dark lords.

But they learn nothing of evil. They are like children who watch the movie *Kung Fu Panda*, and think they know all there is to know about Kung Fu.

And so Lépine was able to continue his slaughter, with ease. Likewise, ISIS, Al Qaeda, Hezbollah, Hamas, and similar enterprises continue their viral spread across the Middle East and Europe, with little resistance.

And why? Because the good guys never got the training manual.

Just Leave the Popcorn on the Floor

People who do not believe in God only see what is *now*... To them, there is no past and no future. There is only here and now. Of course, they understand there has been a past and that there will be a future. But there is no real reason for them to care.

For the atheist, there is—by definition—*only* the here and the now. There's nothing worth fighting or sacrificing for, at least not beyond this present life. Get what you can. And don't forget the sex. You only live once, you know.

For them, life is like a visit to the movie theater: the movie is there to entertain, and there's a beginning and an ending. That is all. You may invest yourself in the characters while the movie is playing but only until the credits roll. You don't know what preceded the story or what will happen after the story, and you don't really care. You're there for the Big Ride.

And you don't know too much about or involve yourself with the other cinema watchers (unless they talk or text during the movie—so annoying). And someone else will clean up the messy popcorn buckets and empty soda paper cups you leave behind.

A nonbeliever is just here for the movie, as it were. He cannot meaningfully say otherwise: why would he care about any legacy? Why have any kids? Why do anything of substance or creative at all? Why give to charity? Why work to be a pillar of your community? Why work hard, fight for your country, be willing to die for anything, or plan ahead for future generations at all?

If all you have in life is the span of your life, and then you become nothing, then what's the point? Why not be a passive player in life and just enjoy the entertainment the movie offers? Because, after all, there's really nothing else. Never mind the generations before you who built the civilization and the goodies that you now consume—safely and at a great price.

It's not just a problem of being passive. It leads to a far worse problem. The problem is that evil lurks everywhere around us. And we noted above, the atheist lacks the passion to fight this evil. And by evil, I mean true evil—the kind that seeks to decapitate, rape, enslave, and set people on fire for not believing just like they do. The evil of those who seek to destroy our civilization, those who despise the very notion of freedom. *Not* the so-called "evil" of those who don't fully embrace transgendered people or the notion of climate change or a fair living wage.

The greater problem is that being passive to evil actually enables more evil. Let's discuss:

Diary of a Wimpy Generation (or "Class, What Are You Willing to Die For? Anyone … Anyone?")

Back in high school in Hawaii, I remember attending a student assembly gathering for Daniel Inouye, who had been the United States senator for Hawaii for a long time. The school had called him to speak of the issues of the day, particularly the prospect of reinstating the draft for military service that Congress was then considering.

Senator Inouye himself had been a hero during World War II, bravely fighting until the moment he lost his arm's use. He had fought in the European theater, and he spoke of the necessity of fighting evil. Evil will always raise its ugly head whenever it can.

He explained it was up to us to recognize evil, and hopefully defeat it before it metastasized to a point where it could destroy us. It was a moving speech, resolute and clear.

A question and answer period followed. Only one student stood up and raised his hand.

"What if I don't want to die?" he asked. "What if I don't want to go to war and die? It's just not what I want to do. I don't want to die." So, in summary, the kid didn't want to die.

I remember Inouye pausing, as he studied the young man. Finally, after a bit of an uncomfortable silence, he rejoined: "Young man, you seem to think that it's a choice between wanting to die and not wanting to die. No one wants to die. None of my friends who died *wanted* to die. But many men who didn't want to die still died. And they died for *you*, my friend—and for all the rights you enjoy today.

"Now it seems you've enjoyed all the benefits of the freedoms they fought for. And you think there is an option to do nothing, and that you can still have all the benefits of this democracy. I'm sad to say, but there is no such option.

"And what if *everyone* thought like you? What then? Or do you expect that only some men will do it for you—the ones who 'want' to die? That *they* should die, but you shouldn't, because *you* don't want to.

"Of course they didn't *want* to die, just like you don't. The difference is that they were *willing* to die, and willing to die for *you*."

The kid—he couldn't have been more than seventeen—sat down, thoroughly chastened. No one clapped, and there were no further questions.

The take-away for me was palpable. I saw in this young student someone who had no connection to his past. He had no idea of what it had taken for him to enjoy his freedoms. He had no montage scene running in his head of the battle cries of hundreds of thousands of men who had dug trenches, had died of wounds or disease. Who had suffered through brutal cold then brutal heat. Who had experienced internal terror before each battle, never knowing if it was to be his final hour. The prospect of torture, of amputation, or suffering paralysis. Of the torment of seeing a cannonball or rocket-propelled grenade, lopping off his buddy's head, right next to him.

He had no sense of any of such things, nor any of the men who had lifted all the rest of us to this very level of self-actualization, a freedom where he and the rest of our generation could pursue any interest we might want, regardless of color, faith, or economic background.

And what made these men willing to die for our life-loving friend? An abiding love of freedom, one they knew only comes from God. And in many cases, a knowledge that God wants us to be free so much that He expects us to fight for that freedom, when we must.

This is what these men believed. And it was this core belief that allowed them to prevail time and time again against tyranny and slavery.

I don't know if that young man was an atheist. But I do know that only somebody who has little or no understanding of God could have said such words.

It is this kind of passivity that allows evil to thrive and grow. This is the "passive" danger of atheism. To this teenager and others like him, they are merely watching a movie from the comfort of their living rooms, air-conditioned, and without threat of any kind. If they are engaged at all, they are at best like the guys from the accounting office enjoying their Sunday off, sitting on the couch and yelling at the TV because the ref made a bad call.

In much the same way, the atheist watches the news and sees how evil continues its march across the globe, and he yells at the TV that fighting never solves everything, that everyone should give peace a chance … and so forth. But at least the guys from the accounting office watching the football game don't pretend they can play better than the players they're watching.

But for most people without God, they simply check out altogether. They're not even really watching that TV; it's just playing in the background. They are no more a part of the world than they are a character in the TV show they're watching. They have detached from life itself.

But they are in fact *in* the show, whether they like it or not. And whether they see it or not, evil is all around them, and it marches toward them.

Passivity is dangerous. And you *enable* evil if you don't take a stand.

You may not want to bring your army to defeat the barbarian hordes coming your way, but for the love of yourself, at least defend your own castle walls. In today's fight against power hungry dictators and Islamo-fascists, we need *fighters*.

But we're discovering that a world without God produces a world of wimps. Why would it be anything else? No amount of technology, weaponry, or manpower can ultimately replace true mission to advance or protect core values. We talked previously about passion, and that it was passion which led to America's victories in the American Revolution and the World Wars. The men who fought these wars were willing to *die* for what they were fighting *for*. In many cases, the odds against them were staggering—particularly in the American Revolutionary War and all the Israeli-Arab wars. There was no willingness to compromise with the evil enemy, and they would make any sacrifice to win. The allies in World War II would not stop until the enemy offered "unconditional surrender," as Franklin Roosevelt insisted.[15]

In short, for any great cause to succeed, you must have people willing to suffer great consequences for it, even the loss of their lives. Those who do not believe in God (or at least have little sense of Him) tend not to have this sense. And so they become, well, ... wimps.

Why? Because people without God do not appreciate the past, which might show how we got here; nor the future, which should show where we are heading. For them, there is only "now." Before and after are less interesting to them.

Where a country's mission becomes unclear, or where the motivation or support from home was lacking, the wars resulted in at best stalemates and flat-out losses: Vietnam (stalemate and then loss), Korea (stalemate); the Second Iraq War of 2003 (victory gives way to stalemate, then to loss), and Afghanistan War (at risk of the same).

In each of these conflicts, America enjoyed much greater firepower, technology, and greater soldier sophistication. In fact, the disparity was far greater in those wars than the disparity between the American army and the German armies of both World Wars. Yet our society didn't seem to rally to give the soldiers a reason to fight, and certainly not one which involved love of God or freedom.

But this is an indictment of Western Civilization's present ethos, a reflection of our apathy—even antipathy—toward God. Why would we expect our soldiers to have the courage to take on the massive risks of war? For them, they have no idea what's on the other end of the proverbial rainbow: In fact, *what* rainbow?

It's even worse in today's Europe. There, the average citizen looks down upon the common soldier. To the average European, aspiring to be a soldier is like aspiring to be an assistant to a bowling alley manager: There's nothing wrong with it, as such. But it's the kind of job you fall into—when all your other options haven't panned out very well.

We have forgotten what gave us the courage to win against the British, the antebellum American South, the Nazis and Imperial Japan. It was our common understanding of our core values.

But we've disconnected from these values, values which were so deep to us only a few decades ago. Those values seem like they belong in the past and should stay there.

There is only one overarching reason: the deconstructing and dismantling of God from our lives. Where God used to be central to the town square, He now seems to be evaporating ever so slowly from it. It's like the famous Da Vinci painting *The Last Supper*, which is suffering a slow fading death, giving way to the elements. Soon we'll only have pictures of the painting to remember it by.

The church no longer serves as the hub of a community, as it once did only a few decades ago. In those days, whether a community had one or many faiths, it generally understood God as its center, and all aspects of life were in some fashion related to God. The local amusement park might have been fun, but it was something you enjoyed after giving respect to God, perhaps after the long workweek. Likewise it was the same for any kind of socializing and even drinking with friends, dating, going to the beach, bowling or camping. All of those things were subservient to God because there was an understanding by most in the community that God made it all possible. God was like the sun which had held all the planets together, and without which we could not enjoy light, heat, or life itself.

But starting in the mid-twentieth century, God's erosion accelerated. In Europe, socialism took hold, which in turn displaced God. In the United States, a series of legal challenges and significant Supreme Court rulings began reinterpreting the First Amendment. The First Amendment soon came to mean *not only* that the state could not establish and impose its own "state" religion (as was common among other European countries at the time), but that we should banish God from the public square altogether, whether in parks, courthouses, public schools, or anywhere else where the public might frequent.

Judicial fiats soon required communities to take down historical crosses. Courts ordered that public ceremonies strike references to God in invocations. On several occasions, courts required civic centers and even courtrooms to remove plaques and other displays of the Ten Commandments.[16] This eventually bled into the culture outside the court system, and many civic public organizations started dismantling and extracting God on their own, either to avoid legal confrontations (imagined or real) or to appear sensitive to different faiths or to those with no faith.

And so here we are. God is now out of sight—at least public sight. For many, God served His purpose but became an unnecessary vestige we could discard—like an old bandage we throw away after the cut heals. Like all the cop movies when the feds come in and tell the local police that "it's our jurisdiction now," science and logic have assumed the role of preserving our society and they'll take it over from here. Thanks for everything you've done so far, but no offense, we're going to rebuild everything from the ground up. Because quite frankly (and again no offense), you boys really screwed this up.

But like those planets that will quickly drift aimlessly into space without its sun, our society will not meaningfully survive without the centrality of God.

Instead of focusing on the hard things which indeed take courage (pursuing liberty, fighting evil and character development), we prefer sideshow issues, all of which have taken on colossal, almost life-or-death proportions: the quest for same-sex marriage recognition. Laws requiring employers and business owners to make sure they do not make transgendered persons feel uncomfortable in restrooms or locker rooms. Laws to punish those who fail to refer to a transgendered person by the pronoun he/she prefers (whew, that was a close one).[17] Animal rights on par with human rights. The mandated teaching of awareness of gay figures in history.[18] Multiculturalism and the insistence that no culture "appropriate" the culture of another. That no one need to learn English for voting or even citizenship. That requiring an ID to vote is a violation of rights (and a racist one at that). The disallowing of any teaching of religion in schools (except perhaps to teach the wonders of Islam). The demonizing of our immigration laws (even creating "Sanctuary" cities and even states). The requirement to teach the oncoming horrors of global warming, and other doomsday "green" teachings. The right of women to go topless in public, for which there were topless marches in the streets[19] (to the credit of men, they showed up in droves to show their support).

None of these issues take *courage* to pursue. They are merely capitulations to those forces which ultimately dismantle society. More to the point, they are nonsensical pursuits which only sidestep the courage we should be summoning to fight real evil—the kind which threatens civilization's very existence.

In short, these are issues for wimps.

Political candidates pay lip service to the bigger issues of God, freedom and America's mission in the world but rarely push them beyond just that—lip service. Instead, Republican and Democrat politicians and candidates alike seem to race toward whatever the social issue of the day demands of them. After all, it's easier. No real courage required.

And the reluctance to confront evil goes straight to the top: former President Barack Obama—on three separate occasions over a year—stated he had "no strategy" when it came to fighting ISIS[20]—a renegade but metastasizing group of Islamic radicals who were gaining more and more territory throughout the Middle East. He had dismissed the group only a year earlier in 2014 as a "J.V. team"—but it soon surpassed Al Qaeda in size, influence, and brutality. While he committed some soldiers to contain the enemy, he lacked enthusiasm for the cause, like the proverbial child whose parents force him to play violin while he looks out the window, watching the other kids play in the street.

Why the lack of gusto? Because even he did not seem to know why he should be fighting them. After all, he believed that America and Christianity had done horrible and "arrogant" things in their respective pasts.[21] So it would be downright hypocritical to sound the bugle and lead the cavalry to charge, like some Joan of Arc, to pursue America's glory. And who knows? Our enemies probably feel the same way, so who's to say who's right?

But if you don't even know what there is to fight for, or that your side believes in core values *worth* dying for, why would you fight at all? It's like a painter who has no idea what he might paint. He just stands in front of the canvas, dabbing globs of color here and there, hoping some subject might one day reveal itself.

Our enemies know when we lack focus, and lack the will to fight. That passivity emboldens them like the wayward sheep emboldens the wolf.

Before World War II, Chamberlain, Hitler, Mussolini and Daladier, the Prime Minister of France, signed the Munich Pact and agreed that all German troops would replace all Czech troops in the Sudetenland.[22]

Hitler was laughing. All Britain and France had shown was their weakness, which only increased Hitler's appetite for more territory. He soon grew his army to such exceptional size and strength that it managed to take over virtually all of continental Europe and northern Africa and to neutralize the once mighty British empire.[23] Only after the Americans entered the war did the tide meaningfully turn around, and that only after great uncertainty and casualties for the next three years. Much of it was a matter of luck in fooling Hitler that the allied invasion (later referred to as D-day) would arrive in Calais, not Normandy, and Hitler's own perplexingly disastrous decision to start a second front to the war, with Russia.

Even in recent times, the West repeats this lack of resolve and refuses to destroy the enemy when it must. This only telegraphed to Osama Bin Laden and others among Islamic terrorist groups that the West lacked the courage to defend its own culture and that it no longer maintained any values. It reaffirmed al Qaeda's own propaganda that Western nations were just "paper tigers." That lack of resolve invited, rather than deterred, their aggression.[24]

As Bin Laden observed: "Look at Vietnam, look at Lebanon. Whenever soldiers start coming home in body bags, Americans panic and retreat. Such a country needs only to be confronted with two or three sharp blows, then it will flee in panic, as it always has."[25] In 1993 Bin Laden called Americans "paper tigers" because they had withdrawn from Somalia so quickly after some of their soldiers had been killed.[26] Another of Al Qaeda's henchmen, Ayman al Zawahiri, wrote to the Iraqis frequently before and throughout the American war in Iraq to "hold on and hold out," that the US was a paper tiger which would cut and run soon enough.[27]

America did quit, pulling out every single American fighter from Iraq in 2011. ISIS soon filled the vacuum. American then sent in forces to assist alongside the Iraqis, resulting in mixed success. ISIS would constantly retake towns. Again, the enemy sensed that the Americans who backed the Iraqi militia had no sense of moral authority and did not have the will to fight. This again only emboldened the enemy.[28] Despite our undeniably greater firepower and technology, our intervening had no meaningful effect.[29] The enemy didn't even have an air force, yet the US and its allies fumbled and struggled.

But there was more: America was not only unable to say that ISIS was wrong, but to *believe* ISIS was wrong, too. Instead, Western leaders could only openly discuss sources of shame (like the Crusades and the Inquisitions), and reasons not to judge others too harshly.[30] A profound self-loathing and refusal to judge what is right and wrong has eaten away at the foundations of the West's moral authority. At a profound level, many thought the fight against ISIS was not worth fighting, because there was nothing worth fighting *for*.[31]

In the meantime, our enemies maintain their focus. They know exactly what they want to achieve—the degradation and ultimate annihilation of Western civilization. *They* have singularity of purpose, as evil as that purpose may be. *They* are willing to die for it.

The West, however, no longer seems to know what or who it is, let alone why Western Civilization even matters. Are we fighting for democracy, the rule of law, free enterprise? For some vague notion of "freedom"—whatever *that* means?

I think that was exactly the mind-set that allowed that young high school student to pose his question in the first place. He didn't understand why *anyone* fought for *any* cause at all. No one taught him to think of God, Western Civilization or freedom as a "cause" —let alone a cause worth dying for.

Without a central understanding of our mission and what makes us different, it is only a matter of time before we become hapless victims to our invaders. It is as if we have a house full of wealth, precious art, and jewelry and we hang up a large sign in the front yard stating we have no intention of defending our home.

God *had* been our purpose and core mission, whether we ever realized it. But we tossed Him out. And then we wonder why we no longer seem to have any interest in fighting.

We must turn yet again to God. A nation's success has never worked without Him.

Wake Me Up When the Clock Chimes Evil

You've encountered it yourself many times: You see something awful happening: perhaps a man beating his dog, a parent humiliating his child, or a bully taunting someone else. Or maybe it's subtler: you see someone stealing from a tip jar.

And you … do nothing. You're already away from the scene, maybe even at home. As you put your groceries down in the kitchen, you realize that maybe you *should* have done something, or at least spoken up.

But you didn't. Now you feel unsettled, even embarrassed. But it had all happened so quickly, and you didn't realize that what was happening was just wrong. The next thing you know, the bully has left the playground or the abusive parent has driven off. The moment of making your great stand against injustice came and went.

But don't feel bad. Like we discussed above, if you've lived in a world without God, chances are that no one has trained you to handle such circumstances. It would be like asking someone to run a 100-yard dash but without him ever having had any practice before. The problem is you didn't even know you were in the race.

The belief in God is one part awe of the universe and life, one part understanding a moral code, but yet another part understanding and recognizing evil, and the obligation to confront it. To know and love God is also to hate evil.

But we live in a world where very few learn of the notion of "evil." They instead teach you there are only "bad choices," and everything is relative to any given moment. So you gave that man the benefit of the doubt when he was beating his dog, humiliating his child, or bullying that kid. You tell yourself that perhaps something else was going on before you got there.

And then time passes, even if it is seconds. And you realize there's no way to spin it: what you saw was wrong, and you should have done something, but you didn't.

Those without God have not received training to recognize evil. Instead, the godless seem to wait for someone—or some movement—to educate them as to what constitutes evil.

If you don't see it yet, imagine you saw someone protesting on a campus *for* Israel, someone arguing that climate change might *not* be a real problem or that perhaps there should be *greater* restrictions on abortion rights. Or imagine a white cop in any altercation with a minority.

That's when you'll hear the godless make their stand. Why? Because those are the circumstances where they've learned to be hyper-vigilant. But the true evils in the world, such as the rise of Islamo-fascism, the treatment of women under Sharia Law, the destruction of the family under welfare and the general collapse of marriage, or any of the small confrontations I mentioned above? Not so much.

We need the Torah, the Bible, to serve as our guide and training manual. We need it to attune us to see evil when it arrives in front of us. That is what will make us vigilant and responsive when real evil presents itself.

Let's again recall Master Sgt. Roddie Edmonds, the brave leader in that German prisoner-of-war camp we discussed in the beginning of this book. He knew instantly to refuse the German commander's orders to give up the Jews among his fellow American prisoners. That's because Edmonds' continuous and consistent learning of God's teachings over many decades gave him that ability to recognize evil, and then to confront it—without hesitation.

Edmonds' lack of fear, his instant and powerful resolve, is likely what made the difference between the commander walking away from Edmonds, and putting the bullet into Edmonds' head.

Those who do not know God cannot rise to such a level of immediate and confident moral clarity, at least not the kind that Edmonds conveyed. But that was what was necessary at the moment. And America's moral certainty requiring unconditional wholesale surrender from both the Germans and the Japanese was what led America to win World War II.

But the godless know very little of moral clarity. In fact, they learn quite the opposite—that one man's terrorist is another man's freedom fighter. Everything is relative for them. They've learned at best to "listen to their heart" or use logic—whatever either of those mean.

The delay is dangerous. The uncertainty of what is good and what is evil leads to protracted wars and confrontations, and therefore to more deaths, and to the weakening of civilization itself.

Hamlet teaches us that hesitation kills. And in this additional, passive way, atheism kills yet again. The godless wait for others to tell them what causes they should fight. The problem is that those causes rarely have anything to do with real evil.

There will be no alarm clock that will conveniently chime for you when evil comes your way. You just have to train yourself for it, ahead of time. You can only do so through the Bible and God.

CHAPTER VIII

HEAR NO GOOD, SEE NO GOOD, AND BUILD NO GOOD

Reality denied comes back to haunt.
— Philip K. Dick,
Flow My Tears, the Policeman Said

There are two ways to be fooled. One is to believe what isn't true;
the other is to refuse to believe what is true.
— Søren Kierkegaard

God as "Fantasy"

When I was a little boy, I remember going to more than several birthday parties and puppet shows. There often was a clown who would entertain the kids with balloons, whacky sounds he would make with a spinning beanie and a kazoo.

And there was one children's party I went to when I was five or so. I remember it being an unusually hot summer day and everyone was sweating. And sure enough, a clown appeared, face-painted with baggy polka dot pants and a frizzy purple wig for hair. We all rushed to sit down and within minutes he was talking about his crazy monkey friend Charlie whom he couldn't find. "Won't you help me find him? I've got to tell him something!"

Well, wouldn't you know it? That silly monkey was right behind him! It was a puppet monkey that somehow climbed up that poor clown's back, appearing with a devilish grin just above the clown's left shoulder. And the clown didn't even know it!

"There he is, there he is!" we all screamed at the clown, pointing. But the clown seemed oblivious. He spun around, trying to find this Charlie. Meanwhile, the monkey just stayed put on the clown's back, spinning wildly with the clown.

"Where? Where?" the clown kept asking the kids ... And wherever he looked, Charlie was always right there but unseen to the clown. What crazy fun it was to see the clown going round and round in circles, always looking for Charlie, never realizing Charlie was *right there on his back. Right THERE!*

How frustrating it was to watch. What a silly clown, I thought. If only he just took a moment, he would find the very monkey he sought.

Now it is decades later. And I have come to believe that the atheist is no different than that clown. The atheist just refuses to look at what's right there for him to find. *Right there.*

But there is one difference with the atheist: He will not only refuse to look at the facts or the science behind God, he will dismiss you. He will mock you. He will contemptuously say belief in God is "fantasy." He will no more dignify a listen to the believer's arguments than he would the arguments of a Scientologist, a Moonie, a Branch Davidian, or any other cultist.

You see, he doesn't believe in fantasy, like you. He believes in *science.* You can blabber all you want with your logic and statistical and mathematical probabilities, but he'll just ignore it all. It's like you've shown up to the baseball game with your team, but the umpire refuses to acknowledge your very presence, looking past you like you're invisible. Next thing you know, he's declaring a forfeit. And you're just thinking, *what the hell is going on here?*

Ironically, *atheists* are the ones who claim to be the scientific ones. Worse yet, they tell you that *you're* not being scientific. You can read books from any major atheist (I've read most of them). They generally boil down to one point: God is just a replacement for those things we don't know. God is merely a "filler" to explain what we don't know (the "God of the gaps" theory). And you, the believer, reject science. To them, it's definitional.

But as we learn more—through the daylight of science—it'll all become clear. You know, like when you realize in the morning that the thing that looked like a monster in your closet was just a pile of clothes. Mystery solved. It'll all be like the end of a very long episode of *Scooby Doo,* when we realize the "monster" was just the owner of the factory, wearing a scary mask to frighten the public away so that he could buy the factory for himself for very little money.

Worse yet, they can't fathom that you believe in science, let alone that science actually might have been the very reason you came to God. They won't let you even present that argument, what with the very notion being so preposterous. You can believe in your fantasies all you want, but don't tell me you're scientific.

Yet I'll show you that it is the atheist who believes in fantasies, not the other way around. And I have come to believe that there is perhaps no greater cause of evil than the desire to believe it isn't there.

Let's return to our friend G. K. Chesterton—the one who observed that when you don't believe in God, you don't believe in nothing; you believe in anything. In fact, the nonbeliever will believe in virtually any absurd offering, so long as the conventional wisdom trumpets it often and loudly enough.

You can show him all the evidence that communism, fascism, and socialism has not only failed horribly but has led to the murder of tens of millions. You can show him that every society that has disavowed the basic structure of the Ten Commandments has either collapsed or at best treaded water. You could show him that every quest for utopia has failed, wherever and whenever anyone tried to practice it.[1] You can show him that belief in God leads to greater happiness and less depression. You can show him the scientifically insane improbabilities of the universe ever forming; of life ever starting, let alone evolving to different species; of the perfection of our Earth's chemical and atmospheric composition and its perfect placement not only in near perfect orbit around the sun, but its perfect placement in our solar system and even within our galaxy. You could show him the perfection of Earth's speed of rotation around its axis or the perfect role that our moon plays in maintaining Earth's spin on its axis.

You could show him how the Bible (the Torah) got every part of its science right (including the Big Bang and the timing of the arrival of the various animal species). You could show him how the fossil record, particularly the Cambrian explosion, utterly discredits the theory of pure evolution as Darwin postulated it. You could show him all the neurological science that shows the separation of the brain and the mind, and how no one can ever explain self-awareness or consciousness.

You could show him all these things and more, and then you can also argue the philosophical points we described above (our instincts for God and a hereafter, for purpose, creativity, beauty, music, humor and so on, none of which have any evolutionary purpose).

You can argue all these things, and how will the atheist respond? He'll say that despite the astronomical odds, well, that's just the way it happened and here we are to discuss it. As to everything that we can't presently explain, the atheist argues "Science will eventually show us."

Imagine a doctor who attempts to diagnose someone who expresses chest palpitations, shortness of breath, sharp shooting pains along his arm from time to time, and complains that he tastes copper in his mouth. The doctor decides that he will rule out the possibility of a heart condition, because he doesn't believe in such a thing as a "heart condition." But Science will eventually figure it out, he says.

So he turns to other possible explanations. Perhaps it's indigestion, perhaps it's back pain or some allergic reaction. But under *no* circumstances will he consider heart disease.

Why does he refuse to consider it? It doesn't really matter, but for some reason, he just has something against heart disease as a possible explanation. Maybe he doesn't believe there can be such a thing as "heart disease" and resents doctors who do. Or maybe he just has no experience in heart disease. Either way, ruling out heart disease is not only unprofessional but dangerous. In a real world situation like that, any patient who might later suffer a heart attack could successfully sue him for millions of dollars for not diagnosing the problem.

Likewise, if someone rejected the notion that the earth revolves around the sun, he would force himself to create a scientific paradigm that would explain the sun revolving around the earth. And scholars of the medieval ages did exactly that, concocting bizarre paradigms and purported rules of the heavens, with myriad exceptions to explain the movements they saw in the sky. That was all they could do in light of their refusal to deal with the much more elegant (and simple) explanation that the earth revolved around the sun.

But that is exactly what the atheist ultimately does when he rejects, from the outset, any possibility of the Creator of the universe. He's like the guy who refuses to consider that the computer might not be working because it's not plugged into an outlet, or that the car is not running because it doesn't have an engine. He's ruled those possibilities out.

And just like ruling out heart disease as a cause for his patient's ailment is dangerous, so too is ruling out God as an explanation to our universe. As we've discussed before, without God there can be no absolute morality. In the end, without true moral absolutes, might will always be the only thing which prevails. And that will change with each new strongman who comes along.

It is the godless who ignore reality. It is they who live in fantasy. And like our patient whose doctor refuses to consider heart disease as a possible explanation of his symptoms, we too must suffer the consequences of that fantasy.

Buying a Stairway to Heaven?

In centuries past, local towns would work to build massive churches which they knew would take not just years or decades to build, but centuries.

Think of what this would mean: that the first generation workers would know that they would live and die while working on the project. They would never experience the joy of completing their product. And likewise with the next generation and the next. It might literally take twenty generations working on the same church project before construction finished—give or take a generation or two.

Have you ever seen a project in today's cities where construction might take twenty years to complete, let alone generations? People would dismiss the very idea.

Also, many of the buildings of today do not necessarily last with time. Ask a real estate developer of most office buildings these days about how many years he hopes his building will last or what "legacy" they hope for, once they complete their project. They'll look at you oddly. You might as well ask what language you think the building will speak, or what flavor you plan to paint the walls.

They're not building the building for future generations. They're building it for practical uses for the next twenty or so years. There's nothing wrong with that, of course; that's business. And whatever the buyer of their building does with the building in ten years is his business.

But the churches of old barely need maintenance. Their builders sought no shortcuts; they devoted only the finest men, resources, planning, and materials to the project. They spared no expense. After all, they were building for time immemorial.

And perhaps that's the point. Are we building *any* buildings in the present day with a sense of their lasting purpose in the future, say for even 100 years from now?[2]

What is the difference? The buildings of old—lasting over generations to build—sought to build *for God*. They sought to build something that might glorify Him. They wanted something which might inspire and awe future generations. There was a sense that God was timeless, and that they had an obligation to advance God's Word for many generations to come.

Like we said: the nonbeliever just watches his own movie. Why would he care about *any* legacy? Why would an atheist seek to do anything of substance or creative at all? Why would he work hard or fight for the liberty of other, or to advance civilization at all? Why would he bother to look beyond the horizon of his own life?

Any efforts he undertakes to "make a mark" in his world would be in defiance of everything he believes (or doesn't believe, to be more accurate). If there is no afterlife and you become nothing upon your death, why would you ever look beyond yourself in *any* way at all?

Without God, there should be only one mission: Get as many prizes, toys, vacations, and sexual and other thrill-seeking adventures along the way as you can. Hopefully, you'll expire at just the moment you've spent all the money you've accumulated throughout your life, like making sure you use all the pre-paid tickets you bought at the local carnival before you leave the park. What a waste otherwise.

I remember Led Zeppelin's classic "Stairway to Heaven" from the early '70s, Like many lyrics of that era and now, the lyrics are somewhat all over the place. There's the line that repeats a few times: "…And she's buying a stairway to heaven."

Why is she "buying" the stairway? I remember wondering. It made no sense. Shouldn't she be helping to "build" it?

Maybe that's it: Heaven is no longer something you work for. You apparently don't build your world toward heaven. It's what someone else is supposed to do for you.

And Now a Word from Atheism....

And now let's talk about the great social contributions of the atheists. They advocate that a world without God would be better, so surely they can show the great contributions of atheists advancing *their* cause. And no doubt it will be far greater than whatever those Jews and Christians ever offered.

Well . . . no, actually: there is nothing. Well, wait: I *did* once see a sign on the freeway that indicated that the group "American Atheists" was sponsoring a section of a freeway. So that was nice. I don't know of much else atheists as a group ever achieved. But there you go: something. It's not a shut-out, after all.

What are you talking about, the atheist will protest: we atheists *love* science. We're all *about* science, they will tell you. Science has all the answers, and your "God" is nothing more than a lazy substitute for all things we don't yet know. Christianity and all that pursuit of "faith" actively *suppressed* science.

The atheist will say science and the scientific method is *his* "messiah," as it were. Look at any atheist and you'll be looking at a person of empiricism, logic, rigorous and skeptical examination, observation and testing, and ultimately debate from the scientific community that takes us from scientific theory to scientific law. In short, he is a relentless pursuer of truth, wherever that may lead him. *That* is what atheism has given to the world.

Here's the problem with this argument: there is no evidence of atheism serving the goals of science. Just as with the judiciary, charity, hospitals, education for all, and for that matter civilization itself, science does not, has not, and cannot come from godlessness. It never has. It has come predominantly from the Judeo-Christian mind-set.

You don't have to like it. You can argue that it somehow would have come about eventually, regardless of faith. But you cannot alter history.

Where is the *good* that atheism has done? On behalf of atheism, there have been *no* inventions, *no* medical advances, *no* universities, *no* schools, *no* judicial systems, *no* scouting program for boys and girls, *no* YMCAs, and *no* charitable organizations for the poor or otherwise. Atheism has not even produced a single anti-alcoholism or rehab program of any consequence, such as Alcoholics Anonymous (quick extra credit question—who created *that* wonderful and highly effective organization?). Atheism did not give the world the Magna Carta, the Constitution, nor even our notion of freedom. Nor did it end slavery or advance civil rights.

Atheists—on behalf of atheism—have not offered virtually any program to advance goodness of any kind in our scientific, cultural, or economic lives. The atheist cannot claim any credit for anything but chaos, or totalitarianism. Neither is good.

But the American Atheist Society did sponsor that freeway. You have to give them that.

But the atheist will retort: That's misleading; the point is that no one ever died *in the name of atheism*. The atheist will announce this as if it has significance. It does not. So what if no one died in the specific *name* of atheism? The godless ideologies, particularly communism, lacked *any* notion of spirituality, let alone God. It was that lack of any core moral principles that unmoored communist and fascist leaders from any sense that they had to answer to anyone higher than them. And so anything was possible.

The atheist will proclaim that such an argument is an unfair correlation. Just because communism was godless does not mean it was the godlessness *in* communism that caused its horrific murder spree of millions.

But that's trying to distinguish the snake from his venom. And wait just one moment: doesn't the atheist have *no* problem asserting that because some agents of the Catholic and Protestant faiths did bad things in the name of God, that therefore all things associated with God must be bad? In fact, for atheists, it's one of the great "proofs" that there must be no God at all.

Remember that?

By contrast, when the believer points out the horrific crimes of communism and fascism and then argues that it was their godlessness which caused wholesale slaughters of hundreds of millions of people and so godlessness is destructive, the atheist cries foul. He'll suddenly insist that the godlessness in communism and fascism had *nothing* to do with communism's evil.

And never mind that there is *nothing inherent or foundational in the teaching of Judaism or Christianity* that mandated anti-Semitism, Inquisitions, or the slaughter of anyone. On the contrary, those faiths at least demand tolerance, hatred of evil, the primacy of family and virtue, and morality in general.

Atheism and godlessness expects no such thing. Such things are irrelevant to atheism, because, as we've established, it is an ideology about nothing.

But that won't stop the atheist from taking offense when you argue that godlessness as a governing ideology leads to horror. But it was just so with communism and fascism—which either *foundationally* required godlessness (communism) or rejected the moral codes of both Judaism and Christianity (fascism).

And that leads us to our second point: it *was* the godlessness part of both communism and fascism that was instrumental to both their central missions. How so? Both sought to unravel all the world's prior moral order and civilization. The Ten Commandments were no longer of any consequence under either ideology. *All* notion of morality, at least as religion developed it, was irrelevant. Only the state and *its* vision of what was proper mattered. Religion was a hindrance to that unbridled pursuit. Just who in the state will lay down those morals and values? Don't worry, we'll figure that out later.

Marx not only referred to religion as the "opiate of the masses" but also stated: "Communism begins where atheism begins." In his famous October 2, 1920, speech, Vladimir Lenin unequivocally stated, "We do not believe in God" and further insisted that "all worship of a divinity is a necrophilia."[3] The description serves a particularly offensive double-whammy: both to show contempt for religion as an odious enterprise doing horrifically perverse things, while also suggesting that religion itself was an archaic or "dead" concept.

Lenin also wrote in a November 1913 letter that "any religious idea, *any idea of any God at all,* any flirtation even with a God is the most inexpressible foulness ... the most dangerous foulness, the most shameful 'infection'" (emphasis added).[4]

Not convinced yet? Lenin wrote in 1913 that "[t]here can be nothing more abominable than religion." On December 25, 1919, Christmas Day, Comrade Lenin issued the following order, in his own writing: "To put up with 'Nikola' [the religious holiday] would be stupid—the entire Cheka must be on the alert to see to it that those who do not show up for work because of 'Nikola' [Christmas] are shot." Under Lenin, this was not an isolated occurrence.[5]

Lenin and his associate Trotsky soon created groups with names like the Society of the Godless, also known as the League of the Militant Godless. Those groups advanced antireligious propaganda in the USSR. This institutionalized hostility to faith continued on with his political progeny, Joseph Stalin, and even Nikita Khrushchev.[6]

Atheism was front and center to the communist experiment. Even those communists unable to secure political power—and thus lacking the ability to persecute believers—still did their best to persecute organized religion and ridicule the idea of the existence of God. Communists were proud and militant about their atheism.[7] Communists did not merely try to block or halt religious faith but to reverse it.[8]

Nor did this communist hostility to God confine itself to Russia. In Romania, the communists not only forbade religious practice and jailed ministers and believers but used torture routinely to beat the faith out of them, as if they were rugs you take outside and pound to get the dust out. And the more degrading it was, the better.

One example was Richard Wurmbrand, a pastor who endured fourteen years in a Romanian prison. He later detailed some of the cruelty he witnessed in testimony before the U.S. Congress and in his famous *Tortured for Christ*, first published in 1967. As he wrote:

> Thousands of believers from churches of all denominations were sent to prison at that time. Not only were clergymen put in jail, but also simple peasants, young boys and girls who witnessed for their faith. . . .
>
> A pastor by the name of Florescu was tortured with red-hot iron pokers and with knives. He was beaten very badly. Then starving rats were driven

into his cell through a large pipe. He could not sleep because he had to defend himself all the time. If he rested a moment, the rats would attack him.

He was forced to stand for two weeks, day and night. . . . Eventually, they brought his fourteen-year-old son to the prison and began to whip the boy in front of his father, saying that they would continue to beat him until the pastor said what they wished him to say. The poor man was half mad. He bore it as long as he could, then he cried to his son, "Alexander, I must say what they want! I can't bear your beating anymore!" The son answered, "Father, don't do me the injustice of having a traitor as a parent. Withstand! If they kill me, I will die with the words, 'Jesus and my fatherland'." The communists, enraged, fell upon the child and beat him to death, with blood spattered over the walls of the cell. . . . Florescu was never the same after seeing this.

Wurmbrand also experienced such torture himself. His captors carved his body into a dozen separate parts. They burned eighteen holes in him. Among the many forms of torture he endured was the "refrigerator cell"—a large frozen icebox. The believer would be locked inside with little or no clothing. Prison doctors would peer through an opening until they saw symptoms of freezing to death, then they would signal the guards, who would rush in and defrost the victims. They would be thawed and then re-frozen within minutes of death. They would repeat this process, over and over again.[9]

All of this, of course, required the captors' considerable effort. As Wurmbrand wrote: "I have seen communists whose faces while torturing believers shone with rapturous joy. They cried out while torturing the Christians, 'We are the devil!'" He called communism "a force of evil" that could only be countered by a greater spiritual force, "the Spirit of God." He added:

> The communist torturers often [told me], "There is no God, no hereafter, no punishment for evil. *We can do what we wish.*" I heard one torturer say, "I thank God in whom I don't believe, that I have lived to this hour when I can express all the evil in my heart."[10] (emphasis added)

In his May 1966 testimony before the Internal Security Subcommittee of the U.S. Senate, Wurmbrand revealed that the communists crucified Christians. They would tie them to crosses for four days and nights. But the communists had a perverse imagination, and sought to ensure that those crucified would suffer *greater* humiliation than even Jesus himself:

> The crosses were placed on the floor and hundreds of prisoners had to fulfill their bodily necessities over the faces and bodies of the crucified ones. Then the crosses were erected again and the communists jeered and mocked: "Look at your Christ! How beautiful he is! What fragrance he brings from heaven!" . . . [A]fter being driven nearly insane with tortures, a priest was forced to consecrate human excrement and urine and give Holy Communion to Christians in this form.

The communists' obsession revealed—ironically—a quasi-religious devotion to the goal of eliminating faith.[11] The destruction of all religion was one of communism's primary offerings, if not its principal one: no less than a great white shark's teeth are primarily for ripping its prey's meat off its bones. Communism's *goal* was to end and unmoor itself of all prior understandings and assumptions of morality. It was to begin anew with a glorious day when the state provided all—and demanded all. The individual, with all his notion of freedom and free will, was to be a thing of the past.

Fascism was no better. It offered a "religion of the state," which meant, in effect, no religion at all. Benito Mussolini's rambling *The Doctrine of Fascism* (1932) explained that individuality and all notions of morality were to give way to the State, which would decide such things. As he explained: "... Fascism is not only a system of government but also and above all a system of thought." As he elaborated:

> The Fascist State, as a higher and more powerful expression of personality, is a force, but a spiritual one. . . . The Fascist State is an inwardly accepted standard and rule of conduct, a discipline of the whole person; it permeates the will no less than the intellect. . . .
>
> Fascism, in short, is not only a law-giver and a founder of institutions, but an educator and a promoter of spiritual life. It aims at refashioning not only the forms of life but their content—man, his character, and his faith. To achieve this [purpose] it enforces discipline and uses authority, entering into the soul and ruling with undisputed sway.[12]

Mussolini upheld tradition instead of spirituality. In fact, tradition in and of itself was the new spirituality, the only kind that now mattered: "We uphold moral and traditional values which socialism neglects or despises." But, he argues, "Fascism has a horror of anything implying an arbitrary mortgage on the mysterious future."[13]

In other words, in fascism, the state will control everyone's destiny, and no ridiculous notion of God can interfere with that. You know—like communism.

While the fascists paid lip-service to the church and Christianity, it was just a ruse to dupe the large Christian population into its godless totalitarianism: In 1929, shortly after the fascists gained the political support of the Roman Catholic Church through the Lateran Treaty, the church threatened to excommunicate Mussolini because of his efforts to silence Catholic newspapers. By the late 1930s, Mussolini became much more hostile to the church, repeatedly denouncing the Catholic Church and discussing ways to get rid of the pope.[14] He took the position that the "papacy was a malignant tumor in the body of Italy and must 'be rooted out once and for all,' because there was no room in Rome for both the Pope and himself."[15] Not surprisingly, Mussolini was an avowed atheist until the very end of his life.[16]

Hitler was quite appreciative of Mussolini's brand of fascism and ended up adopting it wholeheartedly for Germany. Likewise, the National Socialists of Germany employed similar anticlerical policies, but even more aggressively. The Gestapo confiscated hundreds of monasteries in Austria and Germany, evicted clergymen and laymen alike, and often replaced crosses with swastikas.[17] Church leaders who had referred to the swastika as the "Devil's Cross" met swift reprisals: The Nazis banned their youth organizations, limited their meetings and censored or banned various Catholic periodicals.[18] Government officials eventually found it necessary to place "Nazis into editorial positions in the Catholic press." Eventually, the Gestapo arrested up to 2,720 clerics, mostly Catholics, who then sent them to Germany's Dachau concentration camp.[19]

I say that atheism is endemic to communism and fascism, but such totalitarianism is also endemic to atheism. To be an atheist, you ultimately *must believe in some form of totalitarianism*: fascism, communism, or any other form of government domination of society. You reject morality and truth because, after all, what is morality and truth?

So you turn to the state for its offer of all-encompassing mandates on every aspect of life, from how much water and fuel we can use to the monitoring and filtering of speech, to the regulation of how much we can support a political candidate, to ever-increasing mandates regarding sexual education, and to the forced tolerance regarding sexuality and sexual identity out of the norm.

That is just what we see among the leaders of the communist and fascist nations, or more appropriately "statist" nations. They are not so much statists who happen to be atheists. They are atheists who have obtained control, and they have no notions of boundaries to keep them in check. Communism, fascism, and statism are the *result*.

People will argue that there is a difference between communism and fascism. There is a difference, indeed, but it's a difference I suspect very few of their victims care about. It's akin to the difference between an alligator and a crocodile: Sure, we understand there's a technical difference between them, but we don't really care: it's just better not to be near either of them.

And now back to our regularly scheduled program.

The "Good Atheist"

In law school during the late 1980s, one of my professors would proudly declared he was a communist, and that he preferred a communist vision for America.

"How's that working out for you?" one of the cheekier students commented one day during class, after the professor had yet again made a passing reference to the joys of communism.

The professor smiled in dismissive contempt, as if to make clear that he had dealt with this question many times before: "Communism as Stalin and others practiced it was not 'real' communism. Communism, if done correctly, can be and would be very good." He went on to explain that Stalin, Pol-Pot, Ho Chi Minh, Ceauşescu, and every other communist leader managed to twist and distort communism only as a vehicle for their own glory and power. Some of the students nodded their heads as he spoke: Yes, quite right. If only, if only...

So there were good communists, he implied. People like *him*. The theory was more or less: "I'm a communist, and I'm a good person. . . . Therefore, communism is not inherently bad."

And that was that. The flow of the conversation had gotten back to law and he continued with his lecture. But I think I would have asked the obvious follow-up question: Where has communism or godlessness as a governing principle of *any* country ever worked?

At the time, I didn't know enough to challenge him. But I doubt he would've been able to answer meaningfully. Communism worked only in the far corners of his utopian fantasies.

And it dawned on me since then that many atheists make a similar argument: "I am a good atheist, so this shows we don't need religion or God."

First, it forgets the foundation of why the atheist even has a notion of "Good." Such a person is like the bipolar patient who has been taking his medication, and now feels psychologically balanced on a regular basis, but decides he doesn't need the medication anymore. He forgets it was the drugs that stabilized him in the first place.

It is the same with religious wisdom, carried on through approximately a hundred generations. But because it has carried over through so many generations, it gets harder to remember that there was an actual origin to the goodness. If we don't know the history of this baton-passing nature of goodness, we might think civilization was always so, and that goodness is natural in each of us.

But unlike the bipolar patient, who has his own personal history to look back on, we have no immediate Sodom and Gomorrah in our insular Western civilization to see what a world without God might look like. It was just too long ago. But the Judeo-Christian values we created were what brought us *out* of Sodom and Gomorrah, and which continue to keep us from falling back into it. Think of it like a rocket that needs enough escape velocity to keep us from getting sucked back into an evil planet's gravitational pull.

The second fallacy is the notion that goodness is something that can come easily to you, even without God. While of course there are many nice atheists, they're not necessarily nice *because* of their atheism. They don't pause to think that their very notion of kindness, charity, and general community responsibility derives directly from the thousands of years of culture and law that our abiding faith in God has shaped.

The third fallacy is that you can learn God or goodness on your own. This assumes goodness is either natural or instinctive (a notion for which there is no evidence), or that goodness (from God or otherwise) is easy to learn, like learning how to burp.

Thinking so is like thinking you can come up with Calculus on your own. Put more simply, it's like a young teenager who thinks he can operate a car without ever having had a driving lesson. He might end up driving just fine, but it's probably not a good idea.

Not believing in God, the atheist may want to believe there is another natural, nonreligious, source for his desire for good. But he can't find it. If he is honest with himself, he'll appreciate that goodness and civilization wasn't always so. He'll also realize that the Judeo-Christian moral code that most of us live by today is the historical exception.

Atheism does not include a notion of "goodness." Why would it? Goodness is as relevant to atheism as the Magna Carta is to Godzilla.

CHAPTER IX

RADICAL ISLAM

The atheist will point to radical Islam to challenge the notion that religion is a positive force by noting (correctly) that here is a religion where the extremists among them devastate and wreak havoc upon society, precisely *because* of their faith. ISIS engages in systematic rape and torture, burns and beheads its captured, and engages in such horrific cruelty to little children that it truly evokes the Canaanites and other barbaric cultures of the past.[1] Al Qaeda and other Muslim groups have consistently sought the terrorist slaughter of innocents throughout the world, most infamously the attacks of September 11, 2001, in which approximately 3,000 men, women and children met their random deaths after radical Muslim terrorists coordinated crashes of four commercial jetliners into the Twin Towers of the World Trade Center and the Pentagon.

In Europe, Islamists have committed random beheadings and random large-scale attacks, such as the December 2015 simultaneous murder sprees in a concert hall, a soccer stadium, and at restaurants; and still later in Belgium (massive gun attack at the Brussels airport) and Nice (a truck attack plowed over and killed many people) and Berlin (another truck attack).

This is to say nothing of the routine gang-rapes at concerts, routine burning of cars, beatings of ordinary European citizens, and the creation of the so-called "No-Go" zone—meaning areas just around major metropolitan cities even the police don't enter. They are places of horrific living and crimes, where no native European would survive.

And that is just modern-day horrors. The history of Islam is rife with brutal conquest, forced conversions and rapes, and the slaughter of millions in the process.

So this, the atheist argues, must be a big hole in the so-called rule that atheism kills, or that God doesn't kill.

First, remember that the title of this book is *Atheism Kills*. It is not *Only Atheism Kills*. Other things kill, too. And *radical* Islam and the perversion of God kills, too.

Second, and most critically, radical Islam is *not* the pursuit of God, no more than a malignant cluster of cancer cells in your body is the same as the rest of you.

But it is fair for the atheist to bring it up: We should devote discussion to this because radical Islam *does* hold Allah up as its pretext for its horror. It is certainly not atheism.

And the way to respond to it is not simply to say that it is not about God. Clearly these monsters are doing things in the name of Allah (as opposed to the Judeo-Christian God, but let's assume we're talking about the same God for purposes of this chapter).

But this is categorically the opposite of what the Bible teaches and (hopefully) what today's moderate Islam teaches. We've discussed before that human beings can and have abused and distorted just above everything—including God. But that does not render God to be evil Himself.[2] We gave examples earlier of how people and governments have abused the military, the police, and the judiciary and so on. That doesn't mean the very *concepts* of a military, a police force, or a judicial system are inherently wrong or that we should abandon them.

Even if you consider radical Islam to be a big exception to the positive force of religion, it does not indict religion generally, nor undermine religion's usefulness and critical role in civilization generally. Nor does it give godlessness (atheism) points in its column.

And such horror can't be what true Islam teaches. Even many atheists will denounce those who try to paint Islam in such broad strokes. But we can agree on this: Any ideology, or branch of an ideology, that encourages mass torture and murder, rape, wife beating and suppression of women in general, slavery and genital mutilation; demands the death of anyone who converts out of it; and refuses to tolerate the existence of anyone who thinks differently than them, is no good religion at all. And I am confident that the moderate Muslim believes this as well.

The fact that some monsters have used Islam—or any religion, for that matter—as a vehicle to commit mayhem does not change the fact that they are exceptions to religion's ultimate mission of civilization and morality. We have shown from our cursory review of history that the world would be far more cruel, chaotic, and pointless without God.

We have shown that the net-positive of the Judeo-Christian pursuit of God is overwhelming. By contrast, atheism does not promote personal or societal elevation of any kind. Unlike with Judaism and Christianity, such notions of growth are not what atheism is *about*. In fact, an atheist who may believe in any of these things does so *in spite of his atheism,* not because of it. He certainly cannot claim they arose out of atheistic teachings.

Remember: goodness is the exception to atheism, whereas evil is the exception to faith.

Ultimately, the question may boil down to this: would you rather have a country run as a theocracy or a world run without God at all? Just from the numbers of victims alone, a theocracy should be the easy winner. It's not that I am advocating *for* theocracy: far from that. But even between these two undesirable governing alternatives, the theocracy at least would lead to *less* horror, if only because a moral code would still be present—as opposed to one where anything goes, anything can happen, and where there is "logic" for anything.

We need to focus on the neighborhood from which mayhem and horror truly grows: The neighborhood where there is no God. That is the ultimate No-Go Zone.

CHAPTER X

THE END OF DISTINCTIONS

Religion and the Eight-Track Tape

In 2001 a new gadget arrived on the market. Yes, it was another cool product from Apple, but *this* one was different. It completely overtook a fledgling market: the MP3 digital music player.

They called it the *iPod,* and it organized and accessed your digital music simply, cheaply, and with better than "good enough" sound quality. It was cool, small, and convenient. Now you could take your entire music library everywhere with you. It was intuitive and elegant at the same time. Downloads for new music were only a click away.

It would soon wipe out the entire retail music industry. Within a span of only two years, major music retail stores such as Wherehouse, Tower Records, and Virgin Records all came tumbling down. In Britain, by 2010, seventy-five percent of all independent music shops closed.[1] Now, other than collector items stores, there are no stores to visit to buy music.

Likewise, in 2007, Internet-based Amazon introduced its first digital reading device, the Kindle. Amazon soon made book after book available digitally, and more cheaply. The Kindle allowed for all sorts of other conveniences, too. Soon, the retail bookstores had to compete with their own digital readers.

In the end, all this did was hasten bookstores' own demise. It didn't help that people could more easily find traditional books on Amazon, buy them for less, and have them delivered for free. Within four years, mega chain Borders Bookstores would file for bankruptcy. Thousands of other independent bookstores closed by 2012.[2] In the following years, the last remaining mega-bookstore chain, Barnes & Noble, would continue to struggle financially.[3] To the extent consumers even patronize a bookstore today, it's usually a quaint local bookstore where they go more for their attendant coffee houses and intellectual ambiance, but not as a destination to actually buy books. After all, *that* they could do online.

The arrival of Netflix in 1999 tells a similar story. Netflix first offered rentals by mail, with no late fees. The service was quick, reliable, and cheap. Its main rival, Blockbuster, responded too slowly and lost substantial revenues by the time it finally decided to match Netflix's services. By 2008, Netflix offered streaming of its rentals online. The remaining video stores could not compete with such immediate "couch-potato access," not even the goliath and iconic Blockbuster super chain. By late 2013, Blockbuster rented its last video (intriguingly, it was a movie named *This Is the End*, a raw comedy about the Apocalypse).[4]

Soon, Netflix, Amazon, YouTube, Facebook and Google (among many others) were competing for eyeballs seeking movies and other video entertainment. As a consequence, as of 2017, movie theaters have had to make more of an effort to retain customers who can otherwise see most anything they want on their laptops or smartphones.[5]

Likewise, Amazon and multiple other online retailers soon were taking on the world of retail itself. The notion that a store down the street might be out of stock of any product was no longer acceptable. The result? A "bloodbath" for traditional retail stores.[6]

And lest you think such creative destruction only began with the Internet, remember that the cellphone obliterated the car phone *and* the public payphone, the latter which you once could find everywhere. And it wasn't just recent industries that suffered: the car replaced the horse—and all its attendant services (the whip, the saddle, the horseshoe, the buggy, and so on); the airplane replaced travel by ship and train, the light bulb replaced the kerosene lamp (which in turn had replaced the candle), and the refrigerator replaced the iceman. And so on.

Why do we discuss the demise of industries? Hang on; we'll get there.

I remember a passer-by noting the "Going out of Business" sign for a CD music store in the year 2008 or so. He was with his son. The son asked why the store was closing.

"They're no longer relevant," the father explained. "The world changed around them, and they didn't see it coming."

No longer relevant. Remember that now.

Could it be that as secularism overtakes religion as the primary driving force of Western civilization, that so many of the distinctions that we value (good and evil, parent and child, holy and unholy, and so on [see more below]) are becoming just *no longer relevant?*

Without God, could it be that even our quests for democracy, liberty, and our notions of personal freedom are becoming relics of the past? Could it be that they are going the way of buggy whips, books and record stores? Maybe civilization hasn't yet come to realize that the common citizen–or consumer, if you prefer—isn't interested in our wares anymore?

When cars first appeared, horse and buggies still existed; they were still the norm. Cars were just a novelty, the new-fangled contraption that some people had but were not the main form of transportation. But things changed: today horse-and-buggy rides are the novelty (that you pay a lot of money for your kids to ride when you can't think of something better to do). In much faster fashion, e-readers were a novelty, and now they are the norm.

Change happens beyond just matters of innovation. The notion of freedom of speech is changing. Many today understand it's important in the abstract, but it's an esoteric concept for many: Despite the great saying from Evelyn Beatrice Hall—"I may disapprove of what you have to say, but I will defend to the death your right to say it"—I wonder if most people are really willing to defend my right to disagree with them, let alone die for it. Try going on most college campuses these days and see how students "defend to the death" your right to disagree on affirmative action, same-sex marriage, abortion, climate change, the Israeli-Arab conflict, or even the minimum wage.

That passion, that "moxy" for true freedom of expression, was much more real in the past. It's just not there anymore. Not relevant, as it were.

Likewise, churches and church attendance are becoming an old-world novelty, especially in Europe. You'll visit a church on occasion, but more to pass the time because it's something to do before that 10:15 train ride to Florence, and you've heard it may be historical and what not.

There are many more such losses in our society, but if I had to sum up the greatest loss in our civilization over the past 100 or so years, it would be the almost imperceptible *loss of distinctions*—which we discuss next. They seem to happen so slowly, like the snow on your car melting away as the day gets warmer. You don't see it disappear right away, but if you leave to see a movie and come back, you'll see it's gone.

That is, if you care enough to notice.

Cruel to Be Kind? It's All Good.

"He who is kind to the cruel will be cruel to the kind."
— *Talmudic proverb*

You've gotta be cruel to be kind, in the right measure
Cruel to be kind, it's a very good sign
Cruel to be kind, means that I love you baby
— *Nick Lowe, Labour of Lust (1979)*

I have not cited much from the Bible or other ancient religious sources. I have not done so because, as a former atheist, I know how an atheist would dismiss the rest of my discussion the moment I make any such reference. They'll argue that my argument is merely self-referencing and even circular. The atheist argues that the believer's argument is that "the Bible must be real because the Bible says so." And that *would* be circular—*if* that's what we argued.

But the Torah and related Jewish texts convey unique timeless wisdom about human nature, such as the notion above, that if we treat evil as good, we will soon treat good as evil. Or as the Talmud has observed: "Those who are kind to the cruel will be cruel to the kind."

One of the best examples is the never-ending demonizing of religious clergy and Christianity generally, while turning a blind eye to radical Islam, or even excusing it. Or maybe more poignantly, the demonizing of democratic and free Israel while championing Israel's dictatorship enemies.[7] The United Nations routinely condemns Israel, resolution after resolution, while remaining virtually silent on North Korea, Somalia, Syria, Iran, or any other dictatorial regime in history since the creation of the United Nations.[8]

How can the world be so oblivious to such apparent differences? Because without God, distinctions do not matter. Like records and bookstores, they have become less and less *relevant*.

God is in many ways about the observance of distinctions, particularly the distinction of good and evil, the holy and the unholy. In fact, the Hebrew word for holy, *Kadosh*, means "separateness," that which is "set apart"—the opposite of the ordinary and earthly.

When God fades, these distinctions fade, too. But only with such separations and related distinctions can society move forward and improve to become the just society that a God-based society seeks. It cannot occur—despite the best intentions—solely through secular means.

The failure to observe distinctions can lead to great horror. For years the local authorities literally did nothing in Rotherham, England, knowing a ring of mostly Pakistani men were routinely brutalizing and raping over 1,400 underage girls in a virtually open program of sexual slavery, over a period of sixteen years.[9] Police arrested some parents who tried to rescue their children from their abusers. And some police officers even dismissed the claims of the rapes of the children by saying that the sex had been consensual.[10]

That is also why the judicial system in America and abroad routinely lets out murderers sentenced to life, who end up murdering again—sometimes in equally horrific ways and on multiple occasions—only weeks after their release.[11] So, in the name of compassion to those who commit horrific evil, the system ultimately ends up inflicting horror to innocents.

Those who are kind to the cruel will soon be cruel to the kind.

When God fades, there is less and less focus on distinctions, so there are fewer measures to help you judge what is right and wrong, bad and good. Civilization itself becomes less meaningful, because the building blocks of civilization such as churches, synagogues, and even armies and political structures become silly throwbacks of the past, or even frauds, in the eyes of the godless.

Eventually there is no context to what anything is in relationship to anything else. That evisceration of distinctions ultimately leads to great danger. We become like a two-year old child in a petting zoo, but with animals of every kind, including poisonous reptiles and wild carnivores. To him that lion is just as fluffy as that sheep.

To the godless, people are just sophisticated animals, countries are just land masses with people, cultures are just different kinds of food, and churches are merely old buildings. When you have little or no ability to discern the valuable and the holy from the trivial and the unholy, there is nothing to be truly passionate about, nothing to consider meaningful. It's all a meaningless morass, like the strewn rubble of buildings mixed together following an earthquake: yes, it's all the same material, but they're just not what they used to be.

Without God, there can never be any meaningful appreciation of the distinction between good and evil. That is why, when a radical Muslim attacks with the goal of massacring as many innocents as possible by way of knives, semi-automatic weapons, explosions, or trucks they use to plow into crowds, most people race to proclaim that the matter has nothing to do with any interpretation of Islam, and insist that Islam is a religion of peace. Likewise, every time there is a mass-shooting anywhere, such as the horrific 2012 murder melee of children and their teachers at Sandy Hook Elementary in Connecticut, the go-to response is to blame guns, not to deal with evil men who've used the guns.

In short, they do not seek to even address, let alone neutralize, evil. This in turn leads only to a *passive acceptance of evil*, which only invites and emboldens evil to grow and lead to more horrific killing.

And so the cycle is complete: cruelty to the kind and innocent.

Why do they allow this? Why do they not dig deeper? Because recognizing and respecting distinctions involve hard work and vigilance, just as would maintaining a garden or home, or preserving law and order. In the end, it ultimately forces the painful realization that God is the primary creator—and reason—for distinctions.

So many people, the concepts of "good" and "evil" are *not an issue for them*. Those are not serious words in their vocabulary. Just ask your local atheist. Such people instead see everything only in the context of oppressor and oppressed, a paradigm which immediately appeals to their first visceral layer of emotions. They don't want to go deeper. Even though the distinction between good and evil would seem an obvious one, people would rather not think in those terms. After all, if one of God's roles is to judge, that might be a bit … well, judgmental. And who wants that?

There is even a distinction in the afterlife—heaven for those who have engaged in the good, and hell for those who have engaged in evil. But where there is no God, there is no need even for that final accounting.

After all: no God, no judgment.

The end of the distinctions does not stop there. Here are many distinctions in our society which are rapidly disappearing:

1. men and women;
2. entertainment and pornography (the mainstreaming and acceptance of pornography);
3. shame and honor;
4. parent and child;
5. teacher and student;
6. formal and informal (we seem to expect formal attire only at weddings, funerals, and the Oscars; otherwise it's a "leggings" culture, with clothing optional areas and

events in various cities and throughout much of Europe [there is even a new restaurant, Bunyadi, which recently opened in London, where its only unique offering is that you may dine while naked. Upon its first months of opening, there was a wait list of 40,000.[12] Is the food good? Does that matter?]);

7. police and criminals;

8. America and the rest of the world (all cultures are the same; multiculturalism; the call for open borders, the failure to enforce immigration laws);

9. "Life" vs. "not life" (partial birth abortions are increasingly more acceptable; Dr. Kermit Gosnell's murders of late-term and live babies—rendering him the greatest serial murderer in American history—received virtually no mention in the media[13]);

10. art and garbage;

11. talented or athletic versus untalented and unathletic (everyone gets an award; no one keeps score; there are no winners or losers). See related: art and garbage, above;

12. elegant language and profane language (swearing more routinely accepted as part of ordinary conversation). See related: art and garbage, above;

13. people who come from hostile countries and people who come from non-hostile countries ("profiling"). We must treat everyone from every country in the world as if they have an equal likelihood of blowing us up;

14. animals and people (we are just sophisticated animals; eating chicken is like a "holocaust on your plate"[14]);

15. family and all other interpretations of family ("Family" can mean anything now. Any couple of any kind can adopt children; single motherhood is just as valued as a family as a mother and a father);

16. history versus the present (there's a past we can learn from? What past? Ask young people today about the most basic foundations of America; many won't know the significance of the year 1776, or even which country America battled in its War of Independence);

17. science and political or social agenda (climate change; evolution);

18. heroes and those who don't deserve the title "hero" (the heroes of Iraq, Afghanistan, Vietnam, Korea and WWII, and first-responders and law enforcement and Rosa Parks on the one hand; and Edward Snowden, OJ Simpson, Che Guevara and Fidel Castro, sports and entertainment celebrities, or people who come out of the closet or announce that they are transgender [Bruce aka Caitlin Jenner], on the other hand);

19. Cultures of life and cultures of death (all religions are the same; all religions engage in "violent extremism;" all religions seek peace).

Recognizing and maintaining such distinctions are essential to the success of any civilization that aspires to maintain and improve law and order, economic prosperity and more importantly the general betterment of its citizens.

But instead of appreciating these distinctions, we seem to be doing our damnedest to erase them, one social trend or policy at a time: men being allowed into women's bathrooms and locker rooms; non-enforcements at the border; students able to talk back or even swear at teachers; the trivialization of marriage for couples (while in the same breath insisting that marriage is imperative for same-sex couples); the legalization of drugs, the expansion of gambling, the disregard of America's positive role in history, the minimizing of our military, and the mainstreaming of pornography.

Meanwhile, we are starting to create distinctions where there should be none (or in some cases, reviving old ones we hoped to eradicate long ago): minorities versus white people (whites have fared better because of "white privilege"), employee and employer (an obsession with mandating vacation days, sick leave, minimum wage and overtime, leading to increased tensions between them); the many kinds of "genders" beyond just men and women (examples: cis-gender, gender queer, intersex, and pansexual); Muslims (the "vast majority are good" while the "vast majority" of Christians and Christian history are bad; rape victims of those who are raped by Middle Eastern or Northern African descent, and those who are raped by anyone else[15]; those who believe in God (they are bad or ignorant), and those who are secular (good and sophisticated); and, most notably, the so-called separation of Church and State.[16]

Part of our jobs as humans is to learn what we *should* distinguish, and what we should not. It is hard work. But distinguish we must, lest we fail to see evil when it arrives upon our shores, whether as a nation or within our communities, and lest we then forget our obligation to confront that evil, like the men who stood paralyzed in the École Polytechnique while a madman slaughtered their female colleagues. They had no idea that one of their *distinctive* roles as men was to physically fight evil, and to protect women. That this statement might seem out-of-date to some should sadden us all.

It is telling that, in the creation of the world, the Torah describes the creation of the universe and the earth by way of *separation*: there is the dividing of the light from the darkness, earth from the sea and sky, woman from man, and so on. Still later there is the division of clean and unclean, kosher and not kosher. These are the distinctions that allowed the world, and ultimately civilization, to form.

Distinctions—like books, video stores, music stores and just about everything else there is to buy and sell in the age of the Internet—seem no longer relevant in a world where there is no need to plan for future generations, let alone to die for them.

It is the *believer in God* who seeks that different path, the path to elevation. For those who reject God, there is no need for distinctions and elevation, because what's the point? Elevation is not necessary for those who only seek to enjoy the moment, or who see no point beyond their lives, who ultimately just seek a state of perpetual short-term self-gratification.

Those who do not believe in God shun the notion of enrichment through distinctions. That is why they give you a baffled look when you tell them you observe a religious dietary restriction, that you don't work on a Saturday or Sunday, that you set aside time to pray, or that you're not interested in sleeping around or getting stoned. That's not living, at least as far as they see it. And boy what a waste of time all that churchy stuff is.

Distinctions mean very little to those who prefer "you only live once" or "get it while you can" lifestyles. In fact, if you ask them what distinctions they value, most of them will answer you with an absurd blank stare; as if you just asked them what time it is on the planet Jupiter.

They understand the *concept* of distinctions, but cultural changes and the erasing of history have made the notion of distinctions a foreign concept to them.

Better yet, let's say the concept is just no longer *relevant* to them.

And that is why so many do not understand the *need* for distinctions: distinctions are for the fools of yesteryear. You know, the ones who wasted their lives building and creating for some amorphous, unseeable fiction they called "God."

And the irony? The civilization around them wouldn't exist without *precisely* those people who built their world for God;

people who saw themselves as part of a long chain with past and future generations, and who *fought* for distinctions.

It is this very civilization—with all its foundational distinctions—which gave them the streets they can drive so safely on, in the reliable cars they use on those streets, so that they can go to their cafes in which they drink their coffees and eat their biscuits while they listen on the earbuds to the latest music they just downloaded on their smartphone, while they use their hybrid tablet/computers to type their screenplays about how horribly deficient their civilization is.

And they do so, all with the comforting knowledge that none of these products is likely to blow up on them or poison them, and that everyone else has to meet a certain standard of conduct so that they can walk about in reasonable peace among everyone else, in a society that has developed a rule of law over thousands of years that protects them while allowing them to build, innovate, engage in fulfilling endeavors, enjoy entertainment, and make and invest money.

All of it comes from people who worked hard and saw beyond themselves, from people who had a sense that they were struggling but nevertheless participating in a multigenerational relay race, passing a baton to someone else, who would one day turn it over to another someone else, a "someone" they would not know at all.

That sense of baton-passing was what motivated George Washington, Abraham Lincoln, Marie Curie, Franklin Roosevelt, Winston Churchill, Ronald Reagan, Margaret Thatcher, Mother Theresa, Martin Luther King, Jr., Rosa Parks, and so many others who fought for our civilization and freedom, from the days of the Greeks to the American Civil War to World War II to the present.

Each of these great icons of history fought for these distinctions. But we are losing this sense. We don't even seem to recognize a distinction among past, present, and future. No longer do we see ourselves as the next generation, helping to build the ever-growing bridge over the dark waters of chaos. Instead of using a loose piece of wood to build that bridge, we instead just grab it, plop ourselves on top of it, and float along down the river.

Where to? Wherever the current takes us.

The vanishing of society's core distinctions—the very ones that built our civilization—*must* lead to civilization's ultimate collapse. It is hard to imagine a greater cruelty to us all.

The Squishy Believer

I know a little bit about crocodiles. But it's fair to say that, if I go into a cage with a crocodile, I put myself in danger. Likewise, I know little bit about nuclear fission, but if I try to operate a nuclear facility, I will put everyone in danger.

So it is with the learning of God.

We've talked about the atheist and the believer, as though they are binary. But there are those in-between, those who call themselves "spiritual," but who don't really have a deeper sense of God. They don't necessarily know much Scripture, whether from the Torah or the New Testament. They have a sense of the wonder of the universe, but when you probe their beliefs, what they believe seems to come more from Yoda of the *Star Wars* movies. As far as what the Torah or Jesus teaches, they figure it's probably about the same.

These are the "squishy" believers. What seems to move them is Nature, especially when the weather is nice and the animals they see on the trails are really, really cute. They often talk about "oneness" and that "God is love." They believe that most people, if not all of them, are inherently good. War is never the answer, and all conflict is the result of economic issues. There is not so much a distinction between "good" and "evil," as a distinction between those who have a sense of "oneness" with nature and those who do not.

This person is dangerous, too. Since such a person understands Yoda, I will relate the issue in *Star Wars* terms: it's like when Luke Skywalker wishes to abandon his training with Yoda on the planet Dagobah—so that he can help his friends Han and Leia. Yoda warns him not to leave because his Jedi training is not complete, and the Dark Side can easily seduce him.

And just like Luke, the squishy believer does not understand enough. He operates solely out of feelings (feelings which come from the God Impulse), but with no understanding of the tremendous potential for danger in those feelings. It's like having a notion of thirst without having learned to distinguish between drinkable water and muddy water that can kill you. Or more aptly, it's like the way a child might see fire: so bright and magical looking. He might learn the hard way that it's not so much for play.

We must learn about the danger of fire and water. If not, we could very well die. We also learn about how to look both ways as we cross the street, to stay on the right side of the street, to use appropriate language and when not to say what we're thinking to other people. Kids also learn about "stranger danger."

But when it comes to spirituality, the squishy believer seems to think that learning is not necessary. It's all right there in the heart. That's good enough. And when a confrontation comes up, you'll just tap into your inner feelings and your heart will tell you what to do.

You'll just *know*. You know what I mean?

But in truth, the squishy believer, by never studying the fire of the God Impulse, actually places himself in a compromising position. It's a position of neither being here nor there (never "complete," to return to the Yoda reference). He's in the murky danger zone of twilight, or like Hamlet—always hesitating, never making a move, only to have everyone die in the end, including himself.

But the squishy believer still fancies himself to be just as spiritual as the Catholic cardinal or just as deep as a Talmudic scholar. He has enough, what with his appreciation of his nature and all. And, after all, he really *wants* to be good—whatever that might mean.

He's got it all figured out, he nods to himself, as he reaches the beautiful waterfall at the end of his nature walk. Now back to the cabin, where he and his friends will huddle around the fireplace while they all drink port and compare Lou Reed to Bob Dylan.

But for him to believe he's spiritual is like a guy who looks at fashion magazines with pictures of women and thinks he's in a relationship with them, or like a young woman who sees children playing on the swings in a nearby park and thinks she's got parenting all figured out.

But it is never so. God takes time and study; to know Torah involves hard work. It is more than *wanting* to be good. It is understanding *what* good is; why there are distinctions between good and evil; that there *is* evil and why we must hate it and, yes, even pursue war against it; why structure and family is essential; why we need children—and lots of them; why purpose exists; why it is important to *know* God and not just to "feel" His presence.

Without deep study of God, and at least an appreciation that the wisdom of Torah and the Bible has served as the cornerstone of our civilization—we are prone to Yoda's deepest fear indeed: that anything can seduce us so long as it tugs at our spiritual bone.

It is no surprise today we see people trading in God for cults, environmentalism, celebrity (even through pornography), scientology, pseudo-psychology support groups, animal-rights, climate change, so-called "social justice" issues, progressivism, and socialism. They seem to be seeking it out in far greater numbers than ever.

Each of these trends, in their own way, appeal to people's need for "oneness" with the universe, and a sense that they matter (see "What Matters Most," above). They embrace them, not realizing that these trends lead to the opposite of true spirituality.

I suspect that there is a strong correlation between such trends, on the one hand, and the loss of the centrality of God, on the other. Why? Because these trends offer depth to their lives beyond their immediate sense of "spirituality." Such people crave more—maybe not so intense like all those religious guys but something a bit more than just feeling "spiritual."

And there are a lot of people out there waiting to oblige. And that's just where any con man, any cultist, or any pimp wants you.

And as any con man knows, you need only appeal to a person's most basic need for purpose. Tell him that he has all the answers right there in front of him. Let him think that you are just helping him tap into his own instinctive "oneness with the universe" ("just release your inner '*magwa*'" or some meaningless word like that; that's something I just made up) and that you are just showing him how to draw it out. Then you have him ... and all his money.

More disturbing yet, you can make him *do* almost anything in the name of that cause.

The spiritual need is a powerful one. Without understanding it, it is playing with fire. You might as well be the proverbial moth to a flame.

You don't have to know everything in the Bible or the Torah to have an appreciation of God. (I myself certainly don't know all I can know of the Torah, the Gamarah, or the Kabbalah.) But at the very least, *know* that you don't know. And then at some point, you'll at least learn of the purpose of the fire, the real one within you.

It'll still take a long time. But at least no one will play you in the meantime.

R-E-S-P-E-C-T—The Human Distinction

Once there were husband and wife selling dried fruit and nuts in a market bazaar in the local flea market in Iraq. They operated one small stand among many alongside them.

And on this day, a neighbor from the village rushes to them. He has a telegram for them, from their son all the way in America—the one for whom the two of them had saved for years to send to college there.

They open it, only to find that the message is in English. But they don't read English.

"Give it to Mahmoud," the mother says, referring to another stand owner three store shacks away from them. "I think he knows how to read English."

So the mother and father do just that, and hand the telegram to Mahmoud. Mahmoud does read English, just as they had hoped.

But Mahmoud is very busy, and is impatient. He holds up the telegram and quickly translates it for them into Arabic: "Mom, Dad...SEND MONEY!" He practically barks the words. Then he throws the telegram back at them, getting back to his own souvenir business.

The mother and father are taken completely aback. How can this be? Their son couldn't possibly be so rude. The father starts muttering how he'll be damned if they send their boy any money, what with him being so ungrateful and disrespectful.

But the mother just can't believe it. "This makes no sense. I'm sure Mahmoud wasn't reading it right. Let's ask Aboud, two shacks down the other side. I know he can read English, too." The father agrees, and off they go.

Like before, they find and hand Aboud the telegram, asking if he can help them with the telegram from their son. Aboud is very easy-going and pleasant. He's less busy and is happy to oblige:

"Yes, yes, of course! I would be happy to translate!" He holds the paper and studies it.

Very gently, and with a pleasant smile, Aboud translates for them: "Mom… Dad…. Send money?" His words are soft, as if to give a sing-song quality to the son's message.

"Well," the father says to the mother. "Now that he's asking nicely…"

When I was a little boy myself my parents always insisted that I say "please" and "thank you" not only to them but to my relatives, my teachers, the housekeeper, even the toll booth guy.

You name it: my parents made sure I doled out these phrases generously to everyone. They called them the "magic" words. Perhaps you've referred to them the same way with your own children.

But why? Why are they "magic" words? No one ever explained why they should be "magic" to me. They were words we used, but never bothered to ask why.

And perhaps your biggest question right now is: Why is this guy ending his book talking about being polite?

Bear with me. You'll see.

I only figured recently why "please," and "thank you" are so important. It came out of this thought experiment:

Imagine you're at a dining table and you say, "Give me the salt." That's just rude, correct? But what if you said, "Give me the salt, please." A little better, right? But why is it only a little better? After all, you said that "magic" word, didn't you? But we know that that still can come off as rude.

So all right, how about this: "Can you please pass the salt?" Or how about: "Would you mind passing the salt?" I didn't even say "please" in the second sentence there, but somehow it's okay. In fact, it's even better than "Give me the salt, please."

Now imagine yourself telling your dog to roll over. Did you ever say, "Fido, would you mind please rolling over?" or "Trixie, what would you think if you and I hit the park and played a game of 'fetch.' Would that be to your liking?"

Or how about when using the automated digital assistant on your smartphone? Have you ever picked it up and said, "Siri, if you have a moment, would you mind letting me know the weather in Seattle later this afternoon?"

Of course not. We instinctively know the idea as silly.

Why is that? (So what? You are still saying, perhaps a bit annoyed. But again: bear with me on this one).

I think it has something to do with what the great Aretha Franklin sang about in the late '60s: "Respect." You see, saying "please" and "thank you" or similar phrases show *respect*.

But that begs the question: respect for *what*? Why do we even need respect? What is it about us human beings that we require the words "please" and "thank you" so much that we feel a tremendous slight without them? And why is it that we don't express those words to our dogs or to our digital assistants on our smartphones?

Here's why: we use these polite phrases and tones because we recognize that other beings have free will. We recognize they have the ability and the choice *to say no*. We recognize that we are *not* robots or animals.

When you ask someone, "Can you please tell me the time?" you are implicitly recognizing that he has the choice not to stop for you, and not to tell you anything. And that if he does tell you the time, it's because he has chosen to do so. Whether you realize it or not, when you say these "magic" words, you are recognizing God's most important imprimatur upon us: our ability to choose, *the very essence of what makes us human.*

What fascinates me about this is how demonstrable this is, not just among the law-abiding but even among gang members and other criminals. In fact, among the lawless it may even be greater than among the rest of us. We've all heard about someone shooting someone else just for "dissin'" him? I'm not saying it's a proper response for a lack of respect, of course, but it shows that respect is a critical part of their lives, too.

I'll go further: Even the youngest among our children need our respect—even though they're learning to navigate within the boundaries we set for them. As soon as they can communicate, they expect respect—respect for who they are, their individuality, the fact that they are not mere animals.

That doesn't mean you should not discipline your child when necessary and make clear you're the parent and that he still needs to listen to you. But showing respect and disciplining are not at odds with each other. On the contrary, the more you show respect to your child, the more he will listen to you. It is far better to say: "Johnny, what do you think? Do you think you should clean up your room now?" than "Johnny, clean up your room, and I MEAN it! NOW, Johnny."

Johnny will clean up the room under either scenario, but in the first, you've shown him respect, that it would be a good idea to clean up his room. Under the second, he might only be thinking how bossy you are and how he hates you.

Why? Because, in a very real sense, you've ignored—disrespected—his humanity. In the first phrasing, by contrast, you've firmly telegraphed what you want—and what you expect—but without treating him like an automaton. You are helping him with his choice. Just like a child appreciates you helping him to learn how to tie his shoes, you are helping him to exercise his free will, and to let his little human to come out.

Every time your child asks you a question you think he can answer, every time he does something that displeases you, there is a way to answer with "What do you think?" in the response. Your child will love you for respecting him and will want to please you ever more so. You won't ever have to raise your voice with your child.

Does this work, always? Nothing is 100 percent, but it will be the most effective way of getting your child to do or not do as you'd like.

But this chapter is not about child-rearing. I bring it up only to show that kids resonate to respect for a reason: *something* has infused the notion of respect within us, even in children. We seem to demand respect, and we know we need to give it back. Show respect to your child, and it'll dramatically reduce the chances of him saying "I hate you." Show respect even to the thug in the street, and you dramatically reduce your chances of a confrontation.

We study happiness, wealth management, and meditation of the mind. But we don't really study respect. But it is within us all. It shapes our relationships not only with family but with our bosses and fellow employees, our girlfriends and boyfriends. Even the toll booth guy.

But that is not how it is in the animal kingdom. All that matters in the animal kingdom is who is prey and what can outrun what. Even within a pride of lions, or pack of wolves, the strongest has to battle it out for leadership. And when another one challenges that leader and wins, then he's the new leader.

You can think of that as "respect" of sorts if you like, but it's not the same thing. That kind of "respect" is only for the strength of the leader: you know not to mess with him because he's "established" himself as the strongest. And no one else in the pride or pack gets any particular respect.

By contrast, we humans yearn for respect not because of our strength. Brute strength is rarely the sole reason for respect. Our respect to each other stems from the sole fact that we are human beings, first and foremost. That is reason alone to respect your fellow man on the street.[17]

That is the reason we say "please" and "thank you" to everyone, not just to the strongest, most intelligent, or most beautiful among us. We are recognizing that each of us is a creature of God, and he is infinitely valuable in God's eyes, as we believe we are to Him, too. We are recognizing that whatever we ask of them, they have the free will to say no, and that we are not their master nor have any right to exercise dominion over them.

Julius Caesar, perhaps one of the greatest military leaders of all time, recognized this basic principle: while he expected much of his troops, he did not lead by using fear. He led by calling out to his men's unique humanness and their own sense for mission. He took care of their needs at every turn possible.[18] He ate, lived and bled with his men on the front line in battles, working shoulder to shoulder with the legions and spent many years doing the "dirty" work of a soldier.[19] He spent time with his troops, knowing most of his men by name.[20]

Ultimately, he saw them as men first, not as expendable fodder he could throw at the enemy. His men knew that they mattered to Caesar. The men loved him for that and were willing to die for him—even when he returned to fight against Rome itself.

And this is where we revisit atheism.

If he is to be truly intellectually consistent, the atheist cannot accept the notion of free will of men. It is why he has no problem encouraging authoritarian systems of government that rob humans of their individuality, and particularly their free will.

In the atheist's mind, humans are only very sophisticated animals. We are by definition soulless. Worse, we are just clumps of carbon matter that can talk and walk. But when you have that viewpoint, there cannot be anything special about any one of us, whether as a human being or as individual. You do *not* have infinite worth, in anyone's eyes, let alone in the eyes of a creator. You are useful, such as a chicken who gives eggs or a silkworm who produces silk, or you are not. If not, well there is no reason to keep—or respect—you.

If there is no free will and no God who values each of us, then any strongman can do with people as he will. Nothing is forbidden in your treatment of your fellow man, so long as it fosters your notion of what is best for society. Or at least you can justify anything in the name of logic and the common good. And how much easier to do so if you see nothing special, no spiritual spark, in your fellow man. How much easier when there is nothing to *respect* about him.

By contrast, democracy and capitalism were the first systems to appeal to, work with, and respect our innate sense of individualism and God. America's democracy recognized that our rights are inalienable and flow from our Creator. A system like this emphasizes what makes us human and allows us to be what we can all be, individually—for better or for worse. It assumes—also by definition—that we are far more than just clumps of living tissue. It acknowledges and respects that God is within us all.

Atheism is a world *without* respect for the individual. The atheist does not and cannot appreciate the individual because he cannot recognize that everyone's sense of individuality can come *only* from God. A government system without God has no need to respect individuality. To that government individuality is invisible, pointless, and perhaps an obstacle to the greater good on the atheist's merry way to utopia.

And remember my absurd scenarios above, where I contemplated saying "would you mind" and "please" to Fido the dog, and the smartphone digital assistant? Let me add another: The communist, the fascist, or anyone else who subscribes to a command-and-control economy. The very notion of people saying "thank you" and "please" in such societies is laughable to virtually anyone who has escaped such countries. There is no cultural norm to say "please" and "thank you" in such places. The only thing which matters is that everyone follow the Big Plan for Everyone. So just get to work.

Not one godless society has promoted respect for the individual, nor his elevation *as* an individual. The very notion that you are an individual, let alone an individual created in God's image, is alien to them. They have never respected the inherent humanity of any individual. They see only the masses and how the masses can contribute to the big ideas of their elite betters.

To ask society to proceed without acknowledging God's infusion of free will in each of us is like reducing Mozart's role to a piano tuner or Einstein to a bookkeeper. Better yet, it's like expecting Man to think of himself and to act no differently than a silkworm.

Please, thank you, and you're welcome: We know they are magic phrases, but we don't quite know why we feel we should say them. We just do. And not only do we use them, we feel insulted if we don't hear it from others. The words become like the many words and phrases we routinely use in day-to-day life without bothering to wonder their origins.[21]

But "please" and "thank you" and respectful words like them persist in our culture, whether we understand their purpose or not. I think it's because they reveal a great truth about us all, whether we are believers or not: that we know, deep down, that we are creatures of God. Each time we say these words, we show that we recognize the free will in others and that we in turn expect others to recognize it in us. We reveal that we are capable of great choices and that there will be judgment for those choices.

These words are hints and even manifestations of our free will. They reveal also that God expects each of us, with our free will, to help carry out God's mission—a mission which must involve at a minimum just being good to each other.

That can begin only when we recognize the godliness in ourselves and seek to bring it out in others. Saying please and thank you as often as we can is a great way to start.

CONCLUSION

Don't it always seem to go
That you don't know what you've got
'Til it's gone...
> — *Joni Mitchell, "Big Yellow Taxi"*
> *from Ladies of the Canyon (1970)*

Who Are You?
> — *The Who, "Who Are You"*
> *from Who Are You (1978)*

Once there was a Bedouin, an old man who would wander about the desert in the southern part of what is now Israel. Just as his people had done for centuries, he would migrate from place to place, taking care of his small flock of sheep.

One evening, he found a place to sleep that looked particularly inviting. It was a path that had two parallel lines of some durable substance, both which stuck out of the ground, stretching out for as far as the eye could see. Wooden planks seemed to fasten the two lines, also as far as he could see. What a nice place to sleep, he thought to himself, placing himself right between these tracks and making himself comfortable. Soon he fell fast asleep.

About an hour later, the man woke up to a noise. Off in the distance, he heard a whistle, a sound he had never heard before. But it was far away. So he ignored it and fell back asleep.

Five minutes later, he woke up again. This time the whistle sound was a bit louder. Again, he dismissed the noise, and went back to sleep.

Two minutes after that, he woke up not only to hear a huge booming sound of that same whistle but also to see a gigantic monster approaching him at incredible speed. At the head of this monster was a huge light, which got bigger and bigger as it rushed upon him. In a split second, this monster smashed into him, flinging him several feet in the air.

Amazingly, our Bedouin friend did not die instantly, but the impact shattered bones throughout his body. He needed massive rehabilitation. Fortunately, he received immediate medical attention in a hospital in Tel Aviv, where he stayed for months before being released. After some time, the government gave him a large stipend and even a small apartment in a nice part of town. Still, he would need constant care, so they provided him with a nurse who might take care of his needs several hours every day.

After working with him for a few weeks, the nurse thought one day that it would be nice to make some tea. So she went to the kitchen and put the kettle on. Within a few minutes, the water started boiling. The kettle started making a small whistling sound.

The Bedouin, hearing the sound, immediately managed to lift himself out of his bed, grabbed his walker, and struggled his way to the kitchen. There, with all his remaining strength, he lifted up his walker and started furiously smashing the kettle to pieces.

The place was a wreck. His nurse, hearing all the commotion, rushed into the kitchen. Confused, she asked, "Oh my God, what happened here?"

The Bedouin, standing over the kettle, pointed to it, and with wild eyes said, "These you have to destroy when they're small..."

And so it is with atheism. This we must destroy while it's small.

God is disappearing from people's lives every day—not just in China, where the Chinese government itself is officially atheist and where 61 percent are "convinced" atheists (with that number rapidly growing) and only 7 percent consider themselves to be religious—numbers that have grown dramatically in only the past four years. But while the global outlook on atheism is not clear,[1] it may be more probative to examine where atheism is growing in Western civilization countries, particularly America, Europe, Israel and Australia/ New Zealand.

In America, the percentage of self-proclaimed atheists has approximately doubled in the time period between 2007 and 2016.[2] So-called "Nones" make up almost a quarter of the population. In the past decade, U.S. Nones have overtaken Catholics, mainline protestants, and all followers of non-Christian faiths.[3] Not only that, they seem to embrace godlessness with considerable gusto.

Why wouldn't they? Godlessness offers a world without responsibility, without the hard work to figure out each of our individual and collective purposes. And think of the benefits! All the sex you want without guilt (and try every kind of sex while you're at it), gamble and explore drugs to your heart's delight, don't think of your neighbors' needs, and don't worry about any kind of judgment: After all, nothing is really "good" or "bad" anymore. It's *all* good, as it were.

And the numbers bear it out. The "religiously unaffiliated" population will grow from 16 percent in 2010 to 26 percent in 2050.[4] In Europe, church attendance is down dramatically, and atheists have grown so extensively in numbers that the Netherlands now claims 42 percent as nonbelievers.[5] Churches throughout Europe have become *de facto* museums rather than actual places of worship. In one case, the government converted an old church into a skating park (but a young skateboarder using it described as "a gift from God," so maybe there's hope there). In another case, a German church left its doors open twenty-four hours a day to attract whomever they could get.[6]

Exacerbating this trend is a growing hostility toward faith. That hostility comes even from the American government itself. As Martin Castro, chair of the US Civil Rights Commission under President Obama, wrote regarding the state of civil rights in America:

> The phrases "religious liberty" and "religious freedom" will stand for nothing except hypocrisy so long as they remain *code words for discrimination, intolerance, racism, sexism, homophobia, Islamophobia, Christian supremacy or any form of intolerance.* Religious liberty was never intended to give one religion dominion over other religions, or a veto power over the civil rights and civil liberties of others. *However, today, as in the past, religion is being used as both a weapon and a shield by those seeking to deny others equality.* In our nation's past *religion has been used to justify slavery and later, Jim Crow laws.* We now see "religious liberty" arguments sneaking their way back into our political and constitutional discourse ... in an effort to undermine the rights of some Americans. This generation of Americans must stand up and speak out to ensure *that religion never again be twisted to deny others the full promise of America.*[7] (Emphasis added)

The report goes on to recommend a dramatic revision of religious exemptions.[8]

It therefore should come as no surprise that the religiously unaffiliated is growing significantly. It's the second largest religious group in North America and most of Europe.[9] Conversely, while Judaism and Christianity are declining rapidly in Europe, Islam is growing consistently and dramatically.[10]

Put bluntly, Western civilization is literally losing its faith. The primary reason is that we have forgotten God's critical role in our civilization and its attendant values and morality, which we have come to take for granted. We seem to notice only the annoyance of going to church or synagogue and forget the reasons why we have done so for thousands of years. At some point, usually in our adolescent years, we figure that the world will continue on just fine if we don't go to church or synagogue. We conclude we can still be nice to people and people will still be nice to us, even without God.

So at some point, we ask: why bother? What's the point? Eventually, we resent God, not necessarily because He's done anything wrong to us, but because He takes time out of our day. And these rules He expects us to live by; they can be very... inconvenient. Besides, we're basically good, right? That's all that should matter.

We have gotten to the point where we have treated God like a guest who has outworn his welcome. Now we stand at the train podium, waving good-bye to Him and faking a smile as we wish Him a good journey back to wherever He came from. Under our breath, we mutter "good riddance." And He can take His silly distinctions with Him, too.

In a world without a concern for any future, He is no longer necessary. But our need to matter still remains the central driving force in our lives. And so fly-by-night ideologies and strongmen dictators fill the vacuum in this new world without

God. Whether we acknowledge it or not, our need to matter and to belong is so powerful within us that we actually *run* to such monsters because they tell us what we want to hear. But we are only like that runaway girl who has hooked up with a pimp, who seduced her merely be telling her she was beautiful. Soon she's turning tricks on the street, addicted to crack cocaine: things she would never have imagined herself ever doing in her life. But there she is, selling herself along with all the others.

And that's all atheism is, and so many other "isms": It is a pimp that plays off your need to matter in this world, that plays off the God Impulse that you've decided to ignore but which still calls out to you from within.

You can be an atheist, if you like: if you're reading this, chances are you live in a free country that allows you to make such choices. But you choose atheism at great peril to yourself and to society at large. You must accept that you are embracing a world of chaos, of reverting to a world of obscene barbarity.

But the issue is far more concerning when *government* embraces godlessness: China and its former One Child policy and lesser-known but extensive eugenics programs—which it designed to control and reduce its population[11]—are horrific examples. And generally, where the Judeo-Christian mindset for justice and freedom of religion does not inform a country's governing "DNA," such as in China, Russia, Venezuela, Cuba and North Korea, we see rampant suppression of free speech and freedoms as well as a palpable minimizing of the value of life and freedom of their citizens. Even in more benign socialist countries of Western Europe (France, Sweden, Germany, etc.), free speech and privacy rights still entail walking on eggshells: you can say and do whatever you like, so long as it doesn't go against the European Union principles.[12]

A godless government minimizes or even denies human-kind's free will, its quest for goodness and justice and the very notion of the individual. It is a world where there are no distinctions, a world that renders us no different than the animals. Any effort to pursue art, beauty, or innovation becomes ultimately pointless. Worse yet, it invites only a survival of the fittest and "get it while you can" mentality. And it has no true interest in the generations to come.

It ignores the logical reality that *only* with God can we truly hope to elevate ourselves, whether as an individual or as a society. Only with God does creation and innovation make sense. Only a government with God *as its founding premise* can offer a chance to bring out the best in each of us.

The atheist likes the perks of a world with God in it, but doesn't much want its burdens. He seems to think that religion has done its part, and that was nice (and thank you very much), but we no longer need it. Much like that butterfly we mentioned which no longer needs its cocoon.

But that's a false metaphor. It is more like thinking an adult no longer needs food or water, now that he's a grown man. Worse yet, a world without God *must* descend into a world of mayhem, where evil flourishes, whether you are willing to accept that evil exists or not.

How do we know? Because that's what happened in every godless society.

Not all is lost, however. Glimmers of hope are beginning to show up: a very substantial majority of Americans are slowly coming to the realization that churches are good for the individual and for society—even among people who espouse no religiously affiliation, and even those with a college education.[13] In China, Christianity is growing at an incredible rate, at least 7 percent per year (growing from 10 million to 100 million from 1980 to 2015). Officially atheist China, despite its ongoing efforts to restrict religion, could have the largest number of Christians in the world by 2030.[14] The reason? Many Chinese are beginning to understand that the Judeo-Christian mindset embraces and encourages learning of science and seeks answers from the universe.[15] Atheism—and even the more traditional Asian faiths of Confucianism and Taoism—does not.

Likewise in Russia, 70 percent of Russians call themselves Orthodox Christian today, compared to 37 percent in 1991, according to Pew Research.[16] Researchers highlighted the return of religion as a key theme of the survey. Even Vladimir Putin, Russia's President, has been openly facilitating the growth of the church.[17] Russia even invested $100 million to rebuild churches throughout the country.[18] Such a thing is unthinkable in the US, but Putin has passionately embraced the Russian Orthodox Church, and the moral clarity that it espouses. In Putin's world—his Christian world—there are consequences to moral behavior. There is a right and a wrong. There is sin, and there is universal, and not relative, morality. Priests regularly sprinkle Russian space rockets with holy water before liftoff, and the Church has even held a religious service in honor of the nation's nuclear weapons.[19]

In Putin's own words, the West's succumbing to secularism was a trend toward "chaotic darkness" and a "return to a primitive state."[20] His support of the Jews and Israel has become clear as well: In 2016, the president of the World Jewish Congress praised Putin for making Russia "a country where Jews are welcome."[21] Putin even urged Jews suffering the renewed anti-Semitism in Europe to emigrate to Russia, where it would embrace them.[22] Russia's relations with Israel are the warmest in history.[23]

It is ironic that Russia and its new leadership—flawed as it is—now preaches to the West against the evils of godlessness, only twenty-five years after the demise of its atheist communist empire.

It may seem like a strange turnabout: we begin this book by discussing Russia's past as among the most horrific examples of the abuses of godlessness, and now showcase Russia as a fighter *against* godlessness, the standard bearer and champion for Judeo-Christian values.

But in its own way, it somehow makes sense: who would know better the horrors of godlessness than those who had suffered under it? Who would have a keener appreciation of why we must return to God?

In the end, our only *good* choice is to embrace God, and specifically His teachings through Torah and the Bible. We should learn it in the schools (there is no true Constitutional prohibition on the teaching of God in any school; any prohibition is what left-leaning justices have pushed by way of interpretation). More importantly, we as parents must teach it to our children and grandchildren. We must speak of God *as a fact*, not as some hypothetical poetic aspiration or something we might do on the side.

We must utterly reverse the way we've recently approached God since the mid-twentieth century. For God *is* reality—which is why we discussed that reality at length, earlier. Not understanding this reality is like not realizing you are about to drive over a cliff: You can suffer some pretty grave consequences.

Atheism cannot fight evil because atheism doesn't recognize "evil" itself. It is ir*relevant* to atheism. Evil implies moral absolutes, and moral absolutes are nonexistent in atheism.

But we know we must fight evil. We can only do so when we embrace God. As the Holocaust survivor and expert Elie Wiesel famously noted, there is always hope that good can overcome evil: "[But] we must take sides. Neutrality helps the oppressor, never the victim. Silence encourages the tormentor, never the tormented."

That wisdom is timeless. Even where atheism is not destructive, it is at best passive, neutral, and silent in the face of evil. By contrast, only with God can there be the appropriate *active* and prepared attack upon evil when we must confront it.

The specifics and timing may change, but history has shown that the absence of God has always led to the ascent of evil and ultimately the gulags, the gas chambers, and the torture and rape rooms. It can only ultimately lead back to the Sodom and Gomorrah that we've been escaping ever since God first introduced Himself to Abraham.

It is a world back to which we hope never to descend again. As Ronald Reagan put it: If we ever forget that we are one nation under God, then we will be a nation gone under.

And so, we should speak of God, teach of God, and think of God "... when you sit in your house, and when you walk on the way, and when you lie down and when you rise up."[24] Act and think throughout the day with God in mind with every breath and step you take. And be grateful. Be particularly grateful for Judaism and Christianity, which have created the civilization that has bestowed so many blessings and protections to us all, particularly Freedom.

We spoke before about movies, and how we each are living in a movie, whether we realize it or not. We participate in it, and we each have critical roles. But you need to see it, to study it, and to figure out its complex purpose. Not realizing this may be the greatest danger of all. It may very well be that you perceive the story around you is random or even meaningless. If so, you may be that child who just can't see it.

Know this movie, lest someone else tempt you with a different story to satisfy your instinct for structure and meaning. Only by figuring out the story all around you can you escape the chaotic and empty world of the godless.

Remember always that atheism is the empty well, yet our need for purpose is so great that we always seek to fill that well with *something*. We'll do it, even if that something—usually in the form of some utopian vision—may be destructive to us all.

Don't let the godless lead you there. Atheism never elevates. It never creates. Atheism diminishes all that makes us human. It takes away all purpose and all that has allowed us to pursue civilization in the first place: among them the notions of beauty, justice, free will, and freedom itself. Atheism merely robs our humanity and chips away at such things, until one day we will even wonder who we are. It'll be like the elements that continue to lash away at the ever-disappearing painting, *The Last Supper*, to the point one day we'll no longer recognize that painting at all. And atheism will never replace it with another masterpiece.

It is worth asking: who *are* we? where *are* we humans going? Are we going on a vessel, which transports us from one place to another, or are we only here for some ride—like a vacation cruise, enjoying as much booze, sex, and food for the time being, but ultimately ending up in the same port where we began?

As the old line goes: What's it all about, Alfie? Or put more bluntly—*why are we here?*

The believer understands intuitively what our collective mission is: to work together to do God's work on earth, to be the best we can be to each other—one kind step at a time: an apology here, a "how are you today" there, picking up of some litter on the street, holding the door for someone with a lot of groceries, or just asking someone if you can help.

The tools nature has endowed us with (among the many being free will, analysis, abstract thought, a sense of beauty, our unique talents as individuals, and science itself) compels the conclusion *that Someone wants us to find Him*. It's like He's asking us to figure out this elaborate treasure hunt, each stop providing us one more clue to a giant riddle, or perhaps one more piece of a giant puzzle.

And therein—perhaps—lies the path to good news. Despite the title of the book and its subject matter, I am an optimist. We should all feel optimism. How so? Because we know that the answer to so many of our problems lies in something quite simple: the return to the centrality of God in each of our individual lives. It's a recognition that, no matter what our individual languages, interests, talents or careers may be, God is still at the center of everything.

It's like we finally received a diagnosis to so many of our social ills and evils, and it is the disease of godlessness. And once diagnosed, we can start the work to deal with it, to apply the cure.

If we embrace God, the world becomes what we should all want it to be—a world of purpose in all our doings, a world where we seek out God's will and we seek to find Him. If we do so, we can better distinguish between the trivial and the meaningful, the just and the unjust, the beautiful and the ugly, and good and evil. It is a world which blossoms and engages our instinctive senses of beauty, community, humor, art and music, and innovation. It is a world which respects the infinite worth of the individual and that each life possesses its own great promise and purpose. It is a world which enables us to recognize, confront, and fight evil, and therefore not suffer the millions that might die when we don't fight it. It is a world where the various "isms" cannot so easily lure us away to do the bidding of maniacal leaders. In short, we would enjoy a world of true *freedom*, the precious gift that only God can give us.

Sometimes it feels that to appreciate God, we must first become like the despondent George Bailey in that Frank Capra movie, *It's a Wonderful Life*. In that movie, Clarence the angel proceeds to show George what the world would be like had he never been born. The only difference is that in that movie, George sees that in a world without him, just a handful of people would be dead, miserable or financially ruined. But if Clarence the angel was to show us a world without the Judeo-Christian God, we'd see gulags, concentration camps, and rape rooms as commonplace as today's shopping malls, banks and coffee houses; we'd have no sense of purpose in life at all, other than an understanding that might makes right.

Clarence would reveal that we wouldn't have universities, school systems or hospitals. Our notions of science, law and order, and even logic and morality wouldn't exist. There would be virtually no point in many of the values we hold today, such as honor, family, truth, art, or even the concept of progress. And what would they say about freedom? To hell with *that*.

How do we know? Because we know from history that godlessness never advanced such things. And where such things did exist, godlessness has always been there to tear them down.

Without God, there are more than enough people who are happy to tell you what your mission should be, and what you *really* need. They are like sellers at a flea market, hawking their wares from cure-alls to virility pills to stress-relievers. They beckon you. They do it by appealing to your instinctive God impulse, but all the while steering you away from Him. The price in exchange is your freedom. But that is the one gift God expected you never to give up. Without it, you can never come close to Him.

Do not heed these peddlers. They *only* want to misdirect you to what is trivial, confusing, or even evil. They know that the same hand that lights a candle to bless God can also lower to the ground and set fire to the village.

I was an atheist. And thank God indeed that most people still are not. May we always make sure to keep it so.

ACKNOWLEDGMENTS

First and foremost, I thank God, without Whom there would be nothing, and with Whom anything is achievable. God infused in me a passion and quest for truth that sustained me through the approximately nine years it took for me to write this book. His presence was constant.

Nor could I have attained the passion, stamina and energy to write this book without the wisdom of Fyodor Dostoevsky, the great Russian author of *Crime and Punishment* and *The Brothers Karamazov*. It was he who first made me see the dangerous world of my own atheism. I do not know that without him, I would ever have appreciated God's reality. More than any author I have ever read, his books show the consequences of living according to dangerous beliefs, through compelling stories. May we all have such impact on the lives of others.

To acknowledge someone who has died almost a century and half ago may seem odd to some. But those who appreciate true *wisdom*—whether through great literature, art, or the Bible—understand that wisdom is timeless. And, as we explain thoroughly in this book, there is no "time" in any event. And so Dostoevsky sits with me, with his powerful history and wisdom, always pervasive in my life. I thank him for opening my eyes to the truth I had been ignoring—and fighting—for so long, and which impelled me to write this book.

The same goes for Dennis Prager, my friend and mentor who inspired so much in this book. To happen to be friends with Dennis is as fortuitous as having been friends with Shakespeare, Leonard Da Vinci, or the sages of old. Dennis is to wisdom what Albert Einstein was to physics: just as Einstein could simplify and reduce the relationship of matter and energy to a simple formula ($E=Mc^2$), so too does Dennis reduce complex principles of morality, the Bible, and social issues. All of us are fortunate to have him in our lives. Thank you also, Dennis, for helping me in key parts of my book, especially in the historical sections. They were invaluable and have made the book richer and more persuasive as a result.

To my father, Ranan Lurie, the extraordinary political cartoonist and Israeli war hero who taught me the pervasiveness of chess in our lives, and the power of metaphors, good stories, and great long jokes. His primary theory of life, that God wants us to *create*, animated everything he did in his life. That mantra stuck with me, and the more I live on the planet the more I realize how right he is. He also made me realize that I belonged to a long chain of history, a connection that dates to Isaac Luria, the father of the contemporary Kabbalah, and far further back than that. We are a part of a chain of civilization; we all must assume our role. We just need to find it.

To my mother, Tamar Lurie, whose brilliance lies in understanding people and human nature like no other human. It was she who taught me that we must fight evil, that there is nothing new under the sun, and that the world needs *more good people* to counter the bad. I have repeated these words to countless other couples, many of whom decided to have more children as a result. When I was a child, she would tell the stories of the Bible to me in such a way that made the characters come alive, even become friends, and I wanted to learn with them.

To my brother, Rod, who urged me to pursue this book, and who had absolute faith in its reach—despite his own disagreements with much of my premise. *That* is integrity and intellectual honesty. Rod also has an uncanny ability to achieve great things and connect people, and his encouragement for me to pursue this when I doubted myself at times will never be forgotten. Thank you, Rod: you are a true mensch and a great brother.

To Rabbi Brandon (Yitzhak) Gaines and Dr. Drorit Gaines, Ph.D, each of whose erudition in Torah and the Kabbalah echo throughout this book, and each of whom were instrumental especially in the areas of the book dealing with purpose and neuroscience. I thank you both: you have become family to all the Luries. We are brothers and sisters to each other.

To Chet Thompson and Ari David, who painstakingly went through the very first draft of this book, making sure the book was consistent and accurate. And to William Creedon, who would call me and point out paragraph by paragraph arguments that worked, and arguments that did not. Only great friends of many years would agree to undertake such a difficult task. (Of course, they could have each just used the "redline" feature on the Word program, but that was too advanced for them...).

To my children, Max, Sasha, and Alex, young critical thinkers who love to share their proofs of God with me—some of which show up in this book—and who were always there supporting my work. It wasn't easy having to leave them from time to time to write this book. But, in the end, it is for them that I express this urgent call for the centrality of God in our lives.

They tell me they understand.

ENDNOTES

Introduction

1   In 2004, the American Civil Liberties Union (ACLU) pressured the Los Angeles City Council to ban the symbol of the cross on its city seal. They did so because some people convinced them that non-Christians (read: atheists) would feel uncomfortable or unwelcome in the city. The ACLU threatened to deem it unconstitutional, and the Los Angeles City Council didn't want to incur the legal fees to fight it.

    The irony is that Los Angeles' very name is Spanish ("City of The Angels") and obviously far more religious (and therefore "unwelcoming") than the tiny cross in the emblem itself. Never mind that the cross represents California's missionary history. Never mind that the remaining symbols on the emblem contain other spiritual references. The important thing was to eliminate Christianity. In January 2014, City Council members reversed that decision, only to have a court reverse that council decision (back to no cross) in April, 2016.

2   Christina Ng, "California Family Fined for Bible Study in Home," September 22, 2011, http://abcnews.go.com/US/california-family-fined-bible-study-home/story?id=14582868;

3   Teresa Watanabe, "L.A. schools will no longer suspend a student for being defiant," May 15, 2013, http://articles.latimes.com/2013/may/15/local/la-me-ln-lausd-suspensions-20130515.

4   http://www.latimes.com/nation/la-na-supreme-court-american-flag-20150330-story.html. The premise of sending the boys home was that wearing the American Flag on a shirt might be offensive on Cinco de Mayo, where there were hispanic students, and the school was trying to avoid a confrontation. But such banning occurred beyond Cinco de Mayo holidays, too: http://www.theblaze.com/news/2017/03/10/high-schoolers-blasted-for-wearing-american-flag-colors-to-basketball-game-heres-why/ (wearing American flag and colors considered offensive at a routine basketball game; school principal apologized to other team).

5   Or, as Dennis Prager describes it in his "Cut Flowers" theory: You can cut flowers, and they'll look lovely for a few days. But eventually, they'll whither without the soil, the consistent watering and the sunlight that gave them their beauty in the first place. Likewise, morality without God may

appear to last a generation or so, but, ultimately, it too will wither without constant nourishment.

6   See generally, https://en.wikipedia.org/wiki/History_of_atheism.

7   Ibid.

8   Dr. Richard J. Krejcir, "Statistics and Reasons for Church Decline," http://www.churchleadership.org/apps/articles/default.asp?articleid=42346&colum nid=4545 (2007). See also Michael Lipka, "Why America's 'nones' left religion behind," August 24, 2016, http://www.pewresearch.org/fact-tank/2016/08/24/why-americas-nones-left-religion-behind/, which denotes the various reasons that people are leaving religion altogether (sometimes loosely referred to as the "Nones").

9   Ibid.

10   In Dostoevsky's classic *Crime and Punishment*, its main protagonist Raskolnikov, an avid atheist, decides to be intellectually honest and live by his atheist beliefs. He decides that an elderly and cantankerous woman who lives in his apartment building is a drain on society. Employing his dark atheist ideology of utilitarianism, he decides to kill her. Wouldn't the world be a better place? Wouldn't society not have to was time, money and resources in maintaining her useless life? Wasn't killing her the logical and "right" thing to do? Raskolnikov was a *true* "atheist." He wasn't cheating.

Chapter I

1   Account as retold here is from Simon Denyer, "Horrors of One-Child Policy Leave Deep Scars in Chinese Society," the *Washington Post*, October 30, 2015, https://www.washingtonpost.com/world/asia_pacific/horrors-of-one-child-policy-leave-deep-scars-in-chinese-society/2015/10/30/6bd28e0c-7e7b-11e5-bfb6-65300a5ff562_story.html.

2   Philip P. Pan, "Who Controls the Family?," the *Washington Post*, August 27, 2005, http://www.washingtonpost.com/wp-dyn/content/article/2005/08/26/AR2005082601756.html.

3   The accounts referenced above as retold here are all from Denyer, "Horrors of One-Child Policy Leave Deep Scars in Chinese Society," October 30, 2015, https://www.washingtonpost.com/world/asia_pacific/horrors-of-one-child-policy-leave-deep-scars-in-chinese-society/2015/10/30/6bd28e0c-7e7b-11e5-bfb6-65300a5ff562_story.html?utm_term=.a191a1bebd2f

4   Nick Valencia and Devon Sayers, "Florida teens who recorded drowning man will not be charged in his death," July 21, 2017, http://www.cnn.com/2017/07/20/us/florida-teens-drowning-man/index.html

5   The details of the Ecole Polytechnique story as described in this retelling all come from https://en.wikipedia.org/wiki/%C3%89cole_Polytechnique_massacre.

6   Aron Heller, "Late WWII US veteran is 1st soldier honored for saving Jews," December 2, 2015, http://bigstory.ap.org/article/95e629f3cd2b46e6a2 08cf0357f53370/late-wwii-us-veteran-1st-soldier-honored-saving-jews.

7   Ibid.

8   Ibid.

9   Ibid.

10   Not her real name. For more of this horrific story and similar ones, much of which have been incorporated in this anecdote, please see http://fox4kc. com/2014/10/23/young-yazidi-woman-begs-to-be-bombed-ive-been-raped-30-times-and-its-not-even-lunch-time/; Sara Malm, "'The saddest thing I remember was this little girl, 12 years old. They raped her without mercy': Dressed in traditional wedding gowns, Yazidi sex slaves relive their torture by ISIS," DailyMail.com, January 18, 2016, http://www.dailymail.co.uk/news/article-3404894/The-saddest-thing-remember-little-girl-12-years-old-raped-without-mercy-Dressed-traditional-wedding-gowns-Yazidi-sex-slaves-relive-torture-ISIS.html.

11   Ibid.

12   See https://www.hrw.org/news/2015/04/14/iraq-isis-escapees-describe-systematic-rape; See also http://fox4kc.com/2014/10/23/young-yazidi-woman-begs-to-be-bombed-ive-been-raped-30-times-and-its-not-even-lunch-time/

13   See generally https://en.wikipedia.org/wiki/Dechristianization_of_France_during_the_French_Revolution, from which I derived much of this section.

14   Ibid.

15   Ibid.

16   Ibid.

17   Ibid.

18   https://en.wikipedia.org/wiki/Drownings_at_Nantes

19   See generally https://en.wikipedia.org/wiki/Dechristianization_of_France_during_the_French_Revolution

20   Ibid.

21   Ibid.

22   Ibid.

23   Ibid.

24   Ibid.

25   Ibid.

26   Ibid.

27   Ibid.

28   Alexander Hamilton letter from Philadelphia, 1794, as referenced in https://chnm.gmu.edu/revolution/d/593/

29   Ibid.

30   http://www.answers.com/Q/How_many_people_did_Stalin_kill;

31   Ibid.

32   Lucy Ash, "The Rape of Berlin," May 1, 2015, http://www.bbc.com/news/magazine-32529679; for a more full-scale review of the horrors of the Russian occupation of Berlin and Eastern Europe, see generally https://en.wikipedia.org/wiki/Rape_during_the_occupation_of_Germany.

33   Ibid.

34   Anne Applebaum, *Iron Curtain, The Crushing of Eastern Europe* (New York: Anchor Books, 2013), 32.

35   Andrew Roberts, "Stalin's army of rapists: The brutal war crime that Russia and Germany tried to ignore," *Daily Mail*, London, October 24, 2008.

36   Cynthia Haven, "Stalin killed millions. A Stanford historian answers the question, was it genocide?" http://news.stanford.edu/2010/09/23/naimark-stalin-genocide-092310/

37   Ibid.

38   Ibid.

39   Ibid.

40   Ibid.

41   Ibid.

42   See generally, http://www.historyplace.com/worldhistory/genocide/stalin.htm

43   Ibid.

44   Ibid.

45   Ibid.

46   Ibid.

47   See generally http://necrometrics.com/20c5m.htm#Stalin

48   See generally, https://en.wikipedia.org/wiki/Marxist%E2%80%93Leninist_atheism

49   See, generally, https://en.wikipedia.org/wiki/Criticism_of_atheism, discussing at length the state atheism of communism under Stalin, Pol Pot, and Mao.

50   Mao Zedong, "Legacy," Wikipedia, https://en.wikipedia.org/wiki/Mao_Zedong.

51   See https://en.wikipedia.org/wiki/Mao_Zedong

52   "Mass Killings Under Communist Regimes," https://en.wikipedia.org/wiki/Mass_killings_under_Communist_regimes#People.27s_Republic_of_China

53   Ibid.

54   Ibid.

55   Ibid., noting that in August 1966, students in western Beijing murdered more than 100 teachers.

56   Ibid.

57   Ibid.

58   Rod McPhee, "Torture, mass murder, rape and cannibalism ... The horror of Mao's Cultural Revolution 50 years on," May 20, 2016, http://www.mirror.co.uk/news/world-news/torture-mass-murder-rape-cannibalism-8017041.

59 Ibid.

60 Ibid.

61 Ibid.

62 Ibid.

63 "Opium of the people," https://en.wikipedia.org/wiki/Opium_of_
the_people. And while China has changed from the days of Mao, it
appears that Mao's godlessness has persevered firmly through the
generations since. "China has the world's greatest irreligious [or
godless] population. The Chinese government is atheist. . . . In order to
be a member of the Communist Party of China an individual must not
have religious affiliation." While the Chinese government does not ban
religion itself, and the present Chinese constitution nominally protects
religious freedom, the "Chinese government's attitude to religion is one
of skepticism and nonpromotion. According to a 2012 Gallup poll, 47%
of Chinese people were convinced atheists, and a further 30% were not
religious. In comparison only 14% considered themselves to be religious.
Only three years later, another "Gallup poll found the number of
convinced atheists in China to be 61%, with a further 29% saying that they
are not religious compared to just 7% who are religious." If the premise of
our book is correct, watch out for even more callousness from China with
each passing decade. "Irreligion in China," www.en.wikipedia.org/wiki/
irreligion_in_China.

64 "Commanding Heights," https://www.pbs.org/wgbh/commandingheights/
shared/minitext/prof_maozedong.html

65 Malcom Moore, "In China, Chairman Mao Still Bigger than Jesus,"
December 25, 2013, http://www.telegraph.co.uk/news/worldnews/asia/
china/10537651/In-China-Chairman-Mao-still-bigger-than-Jesus.html

66 Malcom Moore, "We should not worship Mao as a god, says China's
president," December 26, 2013, http://www.telegraph.co.uk/news/
worldnews/asia/china/10538324/We-should-not-worship-Mao-as-a-god-
says-Chinas-president.html

67 Fidel Castro Biography, Biography.com, http://www.biography.com/
people/fidel-castro-9241487.

68 Ibid.

69 Ibid.

70 Glenn Garvin, "Red ink: The high human cost of the Cuban revolution,"
December 1, 2016, http://www.miamiherald.com/news/nation-world/
world/americas/cuba/article118282148.html

71 http://en.wikipedia.org/wiki/Fidel_Castro#Religious_beliefs

72 Garvin, "Red ink," referencing July 2015 report, http://www.cubaarchive.
org/files/Blood_Extraction.pdf

73 Sara Miller Llana, "Fidel Castro, excommunicated in 1962,
meets with Pope Benedict," *Christian Science Monitor*, http://

www.minnpost.com/christian-science-monitor/2012/03/
fidel-castro-excommunicated-1962-meets-pope-benedict.

74 See generally, http://www.history.com/this-day-in-history/
che-guevara-is-executed

75 Ibid.

76 https://en.wikipedia.org/wiki/List_of_atheist_activists_and_educators

77 http://www.history.com/this-day-in-history/che-guevara-is-executed.

78 See generally, http://www.cheguevaraonline.com/

79 Roger Williams, "Top 10 Profile: Nicolae Ceaușescu," May 14, 2006, http://
authoritarianism.blogspot.com/2006/05/top-10-profile-nicolae-ceauescu.
html.

80 Ibid.

81 Ibid.

82 "Ceaușescu's Romania," http://politicalpathologies.wikispaces.com/
Ceausescu's+Romania.

83 Williams, "Top 10 Profile," *supra*.

84 Dan Simmons, "Children of the Night," 2012, St. Martin's Griffin, https://
mcpl.monroe.lib.in.us/Mobile/BakerAndTaylor/Excerpt?ISBN=97812500098
52&UPC=&position=1

85 https://en.wikipedia.org/wiki/
Trial_of_Nicolae_and_Elena_Ceau%C8%99escu#cite_note-theday23janu-22

86 Alan Elsner, "Trial and Execution: The Dramatic Deaths of Nicolae and
Elena Ceaușescu," http://www.huffingtonpost.com/alan-elsner/trial-and-
execution-the-d_b_401497.html

87 See generally, https://en.wikipedia.org/wiki/
Religious_persecution_in_Communist_Romania

88 "Nicolae Ceaușescu," More or Less, Heroes & Killers of the 20th Century,
http://www.moreorless.net.au/killers/ceausescu.html (first published 2001,
modified 2011).

89 Raymond H. Anderson, "Giant Among Communists Governed Like a
Monarch," the *New York Times*, May 5, 1980.

90 "Did Yugoslav dictator Tito poison Stalin?," July 18, 2012, http://www.
dailymail.co.uk/news/article-2175385/Did-Tito-poison-Stalin-Historian-
claims-Yugoslav-dictator-killed-rival-target-22-Soviet-assassination-
attempts.html.

91 Ibid.

92 Tomislav Sunic and Nikola Stedul, "Marshal Tito's Killing Fields,"
February 17, 2002, http://www.andrija-hebrang.com/eng/marshal_tito.htm.

93 Ibid.

94 Anderson, "Giant Among communists Governed Like a Monarch."

95 Rudolph J. Rummel, *Statistics of Democide: Genocide and Mass Murder Since
1900* (LIT Verlag Münster, 1998), 164.

96 Vjekoslav Perica, *Balkan Idols: Religion and Nationalism in Yugoslav States*
(New York: Oxford University Press, 2002), 103. Tito has been criticized

for creating a Muslim nation. He had three reasons for doing so. It fit in with his policy of checks and balances to strengthen the Muslims against the stronger power of the Serbs; it went well with his foreign policy of alliance with the Non-aligned Muslim countries of the Middle East and North Africa; and he hoped he could weaken Muslim fundamentalism if it became accepted that it was possible for a Muslim not to be a fundamentalist or indeed any kind of Muslim in religion, but a communist atheist by doctrine and a Muslim by nationality. He knew that he would get no support from Muslim fundamentalism, even before the Ayatollah Khomeini denounced him as an atheist persecutor of Islam. See Jasper Ridley, *Tito: A Biography* (Constable and Company Ltd., 1994), 400.

97 Kallie Szczepanski, "Ho Chi Minh," http://asianhistory.about.com/od/vietnam/p/Biography-of-Ho-Chi-Minh.htm.

98 Charles E. Kirkpatrick, *Vietnam* magazine, February 1990, http://www.historynet.com/ho-chi-minh-north-vietnam-leader.htm#sthash.dFKy3pbq.dpuf.

99 "Ho Chi Minh," http://schools-wikipedia.org/wp/h/Ho_Chi_Minh.htm.

100 Ibid.

101 Ibid.

102 Ibid.

103 Vox Day, *The Irrational Atheist* (Dallas: BenBella Books, 2008), appendix A.

104 The Killing Fields Museum, http://www.killingfieldsmuseum.com/genocide1.html

105 Ibid.

106 Ibid.

107 Ibid.

108 Ibid.

109 https://en.wikipedia.org/wiki/Pol_Pot#cite_ref-NYTi_45-0

110 R. J. Rummel, "Statistics of North Korean Democide, Estimates, Calculations, and Sources," http://www.hawaii.edu/powerkills/SOD.CHAP10.HTM.

111 Ibid.

112 Ibid.

113 Ibid.

114 Bruce Harris, "Kim Il Sung," http://www.moreorless.net.au/killers/kim-il-sung.html, first published October 16, 2003, modified March 8, 2017.

115 Elizabeth Raum. *North Korea. Series: Countries Around the World.* (Heinemann, 2012.) p. 28: "North Korea is an atheist state. This means that people do not pray in public or attend places of worship. Buddhist temples exist from earlier times. They are now preserved as historic buildings, but they are not used for worship. A few Christian churches exist, but few people attend services. North Koreans do not celebrate religious holidays."; see also http://www.conservapedia.com/Kim_Jong-un

116 https://en.wikipedia.org/wiki/
Benito_Mussolini#Expulsion_from_the_Italian_Socialist_Party

117 Anthony James Gregor, *The Faces of Janus: Marxism and Fascism in the Twentieth Century* (2000), p. 20. See generally, https://en.wikipedia.org/wiki/A._James_Gregor.

118 Dinesh D'Souza, "What Hitler Learned from the Democrats," July 31, 2017, http://www.breitbart.com/big-government/2017/07/31/dinesh-dsouza-hitler-learned-democrats/

119 Sullivan, Barry "More than meets the eye: the Ethiopian War and the Origins of the Second World War" pages 178-203 from The Origins of the Second World War Reconsidered A.J.P. Taylor and the Historians, London: Routledge, 1999 page 188.

120 Bruce Strang, *On the Fiery March*, New York: Praeger, 2003 page 27; see generally https://en.wikipedia.org/wiki/Benito_Mussolini#cite_note-Strang.2C_Bruce_page_22-122

121 Ibid.

122 Ibid.

123 Ibid.

124 Dennis Mack Smith. 1982. *Modern Italy; A Political History*. Ann Arbor: The University of Michigan Press. p. 1. See generally, https://en.wikipedia.org/wiki/Benito_Mussolini#cite_ref-dmsmith_1_183-0

125 Ibid.

126 Ibid.

127 Jesse Greenspan (25 October 2012). "9 Things You May Not Know About Mussolini," http://www.history.com/news/9-things-you-may-not-know-about-mussolini.

128 Smith, supra, p. 8.

129 Smith, supra, p. 8.

130 Smith, supra, p. 8.

131 Smith, supra, p. 12.

132 Peter Neville. *Mussolini*. Oxon, England, UK; New York, New York, USA: Routledge, 2005. P. 176.

133 Smith, supra, p. 15.

134 https://en.wikipedia.org/wiki/
Benito_Mussolini#cite_note-rmussolini_129-192

135 Ibid.

136 Ibid.

137 Ibid.

138 Ibid.

139 Ibid.

140 Ibid. and see Smith, supra, pp. 162-163.

141 Ibid., and see Smith, supra, pp. 222-223.

142 "Mosaic of Victims: In Depth," United States Holocaust Memorial Museum (Washington, DC), https://www.ushmm.org/wlc/en/article.php?ModuleId=10007329.

143 Rebecca Onion, "A 1942 List of Hitler's Lies," http://www.slate.com/blogs/the_vault/2016/05/18/a_list_of_hitler_s_lies_compiled_by_the_office_of_war_information_in_1942.html. The list from the Office of War Information is truly breathtaking what Hitler had stated and written. Time has shown these words to be so brazenly false and blatant lies designed solely to lull an otherwise naïve world desirous to believe anyone who told them he did not really want war.

144 "Was Hitler a Christian?," Staff Report, Straight Dope Science Advisory Board, October 30, 1999, http://www.straightdope.com/columns/read/1699/was-hitler-a-christian.

145 Albert Speer, Inside the Third Reich (New York: Simon & Schuster, 1970), 96.

146 http://old.nationalreview.com/shiflett/shiflett012102.shtml, citing speech of March 3,1933, Norman H. Baynes, ed. The Speeches of Adolf Hitler: April 1922–August 1939, vol. 1 (New York: Howard Fertig, 1969), 409.

147 Hermann Rauschning, The Voice of Destruction: Conversations with Hitler 1940 (New York: Kessinger Publishing), 56.

148 Ibid., 57–58.

149 Ibid., 62–63.

150 Yehuda Bauer, "The Trauma of the Holocaust: Some Historical Perspectives," as conveyed during the Twenty-Sixth Annual Scholars Conference, Minneapolis, Minnesota 1996.

151 Adolph Hitler, Hitler Table Talk, 1941-1944: His Private Conversations (Enigma Books; 3rd edition, 2000), Norman Cameron (Translator), R. H. Stevens (Translator), H. R. Trevor-Roper (Preface, Introduction), 625. See also Alan Bullock, Hitler: A Study in Tyranny (Odhams Press; 2nd edition (1952)

152 Anton Gil, An Honourable Defeat: A History of German Resistance to Hitler, 1933-1945 (Henry Holt & Co 1994).

153 "Was Hitler a Christian?," http://www.straightdope.com/columns/read/1699/was-hitler-a-christian.

154 Rauschning, supra, at p. 50, emphasis added. See also Leo Stein, Hitler Came for Niemoeller, The Nazi War Against Religion (Pelican Publishing Company, 2003), 242.

155 Many will point to a couple of passing references in Mein Kampf, his missive from prison, in which he made reference to Jesus, as well as some references to God in various speeches to the masses. But this is virtually all one can point to. One would imagine that if Hitler in fact held a true passion for Christianity, he would attend Church at least on a symbolically regular basis. One would also expect that he would not elevate himself above Jesus or God, as he did.

156 Day, The Irrational Atheist, appendix A. Day notes the top 52 atheist leaders,

all of whom are confirmed to have been responsible for killing at least 20,000 innocents among their own countrymen. There are many more beyond this, of whom it is not known whether they killed at least 20,000 of their own countrymen, but whom were prolific killers nonetheless.

157   We will discuss Islam later, in a separate chapter. There is no denying that Islam—a religion, and one of the three major Abrahamic religions—killed millions throughout its approximately 1400-year presence. Much of Islam's history involves conquest and forced conversions, and imposition of religious dogma through Sharia law, as well as other horrific brutalities, and the suppression of innovation and freedom. Much of the Koran also advocates destruction of all non-believers.

It is true that the atheist can point to Islam, particularly as radical Islamists have applied it, as an example of where religion has gone astray and participated in horrific things. However, remember that I respond to the argument that supposedly *all* "religion" has caused more deaths than anything else. It is just not true: I distinguish the Judeo-Christian faiths from the Islamic faith because the atheist lumps Christianity and Judaism with all other religions when it makes its charge. In the same way not all nations or cultures are the same, not all religions are the same. The focus of this book is on the evils of atheism, in stark relief to Christianity and Judaism.

The fact that Islam has engaged in much killing throughout its history does not change the toxic nature of atheism, nor atheism's horrifically callous history. To argue otherwise is like one mass-murderer (say Charles Manson) arguing that people should consider him a good guy because another mass-murderer (say, Ted Bundy) did horrific things. They were both monsters. Neither of them gets to excuse their monstrosity because another committed similar horrors.

158   Robert P. Lockwood, "History and Myth: The Inquisition," *Catholic League*, August 2000, http://www.catholicleague.org/history-and-myth-the-inquisition/

159   "Salem Witch Trials," 2011, http://www.history.com/topics/salem-witch-trials

160   https://en.wikipedia.org/wiki/First_Crusade#Situation_in_Europe

161   See generally, https://en.wikipedia.org/wiki/Anti-Jewish_pogroms_in_the_Russian_Empire#Casualties, and https://en.wikipedia.org/wiki/Christianity_and_antisemitism.

162   https://en.wikipedia.org/wiki/Spanish_Inquisition

163   Ibid.

164   Roberto Perez, "Myth Busters in Apologetics," http://www.sharefaith.com/guide/christian-apologetics/myth-busters-in-apologetics.html. In the spirit of completeness, some have estimated the deaths to range from 1 million to 9 million but acknowledge the utter lack of records to support the higher numbers. See, e.g., https://www.reference.com/history/many-people-died-

crusades-4483019b5f8684c5; https://www.washingtonpost.com/national/
religion/was-obama-right-about-the-crusades-and-islamic-extremism-
analysis/2015/02/06/3670628a-ae46-11e4-8876-460b1144cbc1_story.
html?utm_term=.d806c4a781b5 (estimating 1.7 million).

165 Ibid.

166 http://www.history.com/topics/salem-witch-trials

167 Dr. Christopher, Probst, "Martin Luther and the 'Jews:' A Reappraisal,"
http://www.theologian.org.uk/churchhistory/lutherandthejews.html

168 See generally, https://en.wikipedia.org/wiki/On_the_Jews_and_Their_Lies;
https://en.wikipedia.org/wiki/Anti-Jewish_pogroms_in_the_
Russian_Empire#Casualties; and https://en.wikipedia.org/wiki/
Christianity_and_antisemitism.

169 Paul Johnson. *A History of the Jews* (HarperCollins Publishers, 1987), p. 242.
However, in fairness to Martin Luther, he was an "equal opportunity"
hater, loathing anyone who disagreed with him in equally foul terms,
including other protestants, the Catholic Church, and the Pope himself—
whom he accused of managing brothels, being the anti-Christ, a murderer,
and even a "werewolf." Eric Metaxas, *Martin Luther* (Viking, 2017), p. 419.

170 See generally, https://en.wikipedia.org/wiki/History_of_the_Jews_
in_Germany. It is not clear how many Jews died during these attacks,
although assuming whole communities perished, the number must be
signficant.

171 For an excellent analysis of the may permutations of Anti-Semitism from
ancient times to the modern era, please see generally, Dennis Prager and
Joseph Telushkin, *Why the Jews: The Reason for Anti-Semitism* (Simon &
Schuster, Inc., 2016).

172 Steven R. Weisman, "In a Tide of Japanese Books on Jews, an Anti-Semitic
Current," February 19, 1991, http://www.nytimes.com/1991/02/19/world/
in-a-tide-of-japanese-books-on-jews-an-anti-semitic-current.html

173 See generally, https://en.wikipedia.org/wiki/
Anti-Jewish_pogroms_in_the_Russian_Empire#Casualties

174 Jay Michaelson, "Was Obama right about the Crusades and Islamic
extremism?" February 6, 2015, https://www.washingtonpost.com/national/
religion/was-obama-right-about-the-crusades-and-islamic-extremism-
analysis/2015/02/06/3670628a-ae46-11e4-8876-460b1144cbc1_story.
html?utm_term=.d806c4a781b5 (stating: "There's a reason the Klan burned
crosses alongside its lynchings and acts of arson, after all.")

175 Penny Starr, "KKK Lynched 3,446 Blacks in 86 Years – Abortion Claims
That Many Black Babies in 'Less Than Four Days,'" May 15, 2013, http://
www.cnsnews.com/news/article/kkk-lynched-3446-blacks-86-years-
abortion-claims-many-black-babies-less-four-days; see also https://www.
quora.com/How-many-people-have-the-KKK-killed.

176 Robert J. Knecht, *The French Religious Wars 1562-1598* (Oxford, England: Osprey Publishing, 2002), 91; see generally, https://en.wikipedia.org/wiki/French_Wars_of_Religion#cite_note-1

177 Ibid.

178 https://en.wikipedia.org/wiki/Fascism. See also https://en.wikipedia.org/wiki/Abortion_in_Germany#History.

179 Ibid.

180 Becky Yeh, "The Abortion Ripple Effect; Russia's tragic abortion tale," June 27, 2014, https://www.liveaction.org/news/the-abortion-ripple-effect-russias-tragic-abortion-tale/. See also, Monica Showalter, "Five Ways Lenin's Propoganda Destroyed Marriage and the Family in Russia," October 23, 2103, http://www.investors.com/politics/viewpoint/bolsheviks-targeted-women-and-children-with-antifamily-antimarriage-propaganda/.

     It should be noted that while Joseph Stalin outlawed the practice in 1936, abortion remained illegal in the country until after his death in 1953, but then reverted to becoming legal. By then the abortion culture had so cemented within Russia that Russia remains the highest abortion producer of the world.

181 Ibid.

182 Ibid.

183 Ibid.

184 Ibid.

185 Ibid.

186 "Abortion Fast Facts," May 28, 2017, http://www.cnn.com/2013/09/18/health/abortion-fast-facts/index.html.

187 Daniel McLaughlin, "Legacy of Romania's Contraception Ban Lives On," August 28, 2007, https://www.irishtimes.com/news/health/legacy-of-romania-s-contraception-ban-lives-on-1.958842. The article describes the chilling relationship of the government with abortion: In Romania, where communism had first allowed abortion liberally along with other communist nations, the population ultimate decreased to alarming levels. To reverse that trend, President Nicolae Ceauşescu enacted "Decree 770" in 1966 to ban abortion and all contraceptives. Women and doctors who performed abortions could be jailed for two years or more. Government agents forced women to mandatory gynecological examinations at work; if they found that they were pregnant, then the Securitate, Ceauşescu's dreaded secret police, would monitor the mother for the term to make sure she kept the child. Securitate agents would even spy on doctors and even examine still-born children to make sure they had not been illegally aborted.

     The result was women dumping over 100,000 unwanted children in Romania's decrepit orphanages, and the death of more than 10,000 women during or after illegal terminations. Still, like their Russian counterparts, Romanian women view abortion as the cheapest and "go-to" form of birth control.

188 Denyer, "Horrors of One-Child Policy Leave Deep Scars in Chinese Society," October 30, 2015, https://www.washingtonpost.com/world/asia_pacific/horrors-of-one-child-policy-leave-deep-scars-in-chinese-society/2015/10/30/6bd28e0c-7e7b-11e5-bfb6-65300a5ff562_story.html?utm_term=.a191a1bebd2f

189 Ibid.

190 Emily Matchar, August 5, 2013, https://www.theatlantic.com/international/archive/2013/08/in-liberal-europe-abortion-laws-come-with-their-own-restrictions/278350/

191 Interestingly, the reason many wanted America not to fight or engage in the Middle East fight against Al Queda or ISIS is that they maintain that Islam is a religion of peace, and the "vast majority" of Muslims love peace, and that to go there and fight might make Muslims think we are seeking war with Islam itself. But if they maintain this "exception" view, then they can't *also* argue that Islam is a general example of how religion is destructive. Even they recognize (or want to recognize) that Islam is inherently peaceful, and that radical Islamists are a "fringe" exception.
   Either they are or they are not. They cannot have it both ways.

192 Ibid.

193 Ibid. Shockingly, when looking at the history of the Progressives through Wikipedia's reference, it states "The Catholics [although favoring collectivism] strongly opposed birth control proposals such as eugenics." Wikipedia gave only the briefest of write-ups regarding the role of "eugenics" in the Progressive movement of the early 1900s. To the Progressives, it was only a form of birth control, perhaps no different than other forms of birth control. Also see http://en.wikipedia.org/wiki/Progressive_Era#Eugenics.

194 Ibid.

195 Ibid.

196 Ibid.

197 Ibid.

198 Jonah Goldberg, *Liberal Fascism: The Secret History of the American Left from Mussolini to the Politics of Meaning* (Doubleday, 2008), p. 9.

199 Ibid.

200 Wolfgang Schivelbusch, *Three New Deals: Reflections on Roosevelt's America, Mussolini's Italy, and Hitler's Germany, 1933-1939* (Picador 2007), p. 23.

201 Ibid.

202 John Griffing, "FDR Praised Mussolini And Loved Fascism," December 13, 2016, http://dailycaller.com/2016/12/13/fdr-praised-mussolini-and-loved-fascism/

203 Ibid.

204 Ibid.

205 Ibid.

206 Ibid.

207 Ibid.

208 Russell Grigg, "Eugenics . . . death of the defenceless," http://creation.com/eugenics-death-of-the-defenceless#r15.

209 Ibid.

210 Ibid.

211 Ibid.

212 Ibid.

213 Ibid.

214 Miller, "Eugenics, American Progressivism, and the 'German Idea of the State.'"

215 Ibid.

216 Ibid.

217 Art Carden and Steven Horwitz, "Eugenics: Progressivism's Ultimate Social Engineering," September 21, 2011, https://fee.org/articles/eugenics-progressivisms-ultimate-social-engineering/.

218 Some will point to a religious spinoff movement from Protestantism at the time, known as the the Social Gospel movement, led mostly by Congregationalist and Unitarian ministers, and which did indeed support the eugenics movement. However, this organization was hardly in line with mainstream Christianity, Catholicism, or Judaism. While every broad movement will find adherents among the millions of pastors, priests, reverends, and rabbis throughout the world, it does not mean that the faiths actually adopted them. It means the eugenics movement was able to contort even some of the faithful to their message.

    Likewise, "the Social Gospel reconceived Christianity as being less about faith and salvation, and more about, as [Christine] Rosen writes, 'ushering in the Kingdom of God on earth through [social] reform and service.' Many Social Gospel adherents viewed eugenics as God's plan to reconcile the truths of science with the Bible. Toward this end, Bible verses were reinterpreted and found to contain what had theretofore been secret eugenics messages. Thus, in one minister's sermon, Noah's flood was God's own eugenics policy for eliminating a human race that had degraded and become inferior." See Wesley Smith, review of Christine Rosen's *Preaching Eugenics: Religious Leaders and the American Eugenics Movement,* http://www.nrlc.org/archive/news/2004/NRL08/preaching_eugenics_religious_lea.htm.

    Sadly, and to their great shame, many "Reform" churches and synagogues, seeking to "get with the times," went along with the eugenics movement, more out of fear of looking like the church might be out of touch with the ever-developing and exciting world of science. In short, such reform churches and synagogues did not wish to see themselves somehow left behind or seemingly irrelevant. Likewise, even today, some pastors have supported abortion as being beneficial to society, and some have embraced same-sex marriage. But one could not meaningfully say that religion institutionally embraces abortion or same-sex marriage.

219 Tiffany Jones Miller, "Eugenics, American Progressivism, and the 'German Idea of the State,'" January 31, 2013, http://www.libertylawsite.org/2013/01/31/eugenics-american-progressivism-and-the-german-idea-of-the-state/.

220 Ibid.

221 Ibid.

222 Ibid.

223 Ibid.

224 David Turner, "Foundations of Holocaust: American eugenics and the Nazi connection," December 20, 2012, http://www.jpost.com/Blogs/The-Jewish-Problem---From-anti-Judaism-to-anti-Semitism/Foundations-of-Holocaust-American-eugenics-and-the-Nazi-connection-364998.

225 Andrea DenHoed, "The Forgotten Lessons of the American Eugenics Movement," April 27, 2016, http://www.newyorker.com/books/page-turner/the-forgotten-lessons-of-the-american-eugenics-movement.

226 Ibid.

227 For more on this, review the disturbing background of Margaret Sanger, founder of Planned Parenthood, who sought not only to advance abortion rights, but also Eugenics (the philosophy of weeding out less desirable "elements" of society—those who are frail or suffer from disease, for example. Or, more ominously, those who don't have the right skin color, particularly African-Americans. https://en.wikipedia.org/wiki/Margaret_Sanger. In spite of such controversies, many continue to view Sanger as a positive force in the American reproductive rights and woman's rights movements. *Ibid.* Horrifically, in her own autobiography, she proudly boasted of her talks to a very receptive Klu Klux Klan in the 1920's. Likewise, that she generated enthusiasm among some of America's leading racists says something about the content and tone of her remarks. *Ibid.* In a famous letter, Sanger wrote: "[Let's not let] word go out that we want to exterminate the Negro population, and the minister is the man who can straighten out that idea if it ever occurs to any of their more rebellious members" (Margaret Sanger commenting on the 'Negro Project' in a letter to Clarence Gamble, Dec. 10, 1939); Arina Grossu, "Margaret Sanger, racist eugenicist extraordinaire," the *Washington Times*, May 5, 2014, http://www.washingtontimes.com/news/2014/may/5/grossu-margaret-sanger-eugenicist/.

Chapter II

1 See John Rennie, "15 Answers to Creationist Nonsense," July 1, 2002, https://www.scientificamerican.com/article/15-answers-to-creationist/,

where the Darwinists claim otherwise and note that "Darwin suggested that even 'incomplete' eyes might confer benefits (such as helping creatures orient toward light) and thereby survive for further evolutionary refinement. Biology has vindicated Darwin: researchers have identified primitive eyes and light-sensing organs throughout the animal kingdom and have even tracked the evolutionary history of eyes through comparative genetics. (It now appears that in various families of organisms, eyes have evolved independently.)" Strangely, they present no actual evidence to support this; however, they imply to the reader that such evidence exists.

The article essentially argues that evidence exists because they say evidence exists. Not only is this reasoning circular, but it ignores that fossil records would show ample evidence of such eye development. They do not. It also ignores the fact that the "eye" has developed so similarly in so many utterly unrelated species.

2   Paul Reber, "What Is the Memory Capacity of the Human Brain?," May 1, 2010, http://www.scientificamerican.com/article/what-is-the-memory-capacity/.

3   I will put aside for now the apparent irony that many among the godless argue that radical Islam is not Islam. In fact, they seem to be apologists for Islam (perhaps because they perceive it as some counterweight to Christianity and Judaism). But this in fact cuts against their argument, since if radical Islam (or "violent extremism" as some have called it) is somehow not the issue, then we can stop our discussion here. However, I pursue this argument for intellectual honesty and consistency.

4   The Catholic Knight, March 17, 2008, http://catholicknight.blogspot.com/2008/03/galileo-inquisition-fully-explained.html.

5   Commentator and national syndicated radio host Dennis Prager has noted that many students routinely state openly they have no moral issue with cheating on tests (as long as they know they can get away with it). And why wouldn't they think this way, without a moral code to tell them otherwise? Logic dictates that they do whatever they can to beat out their fellow classmates. Many people also have no problem with the idea of stealing from a large business enterprise (Walmart, Target, Amazon, Walgreens) because they are "so big" they can absorb the loss easily and it's therefore no big deal. They supposedly "draw the line" only with smaller Mom and Pop stores. Dennis Prager, podcast, "Ultimate Issues Hour—God or Reason?," September 9, 2015.

6   *Buck v. Bell*, 274 U.S. 200 (1927)

7   Dave Andrusko, "Peter Singer: Abortion is justified for population control," October 25, 2012, http://www.lifesitenews.com/opinion/peter-singer-abortion-is-justified-for-population-control, noting Singer "adheres to the position that a child does not attain 'full moral status' until somewhere between one and two, which makes infanticide in some cases

(actually many cases) acceptable." His reasoning turns upon the child being self-aware.

8   Exhibit from Holocaust Museum, Washington D.C.

9   Ibid.

10   https://phys.org/news/2017-08-atheists-thought-immoral-fellow.html, August 7, 2017.

11   Ibid.

12   Ibid. Interestingly, the focus of this study was to express concern for so-called "anti-atheist bias," as if to sound an alarm of growing danger facing atheists. But such "bias" should come as no surprise: a group of people who shun morals worry that others will look at them as people who act without morals. Imagine that.

13   For an excellent appreciation of this, please refer to Joseph Telushkin, *Biblical Literacy* (William Morrow, 2002) which expounds upon this in exceptional detail.

14   See generally, https://en.wikipedia.org/wiki/Science_and_the_Catholic_Church#Galileo_Galilei

15   Christopher Kaczor, "The Church Opposes Science: The Myth of Catholic Irrationality," chap. 1, *The Seven Big Myths about the Catholic Church: Distinguishing Fact from Fiction about Catholicism*, http://www.catholiceducation.org/en/science/catholic-contributions/the-church-opposes-science-the-myth-of-catholic-irrationality.html.

16   https://en.wikipedia.org/wiki/Georges_Lemaitre

17   Ibid, noting that Church patronage of sciences continues through elite institutions like the Pontifical Academy of Sciences and Vatican Observatory.

18   Kaczor, "The Church Opposes Science."

19   Ibid.

20   Scott Locklin, "No Catholic Church, No Scientific Method," New Oxford Review, October 2011, http://www.newoxfordreview.org/article.jsp?did=1011-locklin;

21   Thomas E. Woods, Jr., "The Catholic Church and the Creation of the University, Catholic Education Resource Center, http://www.catholiceducation.org/en/education/catholic-contributions/the-catholic-church-and-the-creation-of-the-university.html.

22   http://en.wikipedia.org/wiki/Role_of_the_Catholic_Church_in_Western_civilization

23   Cameron Atfield, *The Pope's astronomer on space, the Bible and alien life,* The Sydney Morning Herald, October 16, 2014.

24   Pope John Paul II, address, the Pontifical Academy of Sciences, October 22, 1996.

25   Ibid.

26   Fr. Williams, *National Catholic Register*, http://www.defendingthebride.com/pp/sc3/.

27 Ibid.

28 Vatican Council (Sess. III, de fide, c. 4)

29 https://en.wikipedia.org/wiki/Catholic_Church_and_science.

30 https://en.wikipedia.org/wiki/Thomas_Woods

31 Ibid.; see also Thomas E. Woods Jr., "How the Catholic Church Built Western Civilization", LewRockwell.com, accessed March 2, 1010, https://archive.lewrockwell.com/woods/woods40.html.

32 Ronald L. Numbers, ed., "Introduction," *Galileo Goes to Jail and Other Myths About Science and Religion* (Cambridge, MA: Harvard University Press, 2009), 6.

33 "Catholic Church and health care," https://en.m.wikipedia.org/wiki/Catholic_Church_and_health_care

34 https://en.wikipedia.org/wiki/Catholic_Church_and_science

35 "Catholic Church and health care," https://en.m.wikipedia.org/wiki/Catholic_Church_and_health_care

36 Thomas E. Woods, "Commentary: History shows contributions of Catholic Church to Western civilization," *Deseret News*, December 28, 2011, http://www.deseretnews.com/article/700210479/Commentary-History-shows-contributions-of-Catholic-Church-to-Western-civilization.html?pg=all. Also, please refer to Thomas E. Woods Jr., *How the Catholic Church Built Western Civilization* (Washington, DC: Regnery Publishing, 2012).

37 John Coffey, "The Abolition of the slave trade: Christian conscience and political action," Jubilee Centre, June 2006, http://www.jubilee-centre.org/the-abolition-of-the-slave-trade-christian-conscience-and-political-action-by-john-coffey/.

38 https://en.wikipedia.org/wiki/Christian_Abolitionism#cite_note-4

39 Ibid.

40 Ibid.

41 Ibid.

42 Ibid.

43 Ibid.

44 Ibid.

45 Ibid.

46 See http://www.imdb.com/title/tt0041959/quotes

Chapter III

1 http://www.huffingtonpost.com/yalda-t-uhls/kids-want-fame_b_1201935.html

2 http://guardianlv.com/2013/08/studies-show-that-children-just-want-to-be-famous/

3 https://www.attn.com/stories/2058/rashida-jones-documentary-amateur-porn.

4   But then what happens to multiculturalism, which so many liberals embrace, the notion that we should allow as many cultures to flourish everywhere and that no one culture should dominate? Won't this fly in the face of universal governance? So many questions. . . .

5   Mark Lewis and Sarah Lyall, "Norway Mass Killer Gets the Maximum: 21 Years," *New York Times*, August 24, 2012, http://www.nytimes. com/2012/08/25/world/europe/anders-behring-breivik-murder-trial. html?_r=0.

6   Not so fast, according to those who support a different viewpoint. They will argue that the Koran makes a clear exception: "If you fear that you might not treat the orphans justly, then marry the women that seem good to you: two, or three, or four. If you fear that you will not be able to treat them justly, then marry (only) one, or marry from among those whom your right hands possess. This will make it more likely that you will avoid injustice" (Surah Al-Nisa 4:3; www.islamicstudies.info). See also, http://www.alsiraj.net/English/misc/women/html/page16.html for further discussion of polygamy in Islam. But this verse does not *discourage* polygamy. It merely states that you shouldn't do it if you can't show equal justice to each of your wives or can't afford multiple wives.

Chapter IV

1   The car was invented and then mass produced around the turn of the twentieth century. I wonder what would have happened had its inventors created it a hundred years later. I doubt it would have survived today's blistering regulatory scrutiny. It would require the development of roads and traffic laws, but it would have to get over the enormous hurdle of regulator's basic contempt of human individuality. The car is one of the best manifestations of that.

I can just imagine the congressional hearings now: "Are you serious?" the regulators would ask, grilling the inventors' proposal for this latest invention called the "car." "You want us to believe that hundreds of thousands of drivers will drive on this thing you call a 'freeway'—in multiple lanes, no less—all at 50 to 70 miles an hour, and that they'll always dutifully stay in their lanes? You really think that they'll just stop at a stop sign or a stop light? You have way too much faith in your fellow man, sir. They can't be trusted to drive on their own. There'll be pile-ups and crashes every day. What's next, sir? Allowing people to fly in machines in the air? If we allow you to proceed with your car device and give this freely to the people, we will have failed as legislators in the protection of our citizenry from rampant destruction and death. Your machine, sir, is downright irresponsible. Thank goodness we live in a country where we can prevent reckless thinking such as yours. Good day to you, sir . . . good day." [End scene with shameful walkout.]

2   Dennis Prager, "Differences Between Left and Right: It's All about Big Government," July 7, 2015, http://www.nationalreview.com/article/420820/ differences-between-left-and-right-its-all-about-big-government-dennis-prager.

3   Ibid.

4   www.nycga.net/resources/documents/principles-of-solidarity/

5   www.nycga.net/resources/documents/declaration/

6   www.huffingtonpost.com/2011/11/01/occupy-wall-street-security_n_1069597.html. For more information on the details of such crimes, see abcnews.go.com/US/sexual-assaults-occupy-wall-street-camps/ story?id=14873014, www.businessinsider.com/truth-about-crime-at-occupy-wall-street-2011-11, and www.foxnews.com/us/2011/11/09/rash-sex-attacks-and-violent-crime-breaks-out-at-occupy-protests.html.

7   Interview of Michael Moore by Jerry Paxman of the BBC, October 20, 2011, https://www.youtube.com/watch?v=nkumIlD49cg

8   http://en.wikipedia.org/wiki/State_atheism.

9   Ibid.

10   http://townhall.com/columnists/dineshdsouza/2008/01/14/how_christians_ ended_slavery. In the excellent article, Dsouza poignantly notes: "In the American South, Christianity proved to be the solace of the oppressed. .... [W]hen black slaves sought to find dignity during the dark night of slavery, they didn't turn to Marcus Aurelius or David Hume; they turned to the Bible. When they sought hope and inspiration for liberation, they found it not in Voltaire or D'Holbach but in the Book of Exodus." He further notes: "The anti-slavery movements led by Wilberforce in England and abolitionists in America were dominated by Christians. These believers reasoned that since we are all created equal in the eyes of God, no one has the right to rule another without consent. This is the moral basis not only of anti-slavery but also of democracy." See also: https://en.wikipedia.org/ wiki/Christian_views_on_slavery, which discusses the contrast between Christian (and Jewish) belief on the one hand, and the fact that slavery nevertheless existed during the times of the Bible and thereafter, on the other.

11   Ibid. Indeed, in some parts of the world, the campaign to eradicate slavery still goes on.

12   Ibid.

13   Ibid.

14   Walter Olson, "Should Climate Change Deniers Be Prosecuted?" October 1, 2015, http://www.newsweek.com/ should-climate-change-deniers-be-prosecuted-378652

15   In 2006, then Senator John Kerry, who had previously run for the presidency in 2004 against George Bush, commented, "You know,

education, if you make the most of it, if you study hard and you do your homework, and you make an effort to be smart, uh, you, you can do well. If you don't, you get stuck in Iraq." Kerry later tried to argue this was a "botched" joke, and he really meant to apply the comment to George Bush's handling of Iraq itself. Few people accepted this rationale: if he had meant it against George Bush only, it would make no sense for him to argue that if you educate yourself, "you can do well." Achieving the presidency, by most standards, is doing well.

16 "Top political strategist Woody Allen thinks Obama would get much more done as dictator; No, *really*," May 18, 2010, *LA Times* Blogs, http://latimesblogs.latimes.com/washington/2010/05/woody-allen-obama.html.

17 https://www.youtube.com/watch?v=cLNabuovaIg, December 13, 2012.

18 Tim Graham, "Thomas Friedman's Power Lust: Let's Be 'China For A Day,'" MRC News Busters, November 21, 2008, http://www.newsbusters.org/blogs/nb/tim-graham/2008/11/21/thomas-friedmans-power-lust-lets-be-china-day (Thomas Friedman, *Hot, Flat, and Crowded*, "China for a Day [but Not for Two]," chap. 18 [New York: Farrar, Straus and Giroux, 2008]).

19 Ibid.

20 Ibid.

21 Regarding Harry Belafonte, see his interview with Tavis Smiley, December 1, 2011; http://www.pbs.org/wnet/tavissmiley/interviews/actor-activist-harry-belafonte-part-2/. Regarding Woody Allen, see https://whyevolutionistrue.wordpress.com/2015/01/31/woody-allen-on-atheism/ (in which he argues that to survive, one must lie to himself about God, "that one must have his delusions to live.") Regarding Thomas Friedman, see http://www.nytimes.com/2001/11/27/opinion/27FRIE.html. In that article, he doesn't necessarily espouse atheism but expresses a not-so-subtle contempt of all the major faiths. Among other things, he quotes approvingly of a well-known clergy member that each major religion is "totalitarian" in impulse and needs to modernize [whatever that might mean] and not see themselves as holding any absolute truths. Ironically, in dreaming for his coveted "China for a Day" dream, he actually embraces totalitarianism—so long as it secular.

22 Orwell, G., & Dean, M. (2003). 1984 (Book 1, Chapter 7, p. 23). Harlow: Pearson Education.

23 https://www.quora.com/What-are-some-examples-of-doublespeak-used-in-1984

Chapter V

1 For further reading on this subject, the classic thinkers (among many others) include Isaac Newton, René Descartes and the other continental rationalists, Gottfried Leibniz and Baruch Spinoza, Thomas Hobbes, John

Bramhall, George Berkeley, John Locke , Immanuel Kant and David Hume. In particular, Hume believed "a free action generated randomly with no regard for earlier conditions (*sui generis* or self-generated) was *absurd* and *unintelligible*." Gottfried Leibniz even went so far as to state: "Everything proceeds mathematically . . . if someone could have a sufficient insight into the inner parts of things, and in addition had remembrance and intelligence enough to consider all the circumstances and take them into account, he would be a prophet and see the future in the present as in a mirror" (see "History of the Free Will Problem," http://www. informationphilosopher.com/freedom/history/). And yet most of us would reject this thinking. It suggests we are merely highly sophisticated robots. But to think so is to ignore our own instinctive sense that we *do* have free will for most of our decisions, and that we are responsible (http://www. informationphilosopher.com/solutions/philosophers/kant/).

2   While consciousness generally means being aware of one's environment and body and lifestyle, self-awareness is the recognition of that awareness; Ferris Jabr, "Self-Awareness with a Simple Brain," November 1, 2012, www.scientificamerican.com/article/self-awareness-with-a-simple-brain/.

3   For more on the general conundrum of consciousness, see Steven Pinker, "The Brain: The Mystery of Consciousness, January 29, 2007, http:// content.time.com/time/magazine/article/0,9171,1580394-2,00.html; Amir D. Aczel, "Why Science Does Not Disprove God," April 27, 2014, http://time. com/77676/why-science-does-not-disprove-god/; and "Self-awareness," https://en.m.wikipedia.org/wiki/Self-awareness.

4   http://www.bpnews.net/27125/ warden-saw-only-one-answer-for-troubled-la-prison-christ

5   Ibid.

6   Ibid.

7   Dr. Adam Sheck, "New Study: Male Suicide at All Time High," May 7, 2013, The Good Men Project, http://goodmenproject.com/good-feed-blog/ new-study-male-suicide-at-all-time-high/.

8   For a listing of denominations and their varying attitudes toward abortion, please refer to Ernest L. Ohlhoff, "Abortion: Where Do the Churches Stand?" September, 12, 2000, http://www.pregnantpause.org/people/ wherchur.htm.

9   For a brief listing of denominations and their respective attitudes toward religion, please refer to "Which Churches Allow Gay Marriage?," August 3, 2010, http://www.gayweddinginstitute. com/_blog/Gay_Weddings_are_Good_for_Business/post/ Which_Churches_Allow_Gay_Marriage/

10   See https://en.wikipedia.org/wiki/Boy_Scouts_of_America_membership_ controversies. As of the writing of this book, just before publication, the Boy Scouts voted to allow girls as members.

11 See also, Toni Airaksinen, "Why Is Church Still So Popular?" August 18, 2017, https://pjmedia.com/trending/2017/08/18/75-percent-republicans-think-church-good-america/, elaborating on how those who attend church at least once a month are 22 percent less likely to suffer from depression.

12 Lauren Markoe, "Suicide rates among Jewish teens drop as religious devotion grows, study finds," the Washington Post, October 2, 2014, https://www.washingtonpost.com/national/religion/suicide-rates-among-jewish-teens-drop-as-religious-devotion-grows-study-finds/2014/10/02/c8e8f46c-4a71-11e4-a4bf-794ab74e90f0_story.html?utm_term=.dcce7f315653; "Religious and Spiritual Factors in Depression: Review and Integration of the Research," copyright © 2012 Raphael Bonelli et al., https://www.hindawi.com/journals/drt/2012/962860/; Emily Deans, MD, "Brains, Spirituality, and Depression," *Psychology Today*, January 26, 2014, https://www.psychologytoday.com/blog/evolutionary-psychiatry/201401/brains-spirituality-and-depression; ; Clay Routledge, Phd, "Are Religious People Happier Than Non-religious People?, Psychology Today, December 5, 2012, https://www.psychologytoday.com/blog/more-mortal/201212/are-religious-people-happier-non-religious-people.

13 For an excellent analysis of this, please refer to Thomas Cahill's book, which elaborates deeply into perhaps the greatest gift of Judaism: the fiction known as time (*The Gifts of the Jews: How a Tribe of Desert Nomads Changed the Way Everyone Thinks and Feels* [New York: Anchor Books, 1998])..

14 See Dr. Robert Lanza's excellent work on the explanation of biocentrism, which articulates the fictions of time and space in far greater detail than this book can cover. The premise is that all creation, including space, time, and whatever objects exist in the universe, are merely the products of our own perception (*Biocentrism* (Dallas: BenBella Books, 2009).

15 See, e.g., Jeffrey R. Ambrose, "The Human Problem," the *Real Truth*, https://realtruth.org/articles/100510-003-weather.html. There are many other articles in the same vein. Each decries all the horrific destructive actions of Man, mostly environmental, which have negatively impacted animals and plant-life everywhere.

16 Mark Steyn, *After America: Get Ready for Armageddon* (Washington, DC: Regnery Publishing, 2011), 236.

17 See generally, Amir D. Aczel, "Why Science Does Not Disprove God," April 27, 2014, http://time.com/77676/why-science-does-not-disprove-god/; Lisa Zyga, "Free will is an illusion, biologist says," March 3, 2010, http://phys.org/news/2010-03-free-illusion-biologist.html; See also, Robert Lanza, MD, *Biocentrism* (Dallas: BenBella Books, 2009), discussed below.

Chapter VII

1   See, generally http://www.history.com/news/
     history-lists/8-reasons-why-rome-fell

2   Ibid.

3   Ibid.

4   The History of the Decline and Fall of the Roman Empire, Edward Gibbon
     (1737–1794)

5   For a more comprehensive description and analysis of Europe's birth rate
     concerns and their consequences, I commend you strongly to Mark Steyn's
     excellent but chillingly prescient *America Alone: The End of the World As We
     Know It* (Regnery Publishing, 2008).

6   See Sean Flynn, "How Three Americans Prevented the Paris Train
     Attack," December 7, 2015, See http://www.gq.com/story/military-bros-
     foil-french-train-attack; see also Faith Karimi, "Train shooting heroes:
     The men who helped avert a massacre in Europe," August 23, 2015,
     http://www.cnn.com/2015/08/22/europe/france-train-shooting-heroes/
     and Mark Ellis, "Three American heroes on French train are strong
     Christians," August 27, 2015, http://blog.godreports.com/2015/08/
     three-american-heroes-on-train-are-strong-christians/

7   "Civil Rights Pioneer's Book Tells Impact of Religion," January 21, 1995,
     http://articles.latimes.com/1995-01-21/local/
     me-22523_1_civil-rights-movement

8   Searches for "atheist heroes" will point predominantly to famous scientists
     and inventors such as Stephen Hawking, Alan Turing, Thomas Edison, and
     Albert Einstein (although it is dubious to consider Einstein an atheist; the
     record on his religiosity is not clear and at best would suggest agnosticism,
     not atheism). But we are not merely talking about very bright people. We
     are discussing individuals who resisted the status quo at massive risk and
     peril to their freedom or even lives.

     Having said this, one atheist of true heroic stature was Russian
     physicist Andre Sakharov. He developed great scientific advances for
     the Soviet Union and had access to the highest echelons of government,
     including the KGB. But soon he became disillusioned with his country's
     suppressions and wrote extensively against the Soviet system in which he
     lived. Sadly, it is hard to find more brave atheists similar to him.

9   See https://www.cliffsnotes.com/literature/i/in-cold-blood/book-summary
     for an excellent summary, referencing exactly this point. As always, read
     the book for a deeper appreciation.

10   Ibid. See also https://www.cliffsnotes.com/literature/i/in-cold-blood/
     character-list-and-analysis/perry-smith.

11   Anne Speckhard and Ahmet S. Yayla, "ISIS Defector Reports on the Sale of
     Organs Harvested from ISIS-held 'Slaves'," the *Huffington Post*, updated
     January 4, 2017, http://m.huffpost.com/us/entry/8897708.html.

12 See, e.g. "Rotherham child sexual exploitation scandal," https://
    en.wikipedia.org/wiki/Rotherham_child_sexual_exploitation_scandal.

13 In November 2015, US President Barack Obama attended an environmental
    conference in Paris to discuss combating climate change. The summit took
    place only a short time after Jihadi terrorists launched a series of massive
    explosions and killings throughout that same city. In his signature speech
    at the conference, he seemed to say that climate change is the greatest
    threat facing the planet today. In his most telling moment, he stated, "we
    salute the people of Paris for insisting this crucial conference go on . . .
    that proves nothing will deter us from building the future we want for our
    children. What greater rejection of those who would tear down our world
    than marshaling our best efforts to save it?"

    Indeed, he asserted that not postponing the climate change conference
    was an "act of defiance" and a showing of the world's mutual resolve
    against the terrorists who attacked the city. "President Obama wants to
    beat ISIS by fighting climate change" editorial, *New York Post*, December
    1, 2015, http://nypost.com/2015/12/01/president-obama-wants-to-beat-isis-
    by-fighting-climate-change/. The point is not to attack such thinking but to
    showcase this as an example of godless thinking.

14 Mark Steyn, "Excusing the men who ran away," *Macleans*, March 5, 2009:
    http://www.macleans.ca/general/excusing-the-men-who-ran-away/.

15 Roosevelt faced tremendous opposition to his "unconditional surrender"
    stance when he announced it among his fellow allied leaders in
    Casablanca, 1943. Even, Churchill, the Pope and many of Roosevelt's
    cabinet thought it would hurt the chances of peace. But Roosevelt's
    determination soon persevered, and galvanized the allies to complete
    victory only 2 years later. Agostino Von Hassell and Sigrid Macrae,
    "Unconditional Surrender: Questioning FDR's Prerequisite for Peace,"
    January 23, 2013, http://www.thehistoryreader.com/modern-history/
    unconditional-surrender-questioning-fdrs-prerequisite-peace/

16 I do not drill down here into what I believe to be the judiciary's wrong-
    headed interpretation of the First Amendment. Right or wrong, I present
    this history solely to show the godless direction such interpretations have
    taken us, and what I believe will be the consequences.

17 Canada has passed such a law in 2015, as has New York and
    California (the latter, limited to health care practitioners). See
    generally, http://www.snopes.com/transgender-pronouns-fine-nyc/;
    http://dailysignal.com/2017/06/19/canadians-face-hate-crimes-
    using-wrong-gender-pronouns/; http://nypost.com/2016/05/19/
    city-issues-new-guidelines-on-transgender-pronouns/

18 "The new law, SB48, requires the California Board of Education and
    local school districts to adopt textbooks and other teaching materials
    that cover the contributions and roles of sexual minorities, as soon as the
    2013–2014 school year." See "Calif. gov signs landmark law to teach gay

history," *USA Today*, July 14, 2011, http://usatoday30.usatoday.com/news/
nation/2011-07-14-california-teaching-gay-history-schools_n.htm.

19   See https://apnews.com/61588a5642f945289ccec6b7f9b879ab, discussing the
topless rights push in New Hampshire and Los Angeles, and that women
have enjoyed this important right in New York since 1992.

20   Chelsea J. Carter, Catherine E. Shoichet, and Hamdi Alkhshali, "Obama
on ISIS in Syria: 'We don't have a strategy yet'," *CNN*, September 4, 2014,
www.cnn.com/2014/08/28/world/meast/isis-iraq-syria/; Zeke J. Miller,
"Obama Says 'We Don't Have a Strategy Yet' for Fighting ISIS," *Time*,
August 28, 2014, http://time.com/3211132/isis-iraq-syria-barack-obama-
strategy/; Kevin Liptak, "Obama: No 'complete strategy' yet on training
Iraqis," *CNN Politics*, June 9, 2015, www.cnn.com/2015/06/08/politics/
obama-abadi-iraq-germany-g7/. He started by saying at first that he had
"no strategy yet" then ended up the year by confirming he still had no
"complete" strategy.

21   As President Obama stated (in Rhenus Sports Arena, Strasbourg, France,
April 3, 2009), "So we must be honest with ourselves. In recent years
we've allowed our Alliance to drift. I know that there have been honest
disagreements over policy, but we also know that there's something
more that has crept into our relationship. In America, there's a failure
to appreciate Europe's leading role in the world. Instead of celebrating
your dynamic union and seeking to partner with you to meet common
challenges, there have been times where America has shown arrogance
and been dismissive, even derisive." See also generally, Nile Gardiner
and Morgan Lorraine Roach, "Barack Obama's Top 10 Apologies: How
the President Has Humiliated a Superpower," Heritage.org, June 2, 2009,
http://www.heritage.org/research/reports/2009/06/barack-obamas-top-10-
apologies-how-the-president-has-humiliated-a-superpower.

22   http://www.historyguide.org/europe/lecture11.html.

23   Ibid.

24   Larry Diamond, "What is America Fighting For?" December 19,
2015, https://www.theatlantic.com/international/archive/2015/12/
america-freedom-isis/421368/

25   Lawrence Wright, *The Looming Tower: Al Qaeda and the Road to 9/11* (Alfred
A. Knopf, 2006), p. 187, as quoted in https://en.wikiquote.org/wiki/
Osama_bin_Laden

26   "Timeline: Osama bin Laden, over the years," May 2, 2011, http://www.
cnn.com/2011/WORLD/asiapcf/05/02/bin.laden.timeline/index.html

27   "The Mouse that Roared," June 25, 2014, http://www.blackfive.net/
main/2014/06/the-mouse-that-roared.html

28   Tim Black, "Why Can't the West Fight Isis?" June 2, 2015, http://www.
spiked-online.com/newsite/article/why-cant-the-west-fight-isis/17027#.
Wcs2ERNSyRs.

29 Ibid.
30 Ibid.
31 Ibid.

Chapter VIII

1 Many will point to the *Kibbutzim* phenomena in Israel as an example of a utopian—even communist—effort that has succeeded. This deserves greater discussion, but in summary, this argument is weak. First, while socialist ideology was integral to the *Kibbutz*, Jews developed the *Kibbutz* starting in the early 20th Century primarily as a means to collectively provide for themselves and protect against hostile Arab neighbors. Think of it more like a herd of gazelles which travel in herds for the mutual benefit of each individual in the herd.

   Second, *kibbutzim* have not prospered in the decades following Israel's independence. Private enterprise in Israel has far surpassed anything the *kibbutzim* could ever provide (*kibbutzim*, for example, do not hire and fire members who excel or lag behind; they also offer no inherent mechanism or reward for innovation). Not surprisingly, *kibbutzim* are decreasing in number. In short, while the *kibbutzim* served an immediate and important need for the original Jewish pioneers (protection), no one can consider *kibbutzim* to have thrived or grown as a creative institution.

2 And by this I don't mean a general monument, such as the Vietnam Memorial. As interesting as it may be, I have difficulty believing that this memorial—which honors the fallen of that war, and not the valiant fight for freedom that they actually died for—will survive the next fifty years. It will lose its standing as soon as another more "important" event will require the land space. The Memorial offers no tribute to freedom, justice, nor to any sense of any timeless truth. It states only: "In memory of the men and women who served in the Vietnam War and later died as a result of their service. We honor and remember their sacrifice." Really? Sacrifice for what? For their families? For their fellow comrades? For their time? There is no mention that they fought to push back against the monstrosities of communism, to preserve our freedoms and the freedoms of others. There is no recognition of this valiant cause in the inscription—such as you will see in the Lincoln, Jefferson, or Washington Memorials. The monument offers only a sense that these men were victims of an ill-conceived, misguided, and perhaps even imperialist interventionist misstep which America was wrong to have ever pursued in the first place. If that is the message, it ignores the very purpose of the war itself.

3 Paul Kengor, "The War on Religion," Victims of Communism Memorial Foundation, http://victimsofcommunism.org/the-war-on-religion/.

4 Ibid.

5   Ibid.

6   Ibid.

7   Ibid.

8   Ibid.

9   Ibid.

10   Ibid.

11   http://victimsofcommunism.org/the-war-on-religion/

12   Benito Mussolini, "Fundamental Ideas," as compiled in *Twentieth Century Political Reader (2ⁿᵈ ed); a reader*, p. 222; Edited by Stephen Eric Bonner, 2006, Routledge, Taylor & Francis Group.

13   Ibid., citing Dopo due anni, in Diuturna, Milano, Alpes, 1930, p. 242).

14   https://en.wikipedia.org/wiki/fascism

15   Ibid., Denis Mack Smith, *Mussolini*, New York: NY, Vintage Books, 1983, p. 162

16   Ibid.

17   Jochen von Lang, *The Secretary: Martin Bormann, The Man Who Manipulated Hitler*, New York: NY, Random House, 1979, p. 221

18   https://en.wikipedia.org/wiki/Fascism

19   Ibid.

Chapter IX

1   I will put aside for now the apparent irony that many among the godless argue that radical Islam is not Islam. In fact, they seem to be apologists for Islam (perhaps because they perceive it as some counterweight to Christianity and Judaism). But this in fact cuts against their argument, since if radical Islam (or "violent extremism" as some have called it) is somehow not the issue, then we can stop our discussion here. However, I pursue this section of the book for intellectual honesty and consistency.

2   Interestingly, the reason many wanted America not to fight or engage in the Middle East fight against Al Queda or ISIS is that they maintain that Islam is a religion of peace, and the "vast majority" of Muslims love peace, and that to go there and fight might make Muslims think we are seeking war with Islam itself. But if they maintain this "exception" view, then they can't *also* argue that Islam is a general example of how religion is destructive. Even they recognize (or want to recognize) that Islam is inherently peaceful, and that radical Islamists are a "fringe" exception.

Either they are or they are not. They cannot have it both ways.

Chapter X

1   Laura Roberts, "Three quarters of all independent music shops have closed down in the last decade," *The Telegraph*, May 27, 2010, http://www. telegraph.co.uk/culture/music/music-news/7767333/Three-quarters-of-all-independent-music-shops-have-closed-down-in-the-last-decade.html

2   "12 Stats on the State of Bookstores in America Today," Open Education Database, October 29, 2012, http://oedb.org/ ilibrarian/12-stats-on-the-state-of-bookstores-in-america-today/

3   Ramkumar Iyer, "Barnes & Noble sales fall for fifth straight quarter," Reuters.com, September 9, 2015, http://www.reuters.com/article/ us-barnes-noble-results-idUSKCN0R91HH20150909

4   Amanda Kooser, "And the last Blockbuster movie ever rented is . . .," November 12, 2013, CNET.com, http://www.cnet.com/news/ and-the-last-blockbuster-movie-ever-rented-is/.

5   See generally, Michael S. Malone, "Silicon and the Silver Screen," Wall Street Journal, April 17, 2017

6   https://blogs.wsj.com/moneybeat/2017/05/12/ bloodbath-for-retail-stocks-rolls-on/

7   For general facts regarding the overall comparison between Israel and her enemies, see generally http://www.standwithus.com/booklets/IL101/files/ Israel101.pdf and http://www.mefacts.com/cached.asp?x_id=10190 .

8   Eliezer Sherman, "Report: Since Inception, UNHRC Condemned Israel More Than Rest of World's Countries Combined," *The Algemeiner*, June 25, 2015, http://www.algemeiner.com/2015/06/25/report-sido thnce-inception-unhrc-condemned-israel-more-than-rest-of-worlds-countries-combined/#. For a general listing of resolutions either expressly condemning Israel or otherwise making negative findings against Israel, see "List of the UN resolutions concerning Israel and Palestine," https://en.wikipedia.org/wiki/ List_of_the_UN_resolutions_concerning_Israel_and_Palestine

9   Martin Evans, "Rotherham sex abuse scandal: 1,400 children exploited by Asian gangs while authorities turned a blind eye," the Telegraph, August 26, 2014, www.telegraph.co.uk/news/uknews/crime/11057647/ Rotherham-sex-abuse-scandal-1400-children-exploited-by-Asian-gangs-while-authorities-turned-a-blind-eye.html

10 Ibid.

11 For a sampling of such released murderers, see www.dailymail.co.uk/ news/article-2420137/Revealed-The-12-convicted-murderers-freed-licence-kill-AGAIN-past-decade.html. See also Peter Holley, "A convicted murderer was released early for good behavior. Months later, he killed again," *The Washington Post*, April 25, 2016, https://www.washingtonpost. com/news/morning-mix/wp/2016/04/25/he-was-released-early-for-good-behavior-it-took-him-less-than-a-year-to-kill-again/, where it noted that "[a]ccording to a federal recidivism study, more than two-thirds of

prisoners released in 30 states in 2005 were arrested for a new crime within three years of their release. The study, published in 2014 by the Justice Department's Bureau of Justice Statistics, found that 71 percent of violent offenders were arrested for a new crime within five years of their release."

12   Chloe Pantazi, "I had lunch at London's naked restaurant that has a waiting list of over 40,000 people—here's the verdict," *Business Insider*, June 11, 2016, http://www.businessinsider.de/ londons-naked-restaurant-the-bunyadi-2016-6.

13   Conor Friedersdorf, "Why Dr. Kermit Gosnell's Trial Should Be a Front-Page Story," *The Atlantic*, April 12, 2013, http://www.theatlantic.com/national/archive/2013/04/ why-dr-kermit-gosnells-trial-should-be-a-front-page-story/274944/

14   In 2003, the group the People for the Ethical Treatment of Animals (PETA) initiated a promotional campaign with photos of chicken on a plate. On the bottom of the poster, they described it as "the Holocaust on your plate." It argued that eating chicken and other meat was like participating in a Holocaust, like the Nazi Holocaust against the Jews. See generally, "Group blasts PETA 'Holocaust' project," February 28, 2003 http://www.cnn. com/2003/US/Northeast/02/28/peta.holocaust/

15   In Sweden and Germany, and many other European countries, rapes abound now more than ever. Sadly, the vast majority of the men who perpetrate them are from Middle Eastern descent. The police and the prosecutors of these countries often fail to prosecute for fear of the public labeling them racist. See, e.g.., Ivar Arpi, "It's not only Germany that covers up mass sex attacks by migrant men... Sweden's record is shameful," January 16, 2016, www.spectator.co.uk/2016/01/its-not-only-germany-that- covers-up-mass-sex-attacks-by-migrant-men-swedens-record-is-shameful/ (Germany fails to report massive organized molestation attack on New Year's Eve by Muslim immigrants for fear of racism charges); Robert Spencer, "UK: It was 'Racist' to Prosecute Muslim Rape Gangs," November 23, 2014, www.frontpagemag.com/fpm/245898/uk-it-was-racist-prosecute- muslim-rape-gangs-robert-spencer (tragic story of Rotherham, *infra*, where police failed to prosecute years-long Pakistani gang-rapes of teenage girls for fear of racism charges); and Andrew Brown, "This cover-up of sex assaults in Sweden is a gift for xenophobes," January 13, 2016, www.theguardian.com/commentisfree/2016/jan/13/sex-assaults-sweden- stockholm-music-festival (internal memos revealing that the Stockholm police failed to report sex assaults at a festival for fear of worsening ethnic tensions—and also for fear that revealing this would lead to an electoral advantage for the S Vader lDemocrats [the party fighting against increased immigration]).

16   I write "so-called" because the phrase has assumed some air of "official" status, as if the Constitution mandates such a separation. It does not. On the contrary, it states no such thing. Further, every founding father has

made clear that the American experiment cannot work without a core embracing of the Judeo-Christian God. One may decide not to believe that God is necessary for our success as a democracy, but it is a true inversion of the Constitution to suggest that the founding fathers actually sought to "separate" all notion of God from the public square.

17 Naturally, someone can earn even more respect in his community for accomplishing something extraordinary, like a soldier risking his life to save his buddies in combat, or a great CEO who has created new successful products despite all the odds against him. And a person can squander respect through cowardice, or because he was a horrible parent. But that is not the point here: I am talking about the "baseline" of all human beings. I'm talking about the stranger you meet on the street, your waiter or flight attendant. You know nothing of who they are or what they've done in their lives, but we still understand they are human beings. Saying "please" and "thank you" is a constant affirmation of just that.

18 For a detailed review of his leadership and style, see Ethan Leuchter, "What qualities made Julius Caesar such a great leader?," Quora.com, February 24, 2015, https://www.quora.com/What-qualities-made-Julius-Caesar-such-a-great-leader.

19 Dante, "Julius Caesar: A Great World Leader," Ultius.com, September 12, 2014, https://www.ultius.com/ultius-blog/entry/julius-caesar-a-great-world-leader.html.

20 Ibid.

21 Our language and culture contain thousands of words and rituals that we adopt without understanding. Among so many others, why do we have Christmas trees? Why are the words *know* and *neighbor* spelled in those ways? Why does Hebrew read from right to left, and not from left to right? Where do the words *trivia, decimate,* and *right* come from? Why do we say "he wants his pound of flesh?" There are of course origins to all of these and other phrases, but we rarely seek them out.

Conclusion

1 See generally, Nury Vittachi, "Atheism Peaks, While Spiritual Groups Move Toward Convergence," July 13, 2015, http://www.science20.com/writer_on_the_edge/blog/atheism_peaks_while_spiritual_groups_move_toward_convergence-156528. This article focuses on irreligion throughout the world, suggesting a "peak" in atheism in 1970. Still, in other surveys, a rise in atheism is clear throughout some 57 countries, when focused particularly in Asia and Europe: August 9, 2012, http://www.christiantoday.com/article/asia.and.europe.see.rise.in.atheism/30442.htm

2 Michael Lipka, "10 facts about atheists," June 1, 2016, Pew Research Center, http://www.pewresearch.org/fact-tank/2016/06/01/10-facts-about-atheists/.

The same poll interestingly revealed that approximately half of Americans (53%) say it is not necessary to believe in God to be moral, while 45% say belief in God is necessary to have good values, according to a 2014 survey. In other wealthy countries, smaller shares tend to say that a belief in God is essential for good morals, including just 15% in France.

3   Gabe Bullard, "The World's Newest Major Religion: No Religion," *National Geographic*, April 22, 2016, http://news.nationalgeographic. com/2016/04/160422-atheism-agnostic-secular-nones-rising-religion/.

4   Avaneesh Pandey, "Pew Survey Predicts Rise In Atheism In US, Europe Despite Growing Religiosity Worldwide," *International Business Times*, April 4, 2015, http://www.ibtimes.com/pew-survey-predicts-rise-atheism-us-europe-despite-growing-religiosity-worldwide-1869696.

5   Peter Oliver, "European churches struggle to attract worshippers," April 6, 2015, https://www.rt.com/news/246981-europe-atheism-increasing-secularization/.

6   Ibid.

7   "Peaceful Coexistence: Reconciling Nondiscrimination Principles with Civil Liberties," September 2016, http://www.usccr.gov/pubs/Peaceful-Coexistence-09-07-16.PDF. It is notable that despite its substantial accusations against "Christian supremacy" and alleged religious impositions, the report fails to substantiate any of these claims, let alone one instance of how religion "..is being used as both a weapon and a shield by those seeking to deny others equality."

8   Ibid.

9   See Bullard, "The World's Newest Major Religion: No Religion."

10   Conrad Hackett, "5 facts about the Muslim population in Europe," Pew Research Center, July 19, 2016, http://www.pewresearch.org/fact-tank/2015/11/17/5-facts-about-the-muslim-population-in-europe/.

11   https://en.wikipedia.org/wiki/Eugenics

12   http://foreignpolicy.com/2016/07/07/europes-freedom-of-speech-fail/

13   Toni Airaksinen, "Why Is Church Still So Popular?" August 18, 2017, https://pjmedia.com/trending/2017/08/18/75-percent-republicans-think-church-good-america/

14   Sutirtho Patranobis, December 25, 2016, "Atheist China could have largest number of Christians in the world by 2030," http://www.hindustantimes.com/world-news/in-atheist-china-christians-outnumber-communist-party-members/story-dNG9fAuLrPvSvoAwbWYL0K.html. See also, Ian Johnson, "In China, Unregistered Churches Are Driving a Religious Revolution," April 23, 2017, https://www.theatlantic.com/international/archive/2017/04/china-unregistered-churches-driving-religious-revolution/521544/, discussing the underground Christian movement and tension with China's officially atheist government.

15   Carl Bunderson, "Why is Christianity growing so quickly in mainland China?" http://www.catholicnewsagency.com/news/why-is-christianity-growing-so-quickly-in-mainland-china-57545/

16   Kelsey Dallas, "Russia is 'much more religious' than it was 25 years ago. So why is religious freedom under attack?" May 11, 2017, http://www.deseretnews.com/article/865679764/Why-religious-tensions-are-rising-in-Russia.html

17   Stephen Ryan, "The Surprising Rise of Christianity in Russia," December 21, 2015, http://www.patheos.com/blogs/mysticpost/2015/12/21/the-surprising-rise-of-christianity-in-russia/

18   Ibid.

19   Ibid.

20   Franklin Foer, "It's Putin's World," March, 2017, https://www.theatlantic.com/magazine/archive/2017/03/its-putins-world/513848/

21   https://en.wikipedia.org/wiki/Vladimir_Putin#Religious_policy, fn. 209.

22   Sam Sokol, "Putin Calls on European Jews to Take Refuge in Russia" January 20, 2016, http://www.jpost.com/Diaspora/Putin-calls-on-European-Jews-to-take-refuge-in-Russia-442175

23   Seth J. Frantzman, "Despite Syria, Israel-Russia Relations Are the Warmest in History," March 25, 2017, http://www.jpost.com/Israel-News/Despite-Syria-Israel-Russia-relations-are-the-warmest-in-history-485062.

It is fair to ask whether Putin's embrace and preaching of Christianity and its morals could all be a ruse merely to manipulate his people to solidify the religious base of his power. After all, Hitler (at least in his earlier life) said some favorable words about Christianity, too.

Although anything is possible, I am less inclined to believe this about Putin, as the comparisons to Hitler's passing lip service to Christianity are weak. First, Hitler's lip service was exactly that: lip service and he very quickly revealed his contempt for the weakness of Christianity. Putin talks about Christianity consistently and often. Second, Putin actually pursues the advance of Christianity, including the building of churches far and wide through Russia. Third, Putin jabs his fingers at other leaders for losing their Christian values. Fourth, Putin encourages European Jews—that's right, Jews—to emigrate to Russia, in light of his belief in the Judeo-Christian value set. Fifth: Russia's embrace of Israel as an ally is telling—especially in a world where supporting Israel only serves as a lightning rod for much of the world's ire. From a pure geo-political perspective (not a moral one), a relationship with Israel can be seen as toxic. Why pursue it? Finally, Putin's Christianity goes to the core of his belief in Russia itself: he saw Russia and Russian Orthodoxy as inextricably part and parcel of each other. Unlike Hitler, there are no secret missives from Putin expressing his preference for some other system (godless or not), nor secret disdain for Christianity.

24   See Deuteronomy 6:4-9.

About The Author

BARAK LURIE is a managing partner of the firm Lurie & Seltzer in Los Angeles, California. Barak obtained his BA with honors at Stanford University in 1985, and his JD and MBA at the UCLA School of Law and Anderson School of Business in 1989. He is the host of The Barak Lurie Show, a popular and riveting radio program heard Sunday mornings on AM870, KRLA in Los Angeles. He was born in Israel and serves on many pro-Christian and pro-Israel boards.

Barak is a former atheist who turned to God after using logic, science, and probabilities. Barak pulls no punches as he makes the case for the existence of God—and shows the dangers of atheism. He beats down atheists with a club of reason, history, and science, and exposes atheists' flawed assumptions. Barak's many articles, podcasts, and speeches on atheism and its dangers have made him a declared and decorated champion of Christianity and Judaism, and their crucial roles in all the values we hold dear in Western civilization.

Barak is a lover of God, America, and Israel, and an avid mountain biker and vegan. He and his wife Stacey have three children and live in Brentwood, California.